MS. MARVEL

writer
G. WILLOW WILSON

artist
ADRIAN ALPHONA

color artist
IAN HERRING

letterer
VC'S JOE CARAMAGNA

cover art
SARA PICHELLI & JUSTIN PONSOR (#1),
JAMIE McKELVIE & MATTHEW WILSON (#2-3 & #5)
and **JAMIE McKELVIE** (#4)

assistant editor   editor
DEVIN LEWIS   **SANA AMANAT**

senior editors
STEPHEN WACKER & NICK LOWE

collection editor
JENNIFER GRÜNWALD
assistant editor
CAITLIN O'CONNELL
associate managing editor
KATERI WOODY
editor, special projects
MARK D. BEAZLEY
vp production & special projects
JEFF YOUNGQUIST
svp print, sales & marketing
DAVID GABRIEL
book design
JEFF POWELL

editor in chief
C.B. CEBULSKI
chief creative officer
JOE QUESADA
president
DAN BUCKLEY
executive producer
ALAN FINE

S. MARVEL VOL. 1: NO NORMAL. Contains material originally published in magazine form as MS. MARVEL #1-5 and ALL-NEW MARVEL NOW! POINT ONE #1. Eleventh printing 2019. ISBN 978-0-7851-9021-9.
blished by MARVEL WORLDWIDE, INC., a subsidiary of MARVEL ENTERTAINMENT, LLC. OFFICE OF PUBLICATION: 135 West 50th Street, New York, NY 10020. © 2014 MARVEL No similarity between any of the names,
aracters, persons, and/or institutions in this magazine with those of any living or dead person or institution is intended, and any such similarity which may exist is purely coincidental. **Printed in Canada.** DAN BUCKLEY,
esident, Marvel Entertainment; JOHN NEE, Publisher; JOE QUESADA, Chief Creative Officer; TOM BREVOORT, SVP of Publishing; DAVID BOGART, Associate Publisher & SVP of Talent Affairs; Publishing & Partnership;
VID GABRIEL, VP of Print & Digital Publishing; JEFF YOUNGQUIST, VP of Production & Special Projects; DAN CARR, Executive Director of Publishing Technology; ALEX MORALES, Director of Publishing Operations; DAN
INGTON, Managing Editor; SUSAN CRESPI, Production Manager; STAN LEE, Chairman Emeritus. For information regarding advertising in Marvel Comics or on Marvel.com, please contact Vit DeBellis, Custom Solutions &
egrated Advertising Manager, at vdebellis@marvel.com. For Marvel subscription inquiries, please call 888-511-5480. **Manufactured between 9/4/2019 and 9/24/2019 by SOLISCO PRINTERS, SCOTT, QC, CANADA.**

19 18 17 16 15 14 13 12 11

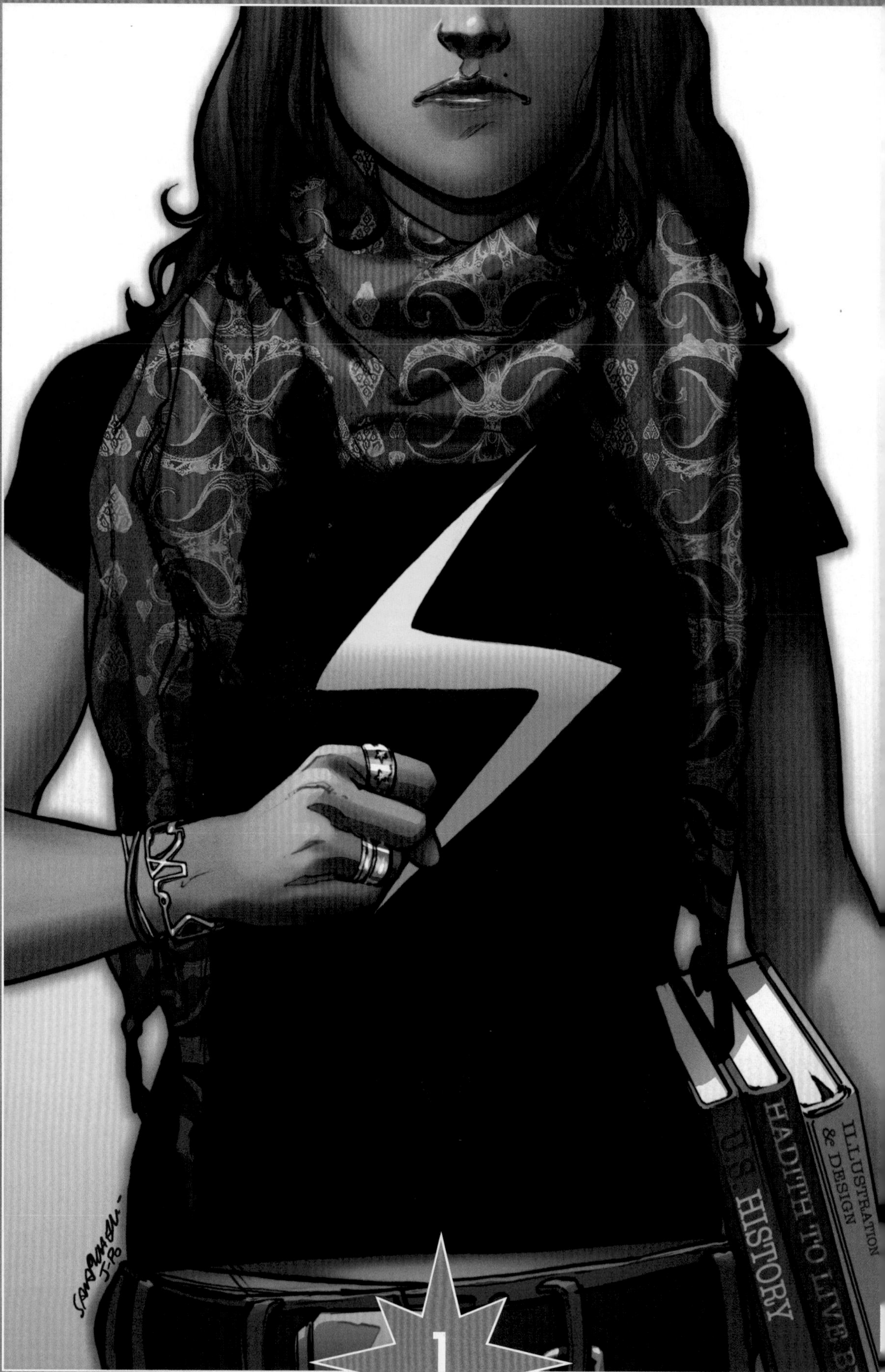

U.S. HISTORY
HADITH TO LIVE B
ILLUSTRATION & DESIGN
1

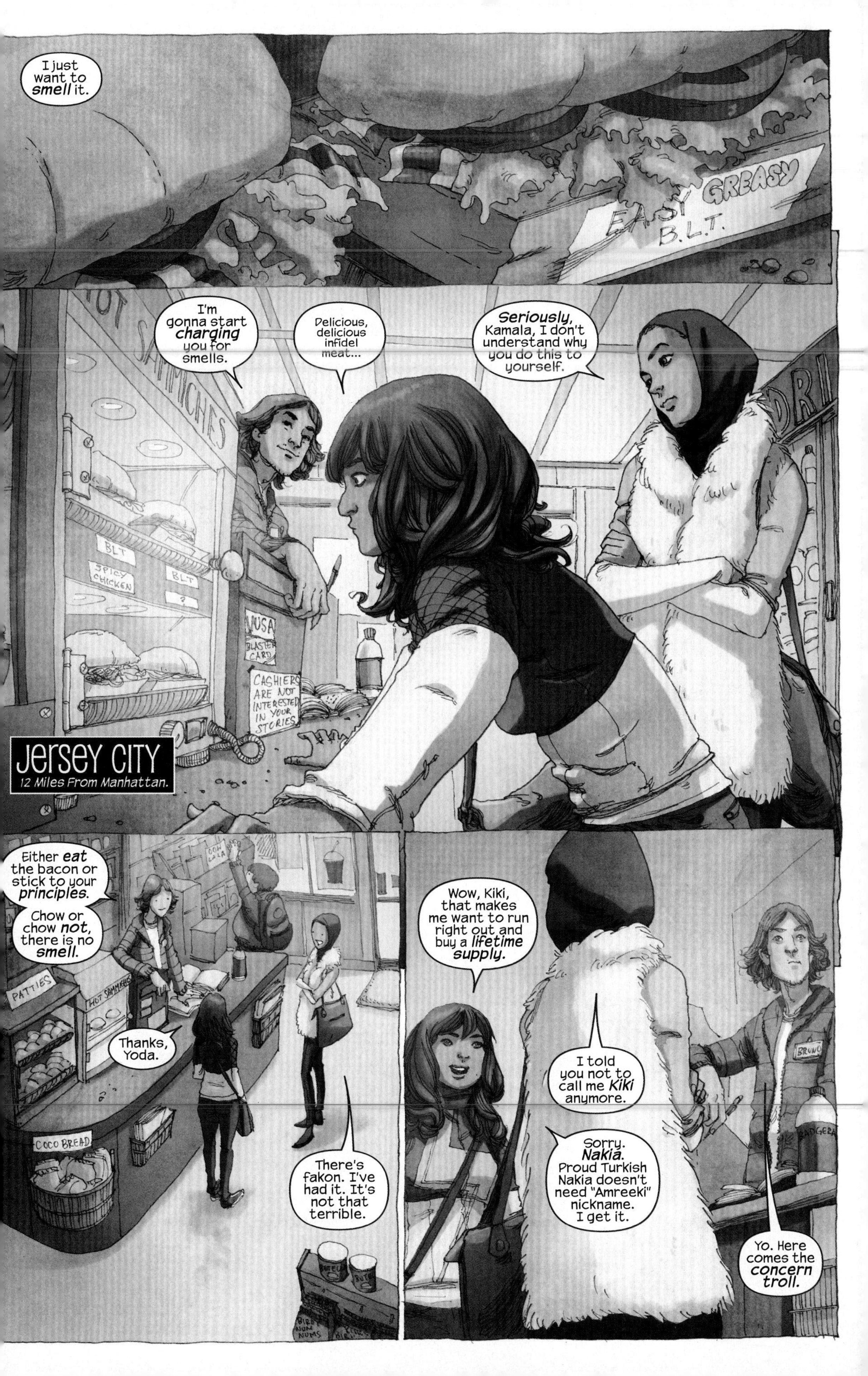
I just want to smell it.
EASY GREASY B.L.T.
HOT SAMMICHES
I'm gonna start charging you for smells.
Delicious, delicious infidel meat...
Seriously, Kamala, I don't understand why you do this to yourself.
BLT
SPICY CHICKEN
BLT
CASHIERS ARE NOT INTERESTED IN YOUR STORIES
JERSEY CITY
12 Miles From Manhattan.
Either eat the bacon or stick to your principles.
Chow or chow not, there is no smell.
Thanks, Yoda.
PATTIES
COCO BREAD
There's fakon. I've had it. It's not that terrible.
Wow, Kiki, that makes me want to run right out and buy a lifetime supply.
I told you not to call me Kiki anymore.
Sorry. Nakia. Proud Turkish Nakia doesn't need "Amreeki" nickname. I get it.
BRUNO
Yo. Here comes the concern troll.

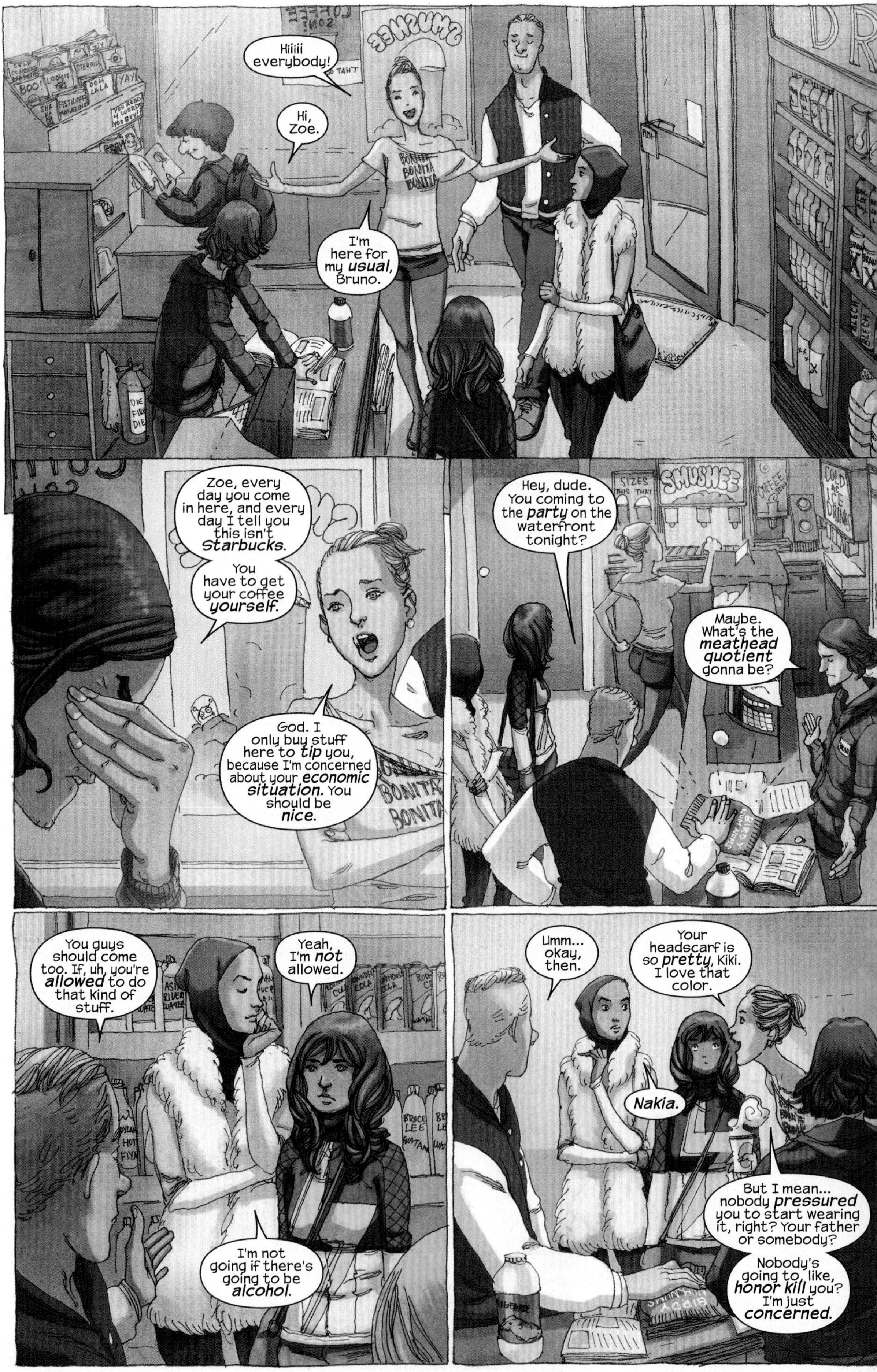

Hiiiii everybody!
Hi, Zoe.
I'm here for my *usual*, Bruno.
BONITA BONITA BONITA
Zoe, every day you come in here, and every day I tell you this isn't *Starbucks*.
You have to get your coffee *yourself*.
God. I only buy stuff here to *tip* you, because I'm concerned about your *economic situation*. You should be *nice*.
SIZES THIS THAT
SMUSHEE
COLD AS ICE DRINKS
Hey, dude. You coming to the *party* on the waterfront tonight?
Maybe. What's the *meathead quotient* gonna be?
You guys should come too. If, uh, you're *allowed* to do that kind of stuff.
Yeah, I'm *not* allowed.
I'm not going if there's going to be *alcohol*.
Umm... okay, then.
Your headscarf is so *pretty*, Kiki. I love that color.
Nakia.
But I mean... nobody *pressured* you to start wearing it, right? Your father or somebody?
Nobody's going to, like, *honor kill* you? I'm just *concerned*.

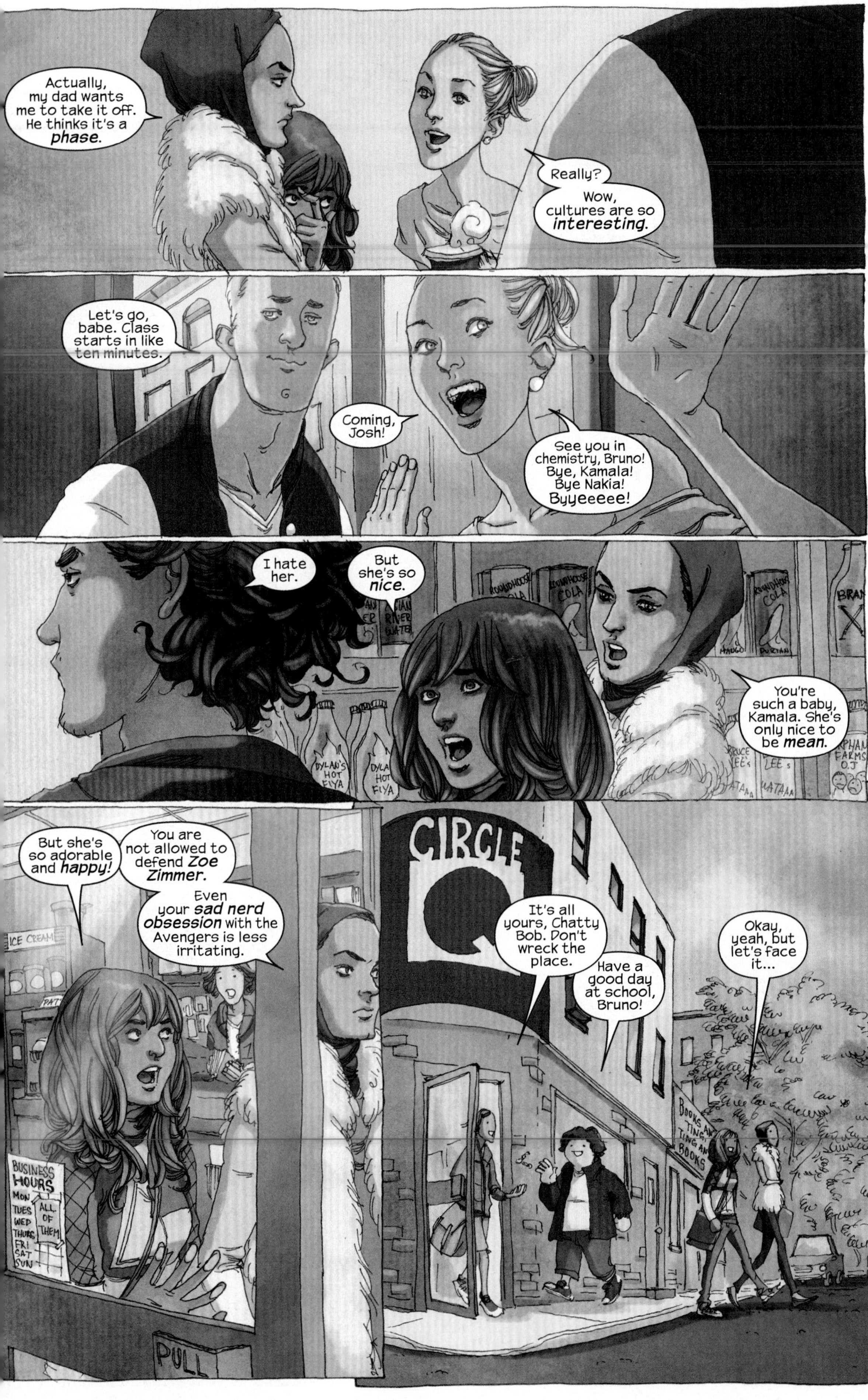
Actually, my dad wants me to take it off. He thinks it's a *phase*.
Really?
Wow, cultures are so *interesting*.
Let's go, babe. Class starts in like ten minutes.
Coming, Josh!
See you in chemistry, Bruno! Bye, Kamala! Bye Nakia! Byyeeeee!
I hate her.
But she's so *nice*.
You're such a baby, Kamala. She's only nice to be *mean*.
But she's so adorable and *happy*!
You are not allowed to defend *Zoe Zimmer*.
Even your *sad nerd obsession* with the Avengers is less irritating.
CIRCLE Q
It's all yours, Chatty Bob. Don't wreck the place.
Have a good day at school, Bruno!
Okay, yeah, but let's face it...
BUSINESS HOURS
MON TUES WED THURS FRI SAT SUN
ALL OF THEM
PULL
ICE CREAM

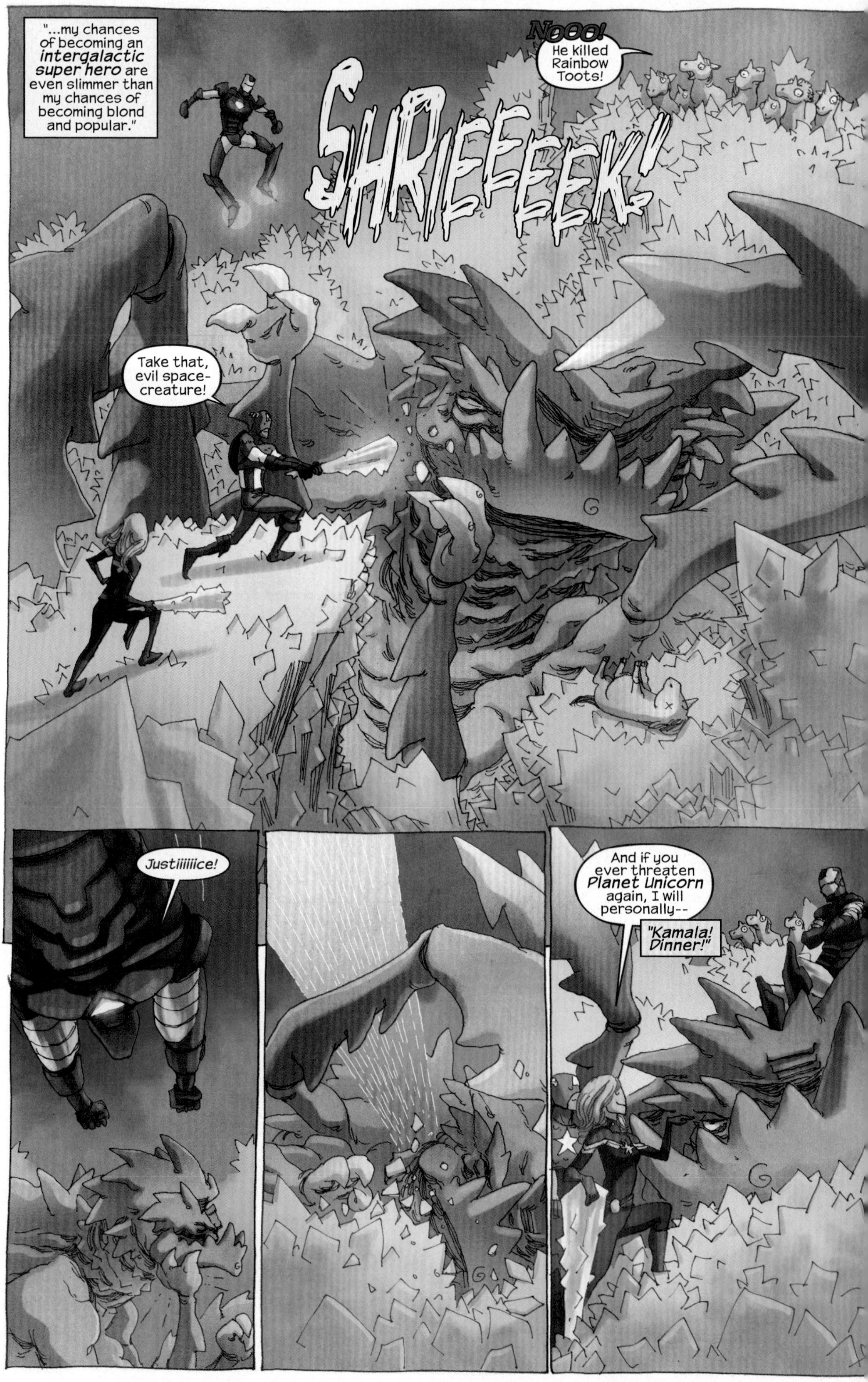
"...my chances of becoming an *intergalactic super hero* are even slimmer than my chances of becoming blond and popular."
NOOOO!
He killed Rainbow Toots!
SHRIEEEEK!
Take that, evil space-creature!
Justiiiiiice!
And if you ever threaten *Planet Unicorn* again, I will personally--
"Kamala! Dinner!"

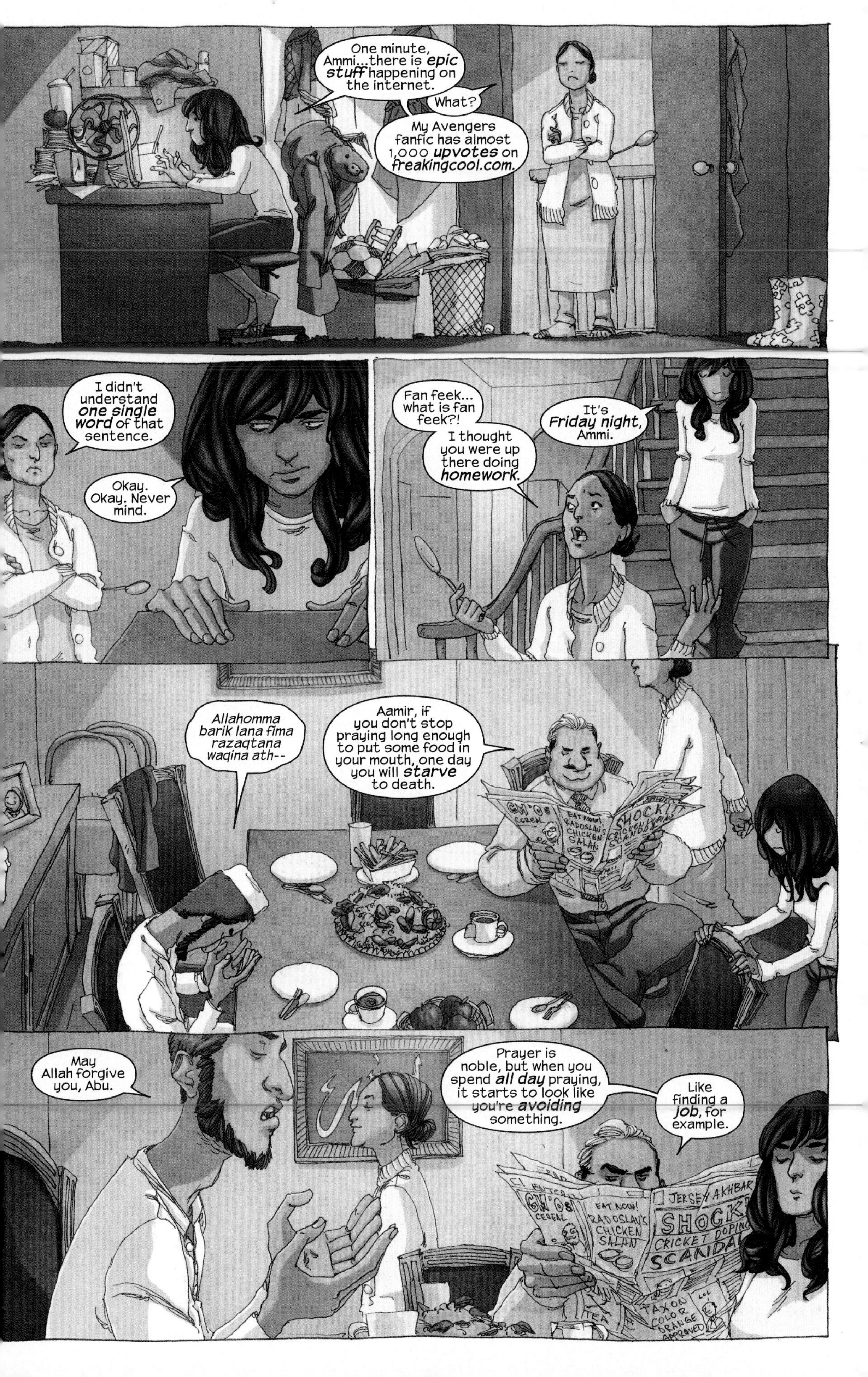

One minute, Ammi...there is *epic stuff* happening on the internet.
What?
My Avengers fanfic has almost 1,000 **upvotes** on ***freakingcool.com***.
I didn't understand ***one single word*** of that sentence.
Okay. Okay. Never mind.
Fan feek... what is fan feek?!
I thought you were up there doing ***homework***.
It's ***Friday night***, Ammi.
Allahomma barik lana fima razaqtana waqina ath--
Aamir, if you don't stop praying long enough to put some food in your mouth, one day you will ***starve*** to death.
May Allah forgive you, Abu.
Prayer is noble, but when you spend ***all day*** praying, it starts to look like you're ***avoiding*** something.
Like finding a ***job***, for example.
JERSEY AKHBAR
SHOCK!
CRICKET DOPING SCANDAL

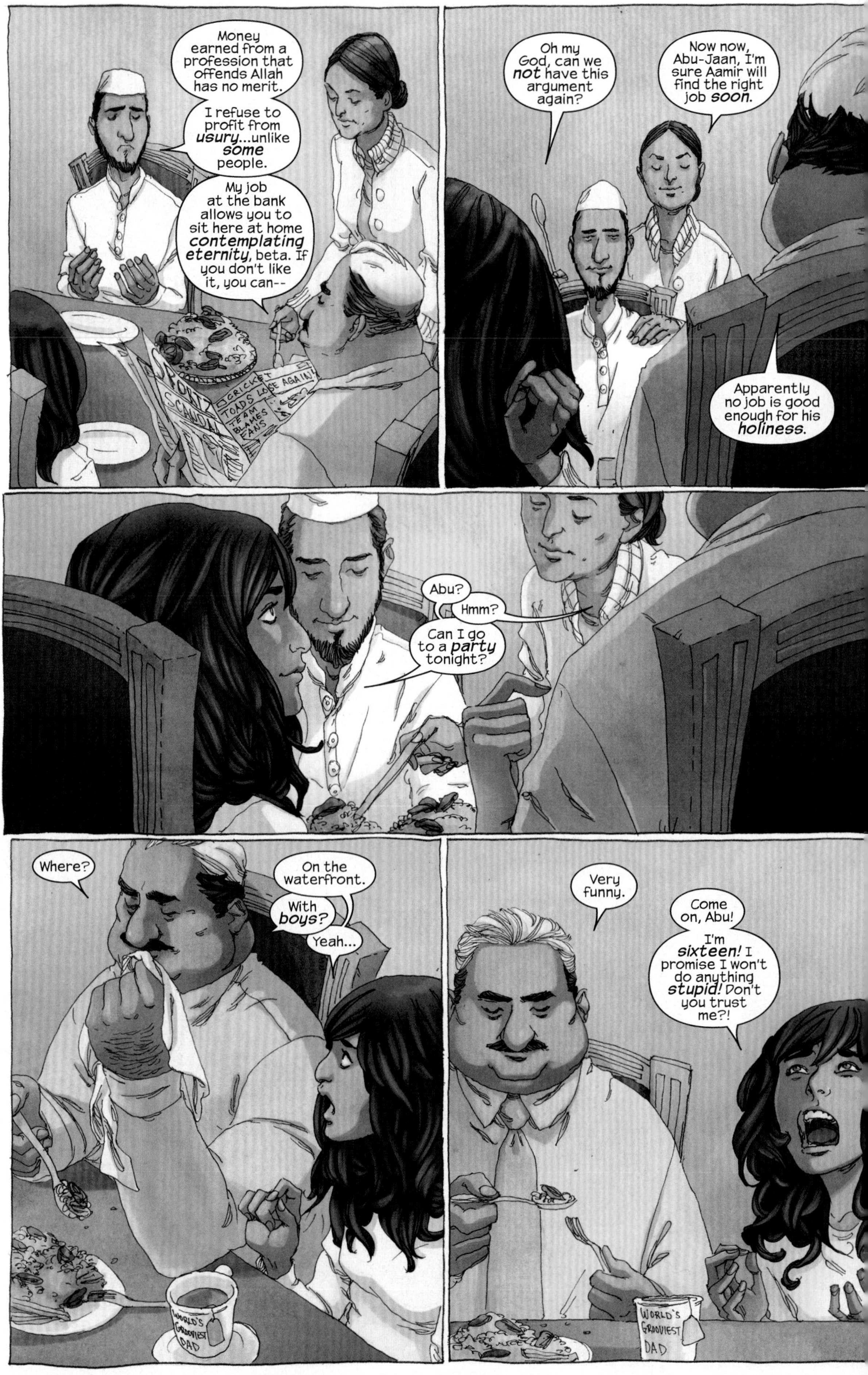

Money earned from a profession that offends Allah has no merit.
I refuse to profit from usury...unlike some people.
My job at the bank allows you to sit here at home contemplating eternity, beta. If you don't like it, you can--
SPORTZ
SCANDAL
CRICKET TOADS LOSE AGAIN!
TEAM BLAMES FANS
Oh my God, can we not have this argument again?
Now now, Abu-Jaan, I'm sure Aamir will find the right job soon.
Apparently no job is good enough for his holiness.
Abu?
Hmm?
Can I go to a party tonight?
Where?
On the waterfront.
With boys?
Yeah...
WORLD'S GROOVIEST DAD
Very funny.
Come on, Abu!
I'm sixteen! I promise I won't do anything stupid! Don't you trust me?!
WORLD'S GROOVIEST DAD

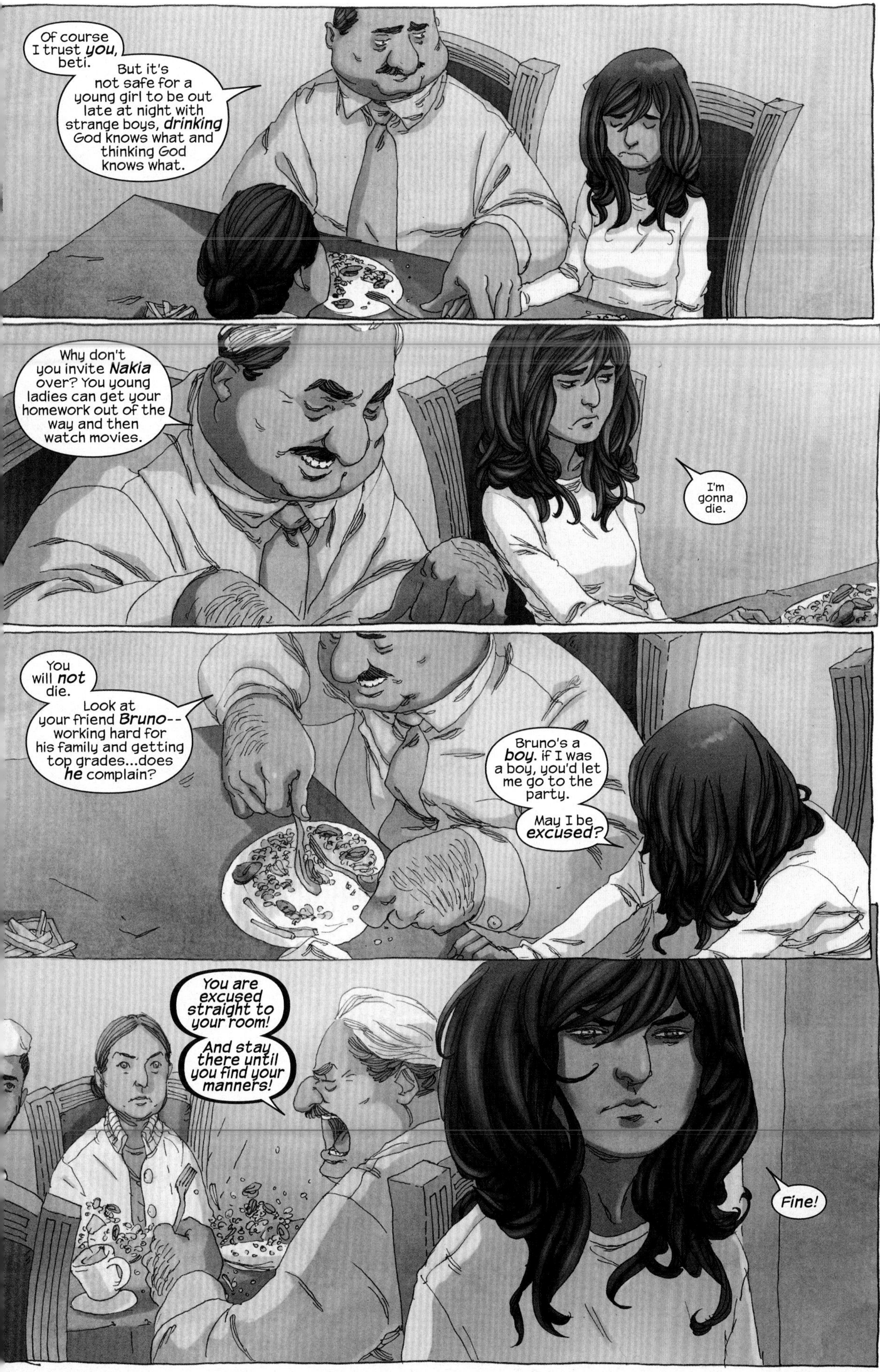

Of course I trust *you*, beti.
But it's not safe for a young girl to be out late at night with strange boys, *drinking* God knows what and thinking God knows what.
Why don't you invite *Nakia* over? You young ladies can get your homework out of the way and then watch movies.
I'm gonna die.
You will *not* die.
Look at your friend *Bruno*--working hard for his family and getting top grades...does *he* complain?
Bruno's a *boy*. If I was a boy, you'd let me go to the party.
May I be *excused*?
You are excused straight to your room!
And stay there until you find your manners!
Fine!

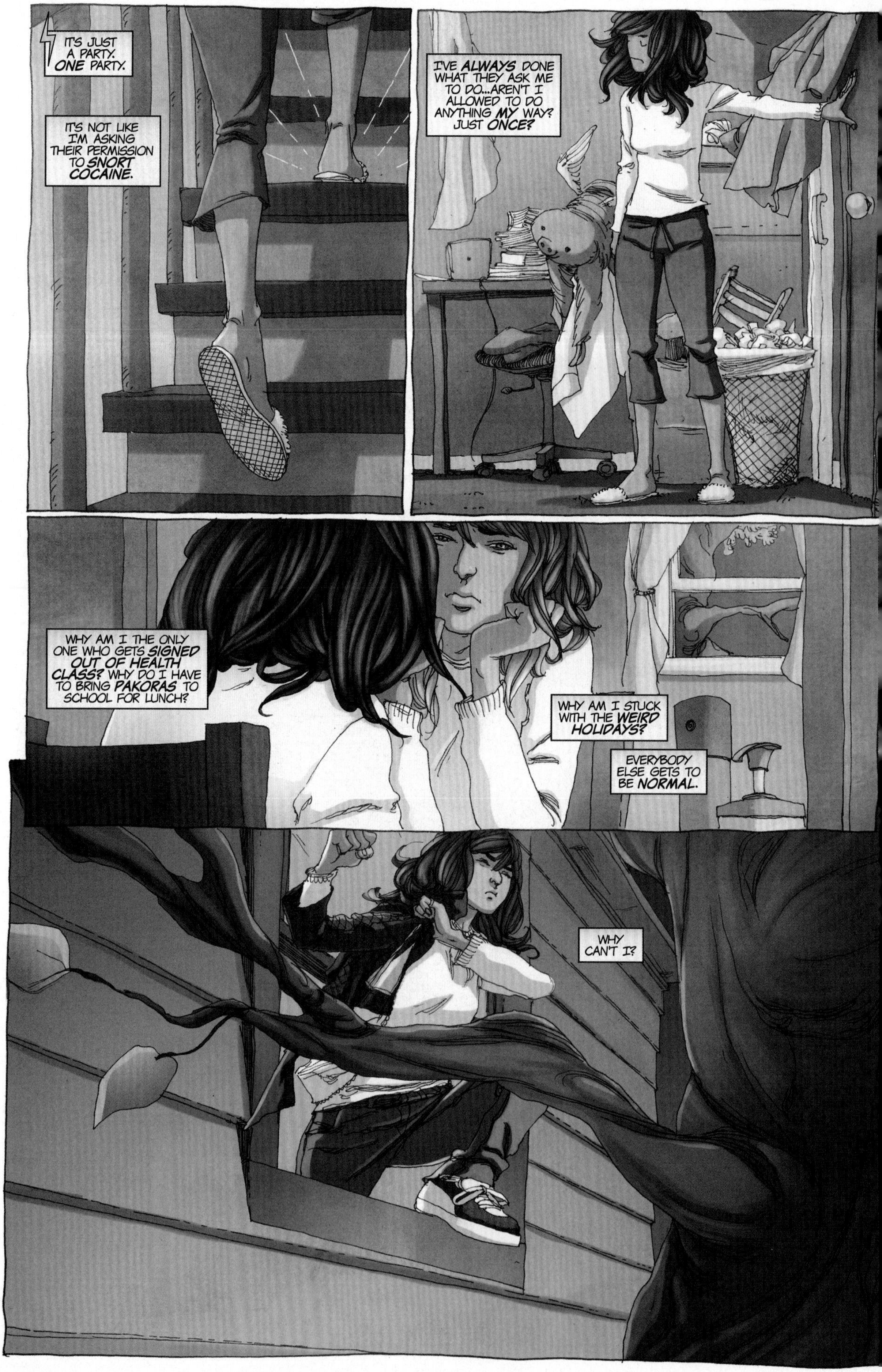
IT'S JUST A PARTY. ONE PARTY.
IT'S NOT LIKE I'M ASKING THEIR PERMISSION TO SNORT COCAINE.
I'VE ALWAYS DONE WHAT THEY ASK ME TO DO...AREN'T I ALLOWED TO DO ANYTHING MY WAY? JUST ONCE?
WHY AM I THE ONLY ONE WHO GETS SIGNED OUT OF HEALTH CLASS? WHY DO I HAVE TO BRING PAKORAS TO SCHOOL FOR LUNCH?
WHY AM I STUCK WITH THE WEIRD HOLIDAYS?
EVERYBODY ELSE GETS TO BE NORMAL.
WHY CAN'T I?

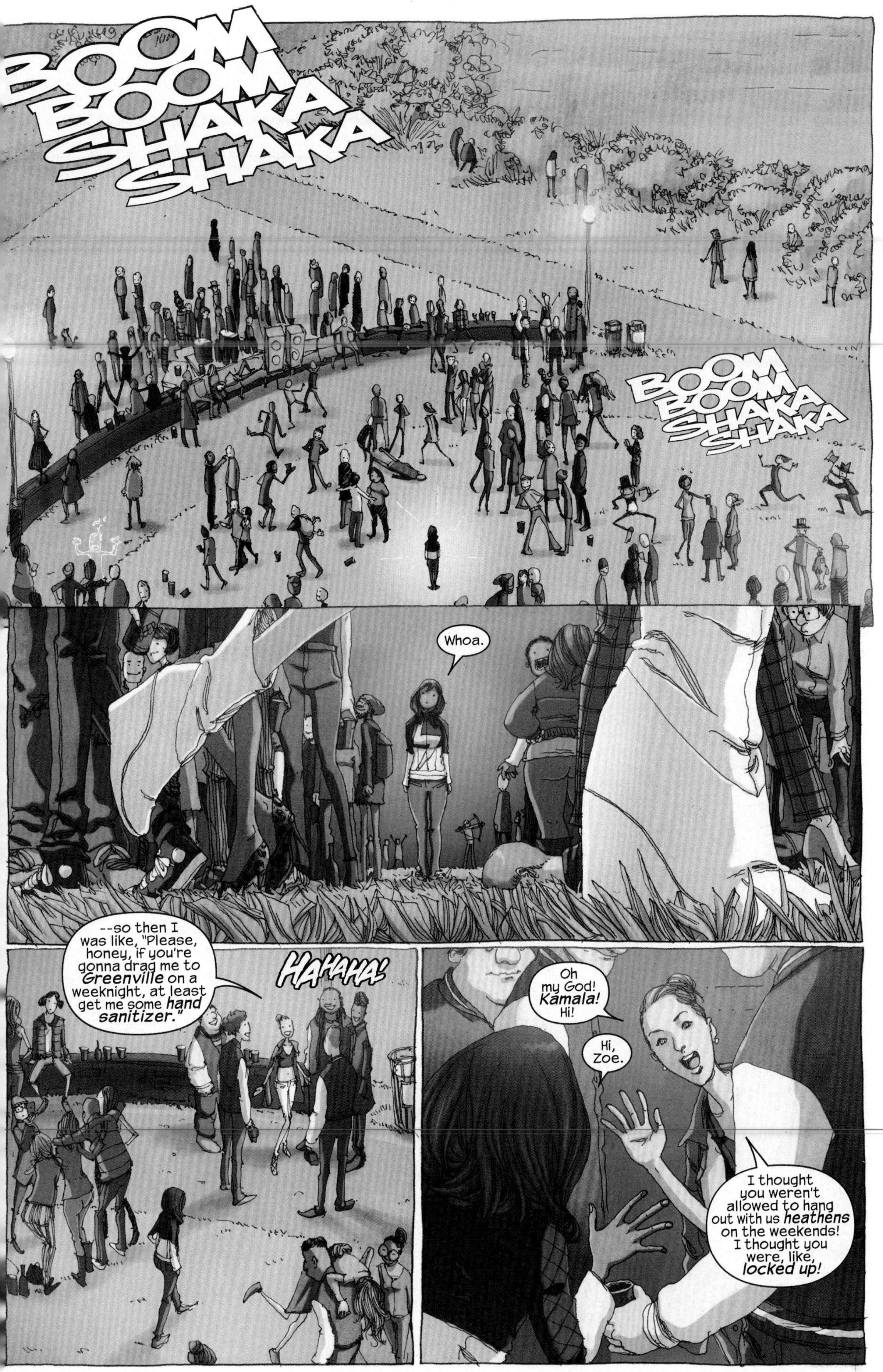
BOOM BOOM SHAKA SHAKA
BOOM BOOM SHAKA SHAKA
Whoa.
--so then I was like, "Please, honey, if you're gonna drag me to Greenville on a weeknight, at least get me some hand sanitizer."
HAHAHA!
Oh my God! Kamala! Hi!
Hi, Zoe.
I thought you weren't allowed to hang out with us heathens on the weekends! I thought you were, like, locked up!

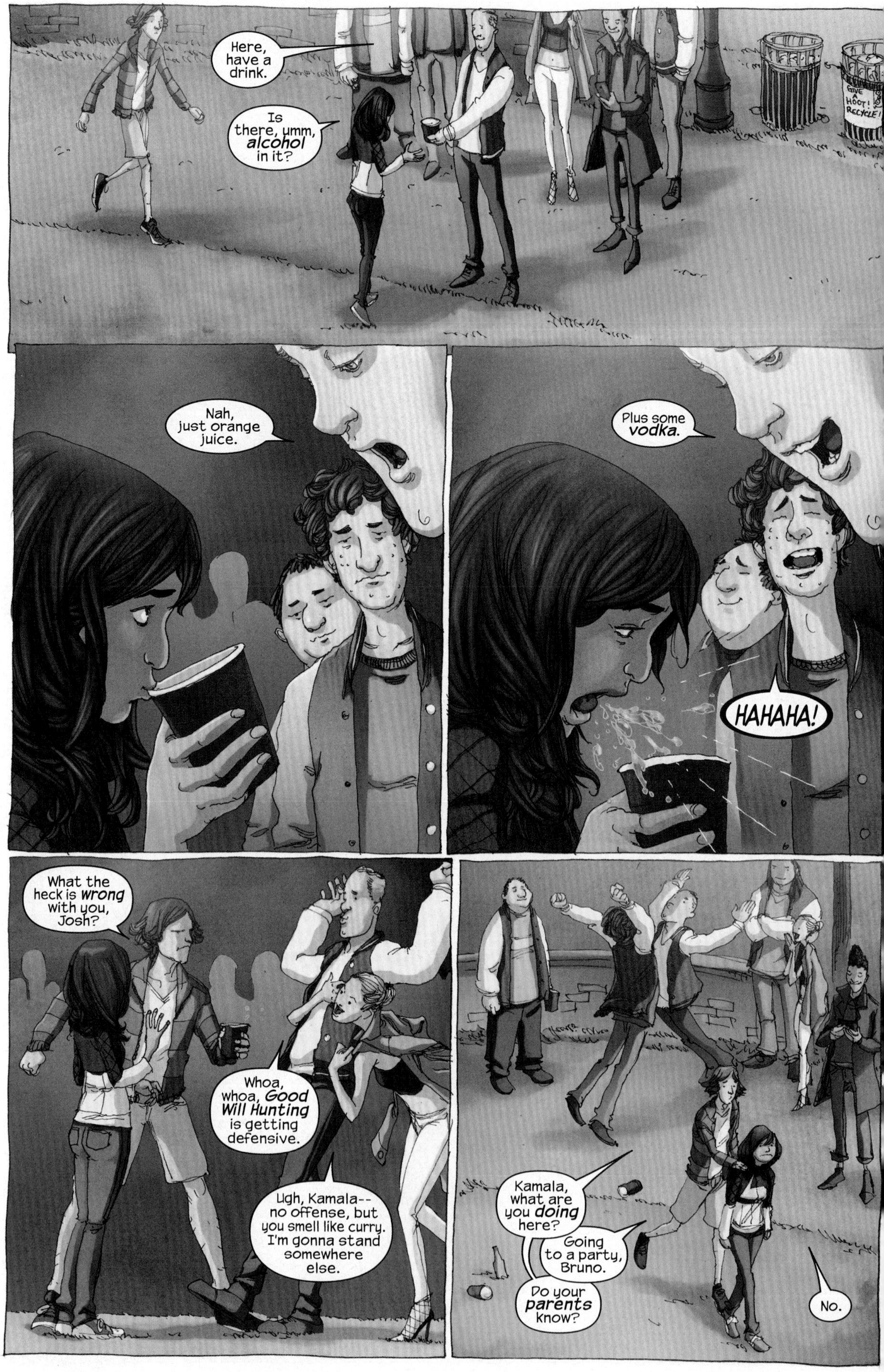
Here, have a drink.
Is there, umm, alcohol in it?
GIVE A HOOT! RECYCLE!
Nah, just orange juice.
Plus some vodka.
HAHAHA!
What the heck is wrong with you, Josh?
Whoa, whoa, Good Will Hunting is getting defensive.
Ugh, Kamala-- no offense, but you smell like curry. I'm gonna stand somewhere else.
Kamala, what are you doing here?
Going to a party, Bruno.
Do your parents know?
No.

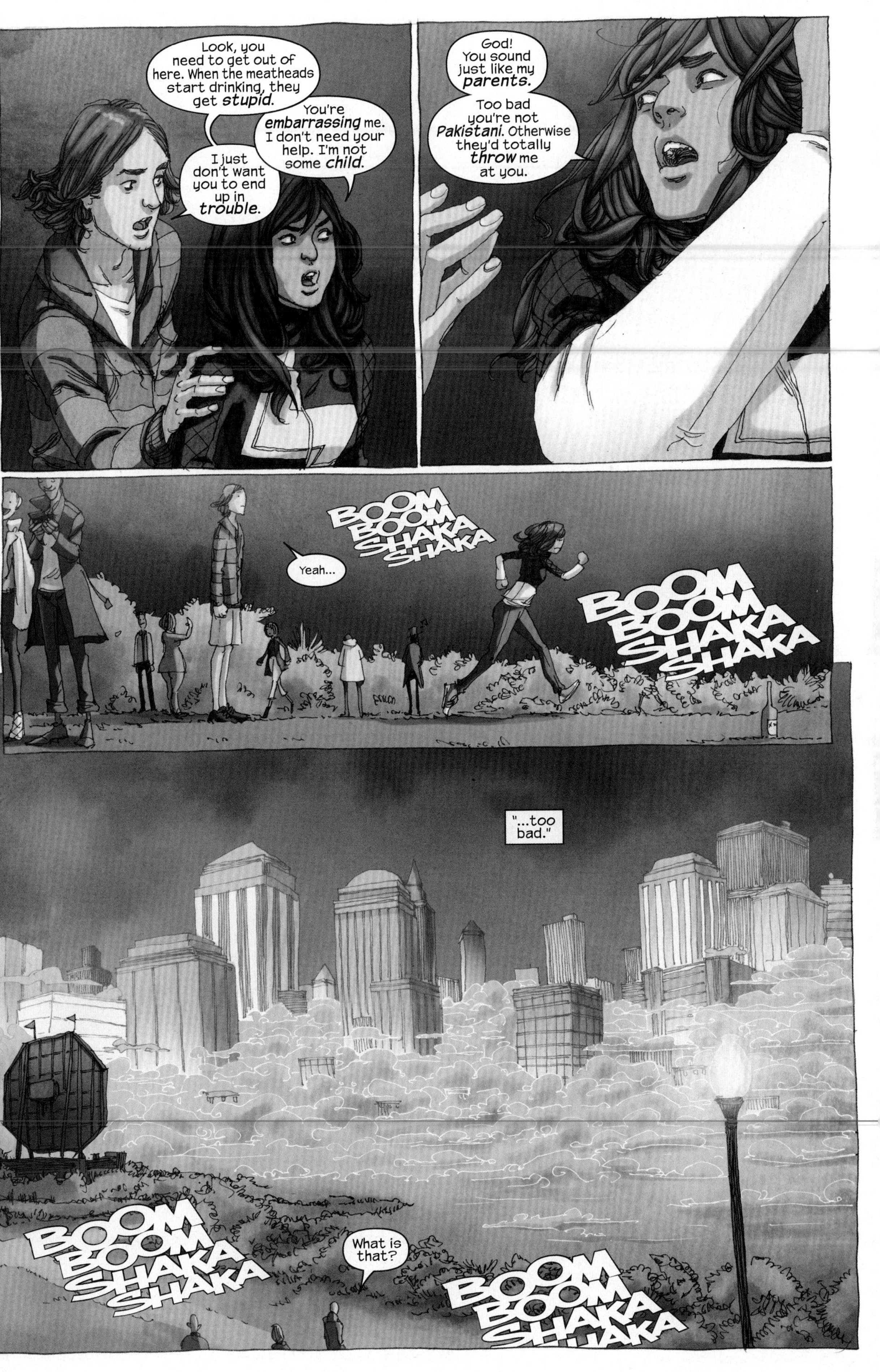

Look, you need to get out of here. When the meatheads start drinking, they get stupid.
You're embarrassing me. I don't need your help. I'm not some child.
I just don't want you to end up in trouble.
God! You sound just like my parents.
Too bad you're not Pakistani. Otherwise they'd totally throw me at you.
BOOM BOOM SHAKA SHAKA
Yeah...
BOOM BOOM SHAKA SHAKA
"...too bad."
BOOM BOOM SHAKA SHAKA
What is that?
BOOM BOOM SHAKA SHAKA

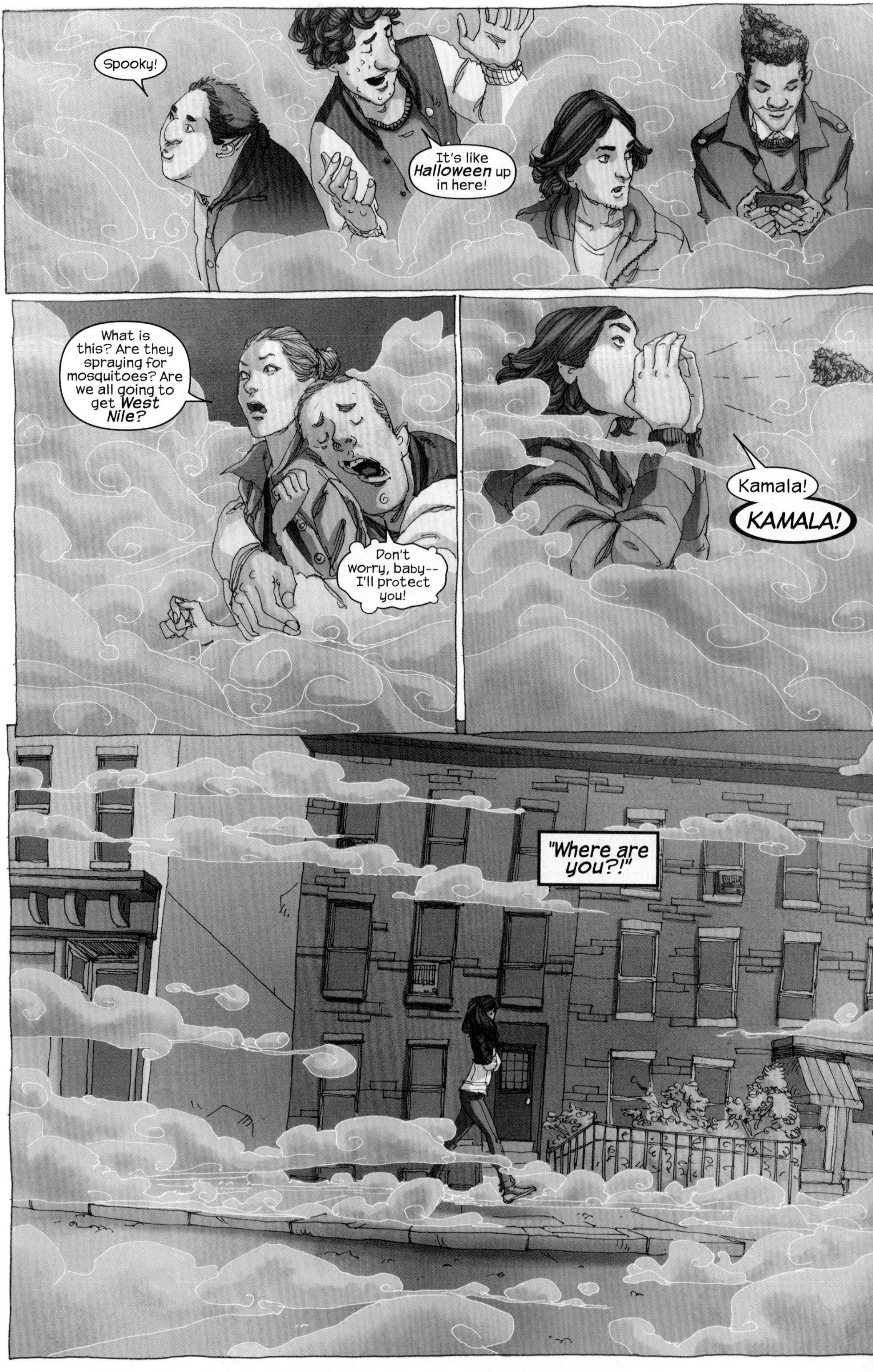
Spooky!
It's like Halloween up in here!
What is this? Are they spraying for mosquitoes? Are we all going to get West Nile?
Don't worry, baby-- I'll protect you!
Kamala!
KAMALA!
"Where are you?!"

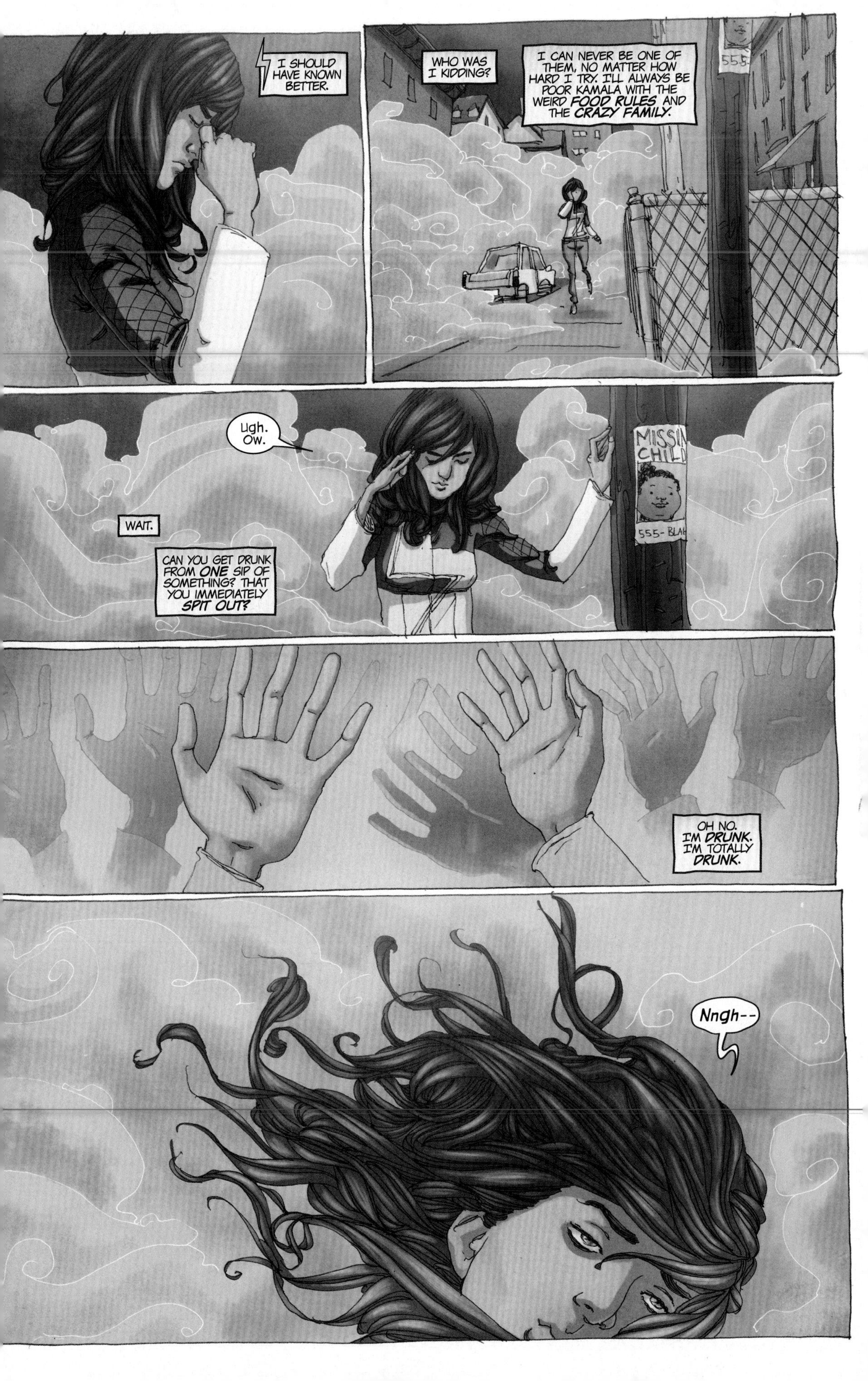
I SHOULD HAVE KNOWN BETTER.
WHO WAS I KIDDING?
I CAN NEVER BE ONE OF THEM, NO MATTER HOW HARD I TRY. I'LL ALWAYS BE POOR KAMALA WITH THE WEIRD FOOD RULES AND THE CRAZY FAMILY.
555
Ugh. Ow.
MISSIN CHILD
555- BLAH
WAIT.
CAN YOU GET DRUNK FROM ONE SIP OF SOMETHING? THAT YOU IMMEDIATELY SPIT OUT?
OH NO. I'M DRUNK. I'M TOTALLY DRUNK.
Nngh--

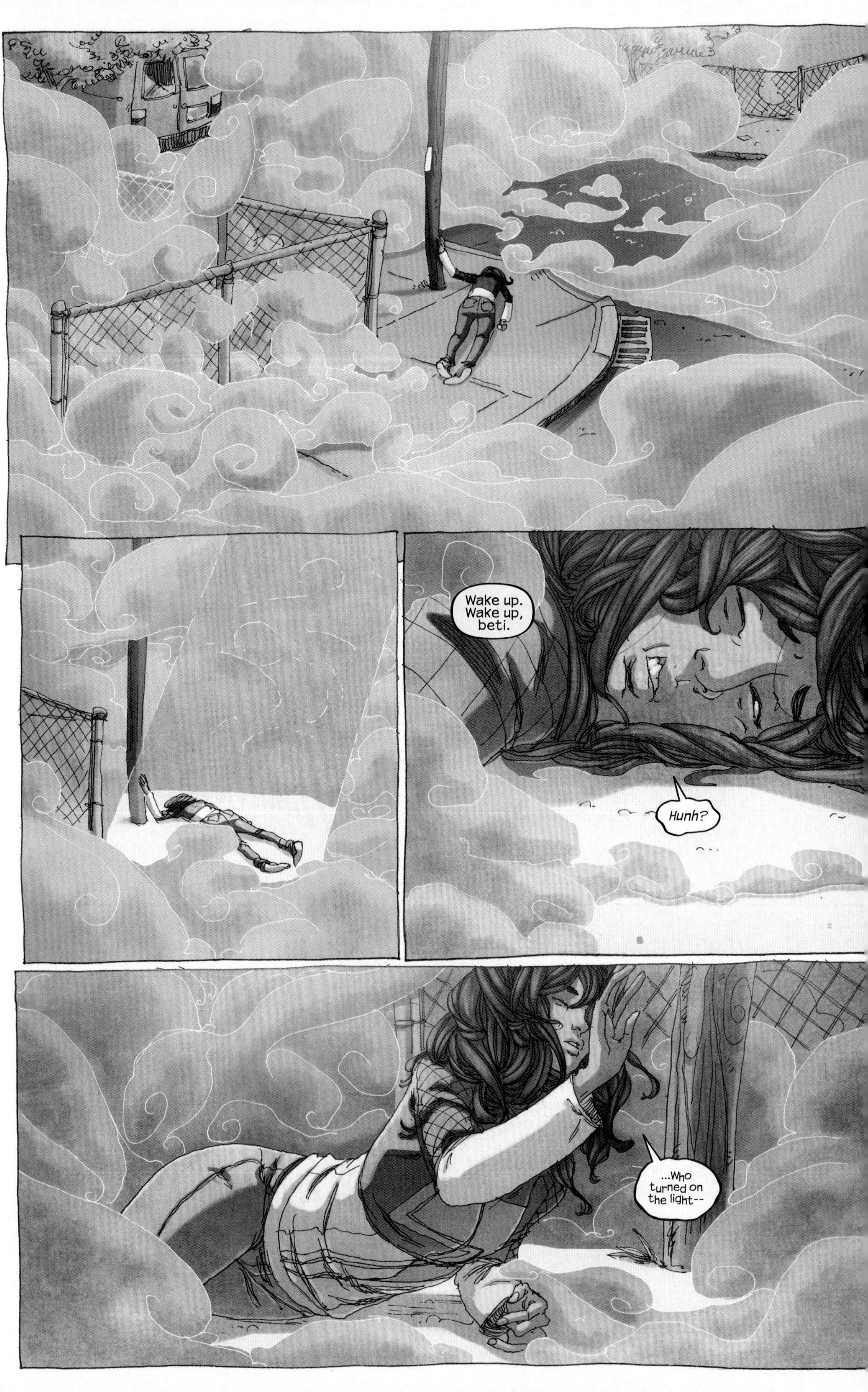
Wake up. Wake up, beti.
Hunh?
...Who turned on the light--

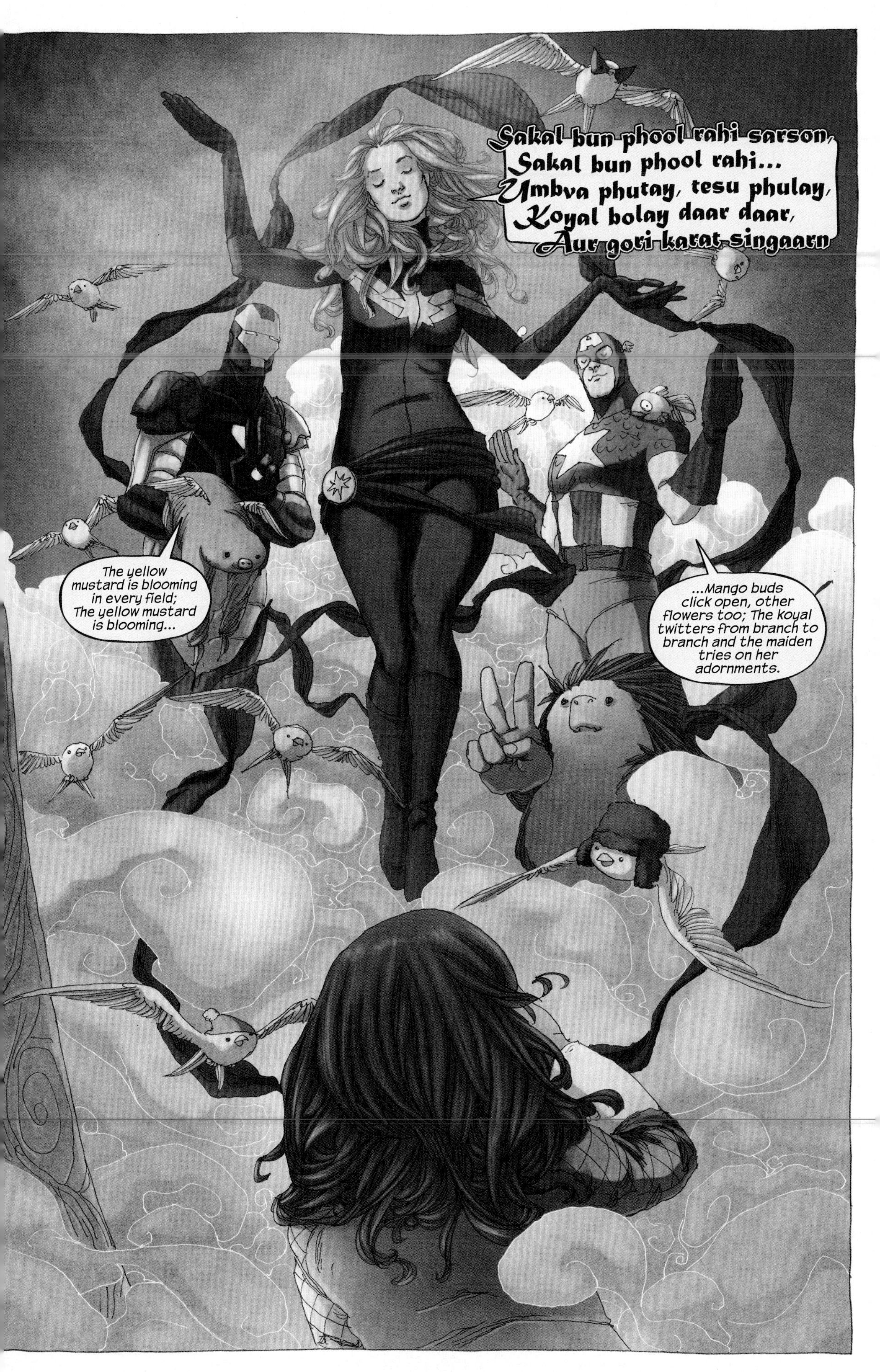
Sakal bun phool rahi sarson, Sakal bun phool rahi... Umbva phutay, tesu phulay, Koyal bolay daar daar, Aur gori karat singaarn
The yellow mustard is blooming in every field; The yellow mustard is blooming...
...Mango buds click open, other flowers too; The koyal twitters from branch to branch and the maiden tries on her adornments.

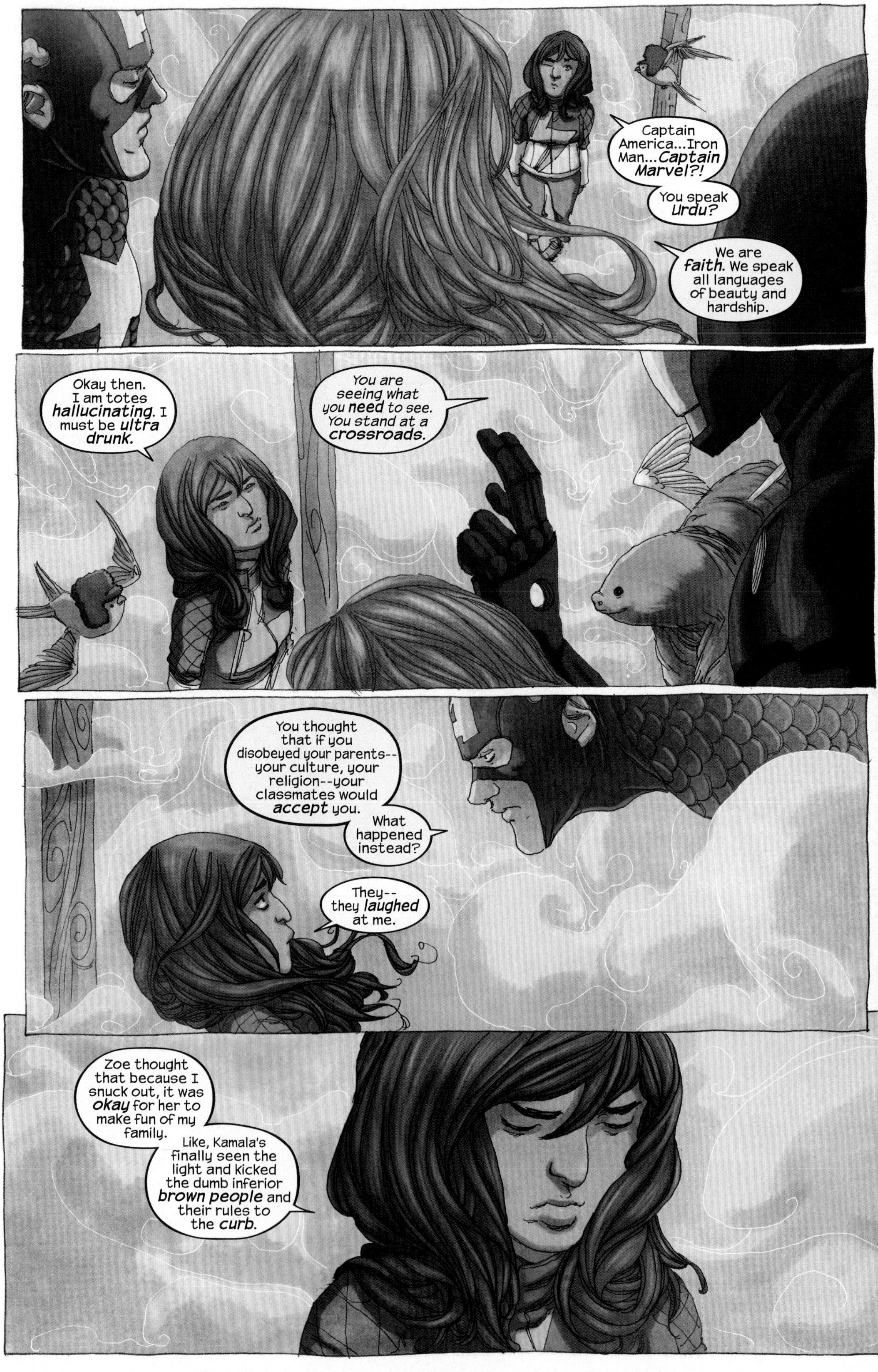
Captain America...Iron Man...Captain Marvel?!
You speak Urdu?
We are faith. We speak all languages of beauty and hardship.
Okay then. I am totes hallucinating. I must be ultra drunk.
You are seeing what you need to see. You stand at a crossroads.
You thought that if you disobeyed your parents--your culture, your religion--your classmates would accept you.
What happened instead?
They--they laughed at me.
Zoe thought that because I snuck out, it was okay for her to make fun of my family.
Like, Kamala's finally seen the light and kicked the dumb inferior brown people and their rules to the curb.

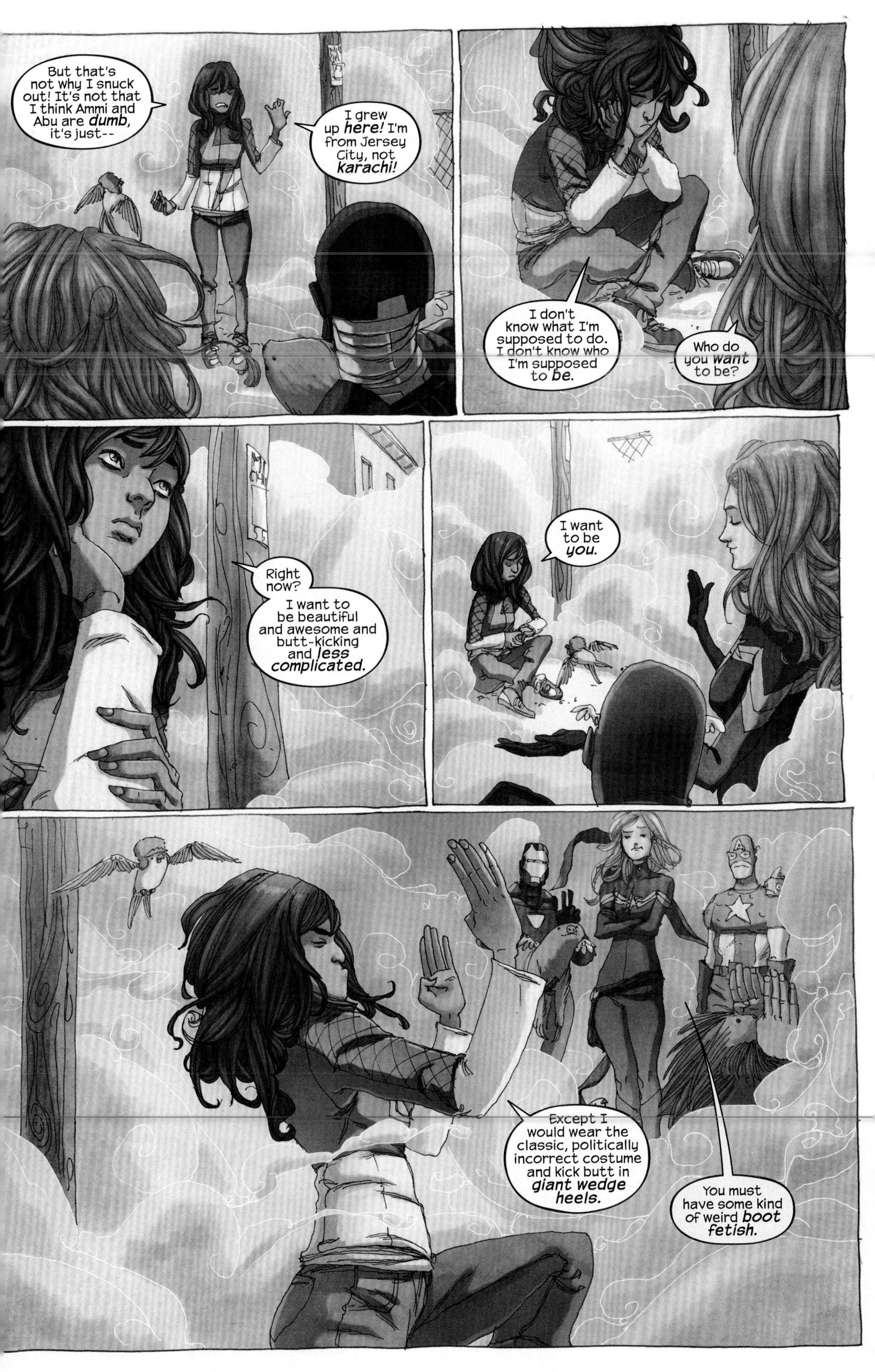

But that's not why I snuck out! It's not that I think Ammi and Abu are *dumb*, it's just--
I grew up *here!* I'm from Jersey City, not *karachi!*
I don't know what I'm supposed to do. I don't know who I'm supposed to *be*.
Who do you *want* to be?
Right now?
I want to be beautiful and awesome and butt-kicking and *less complicated.*
I want to be *you*.
Except I would wear the classic, politically incorrect costume and kick butt in *giant wedge heels.*
You must have some kind of weird *boot fetish.*

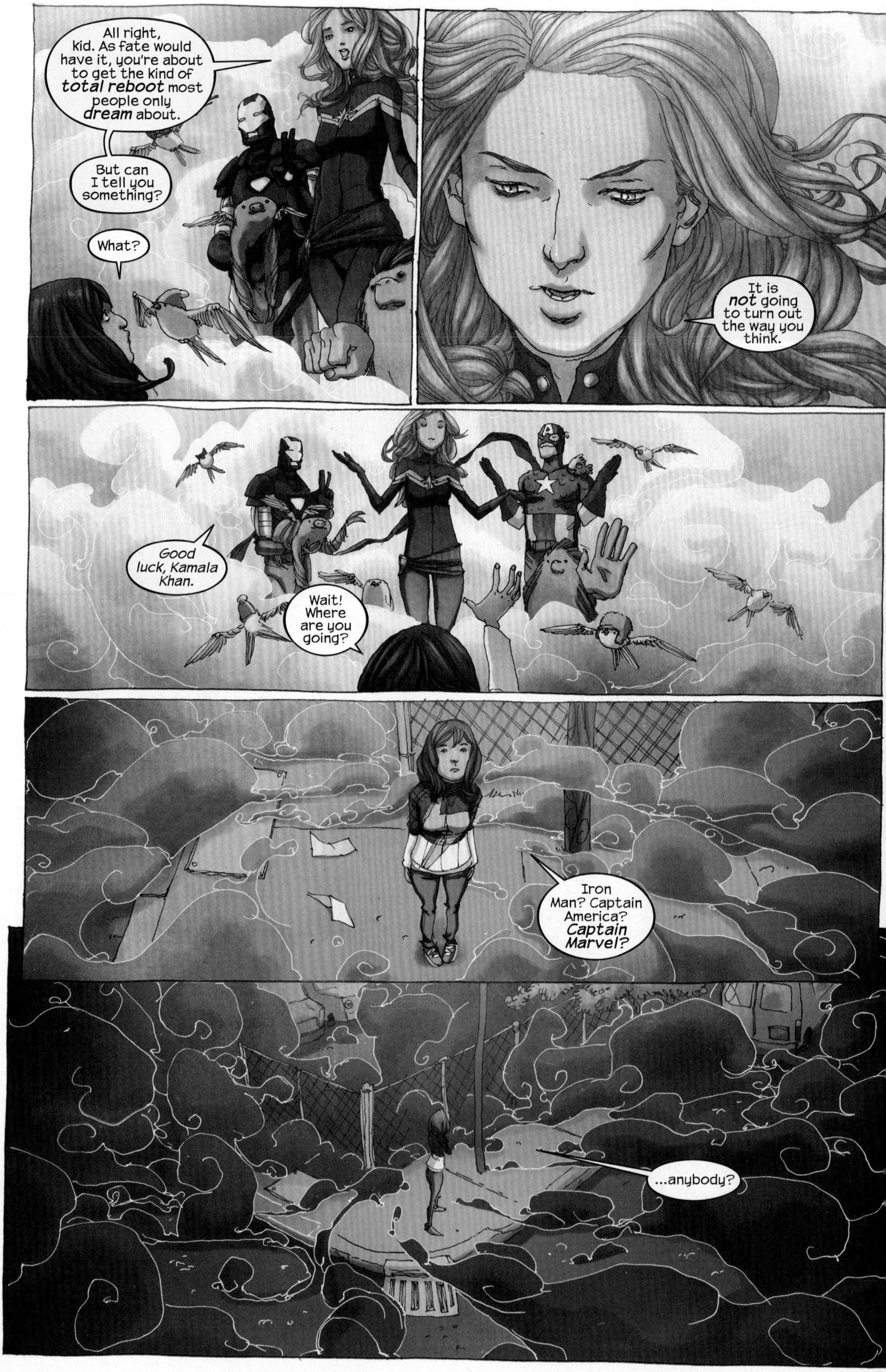
All right, kid. As fate would have it, you're about to get the kind of **total reboot** most people only **dream** about.
But can I tell you something?
What?
It is **not** going to turn out the way you think.
Good luck, Kamala Khan.
Wait! Where are you going?
Iron Man? Captain America? **Captain Marvel?**
...anybody?

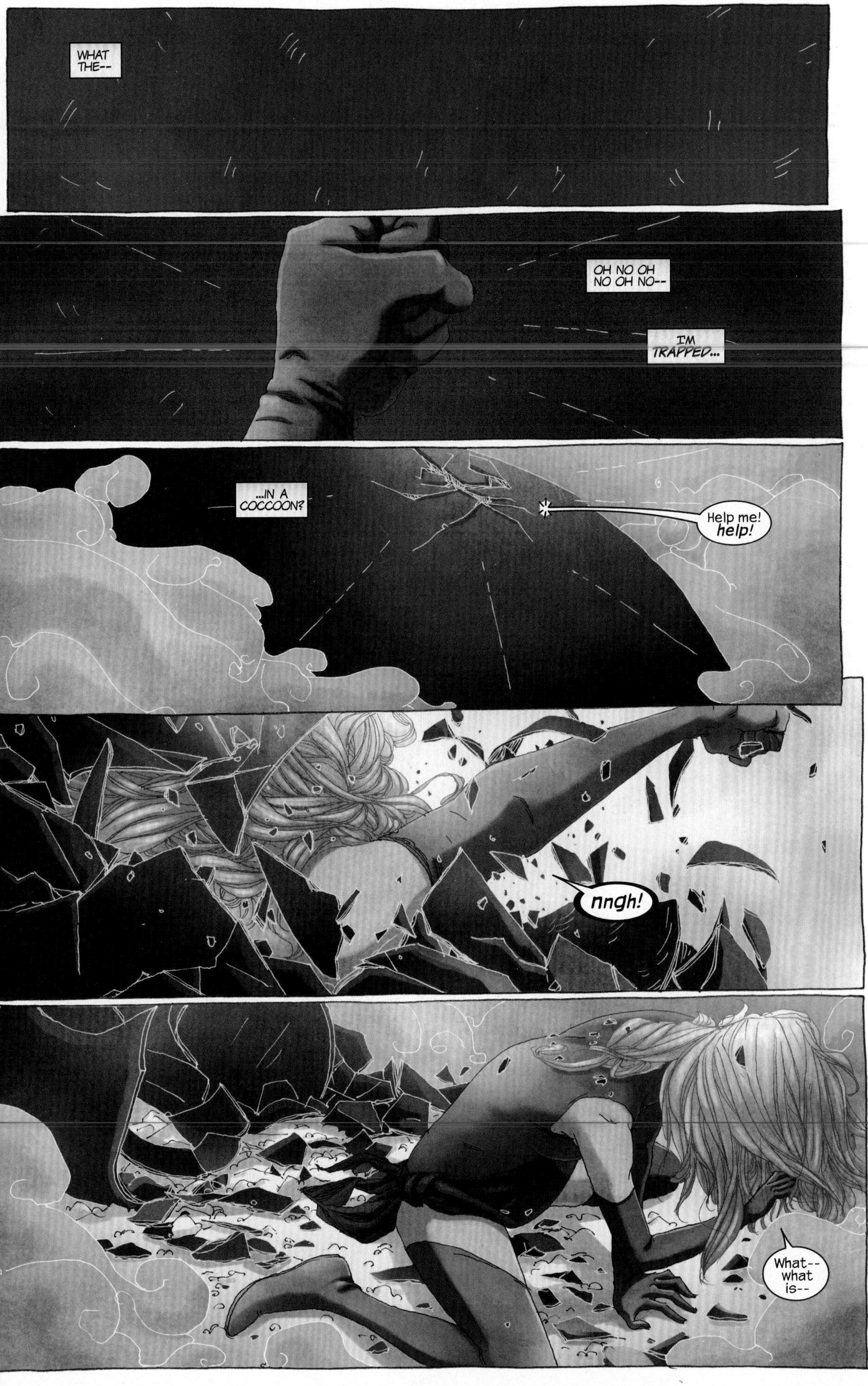
WHAT THE--
OH NO OH NO OH NO--
I'M TRAPPED...
...IN A COCCOON?
Help me! help!
nngh!
What-- what is--

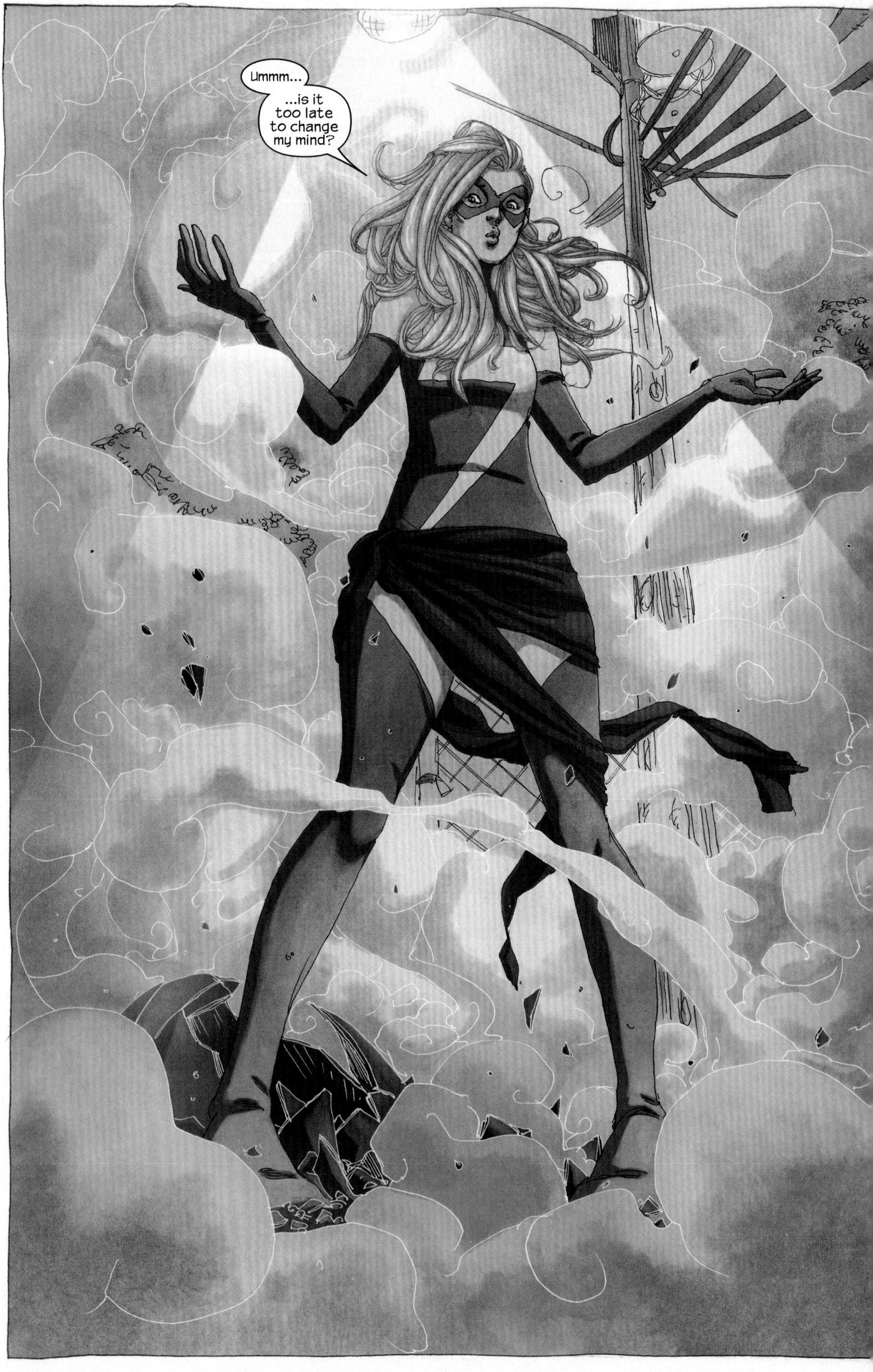
Ummm...
...is it too late to change my mind?

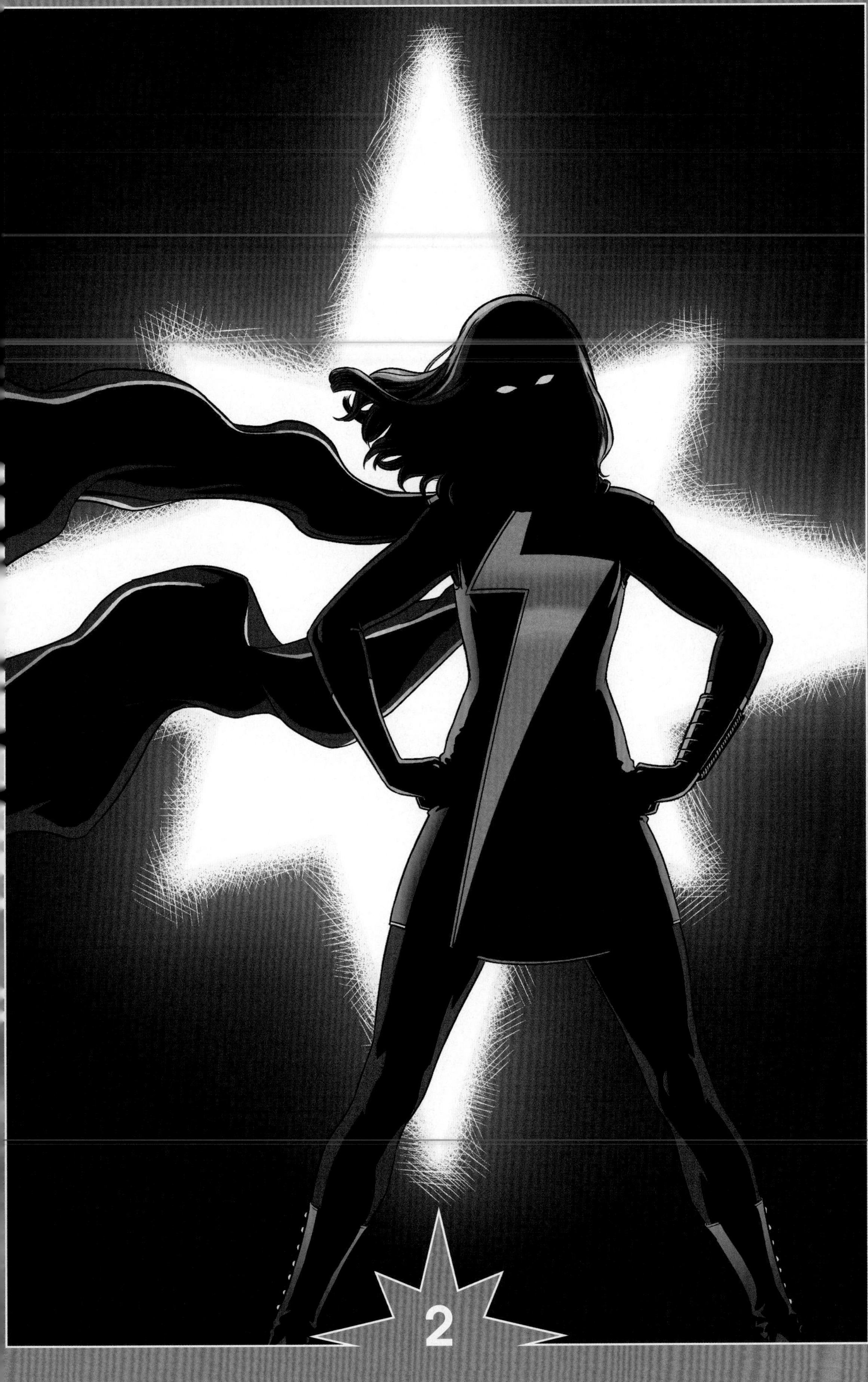
2

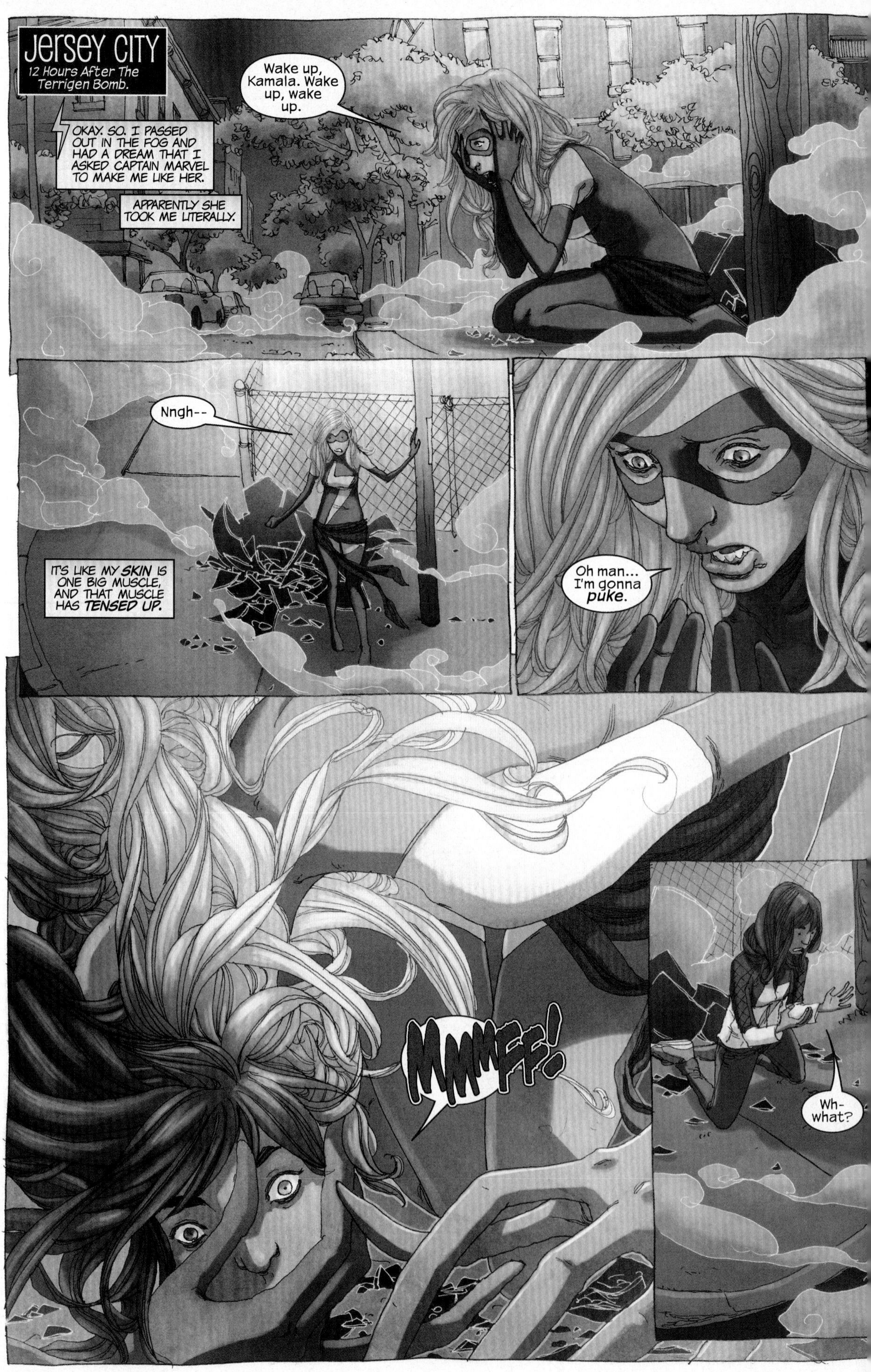
JERSEY CITY
12 Hours After The Terrigen Bomb.
Wake up, Kamala. Wake up, wake up.
OKAY. SO. I PASSED OUT IN THE FOG AND HAD A DREAM THAT I ASKED CAPTAIN MARVEL TO MAKE ME LIKE HER.
APPARENTLY SHE TOOK ME LITERALLY.
Nngh--
IT'S LIKE MY SKIN IS ONE BIG MUSCLE, AND THAT MUSCLE HAS TENSED UP.
Oh man... I'm gonna puke.
MMMFF!
Wh-what?

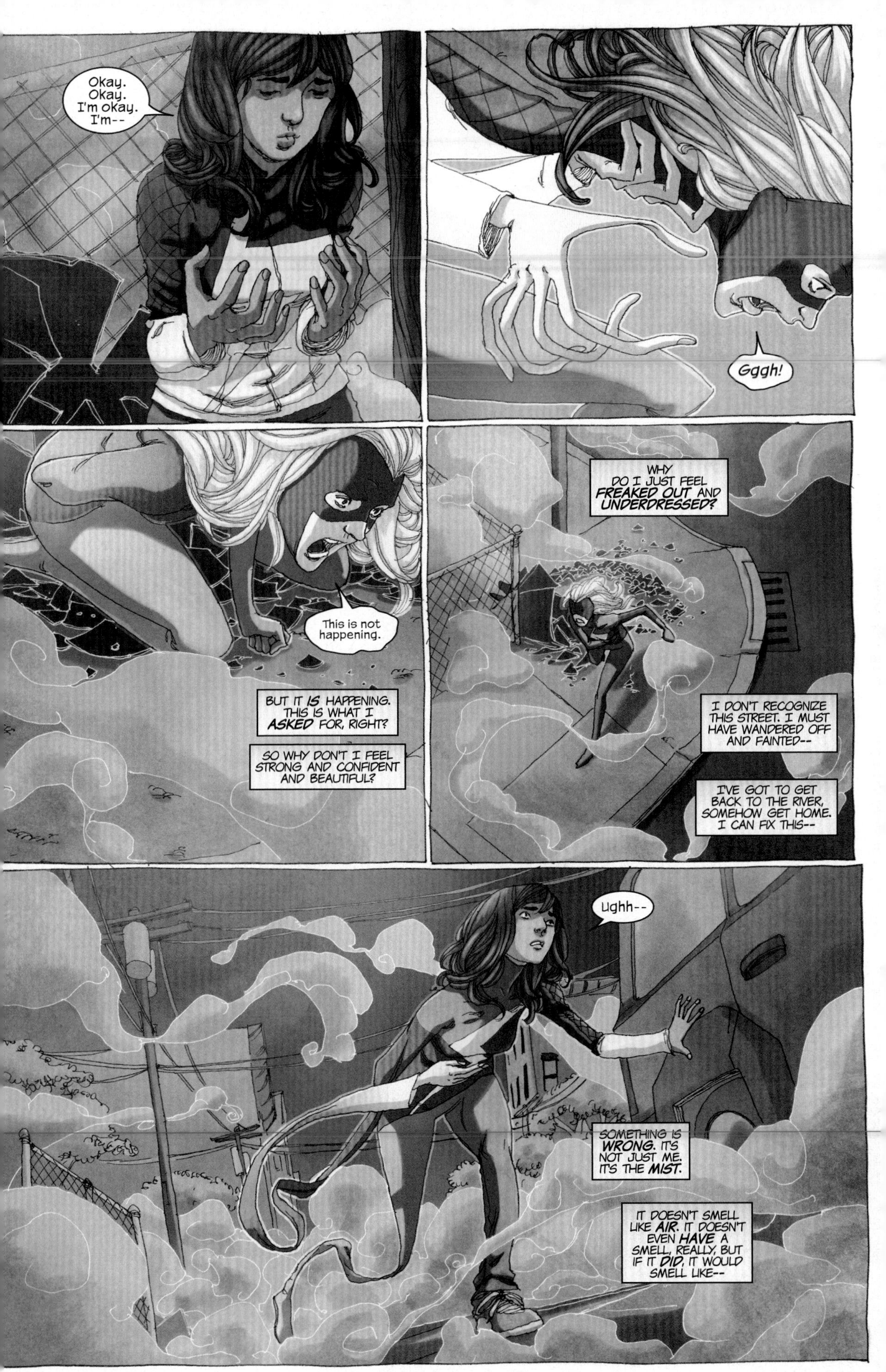
Okay. Okay. I'm okay. I'm--
Gggh!
This is not happening.
BUT IT IS HAPPENING. THIS IS WHAT I ASKED FOR, RIGHT?
SO WHY DON'T I FEEL STRONG AND CONFIDENT AND BEAUTIFUL?
WHY DO I JUST FEEL FREAKED OUT AND UNDERDRESSED?
I DON'T RECOGNIZE THIS STREET. I MUST HAVE WANDERED OFF AND FAINTED--
I'VE GOT TO GET BACK TO THE RIVER, SOMEHOW GET HOME. I CAN FIX THIS--
Ughh--
SOMETHING IS WRONG. IT'S NOT JUST ME. IT'S THE MIST.
IT DOESN'T SMELL LIKE AIR. IT DOESN'T EVEN HAVE A SMELL, REALLY, BUT IF IT DID, IT WOULD SMELL LIKE--

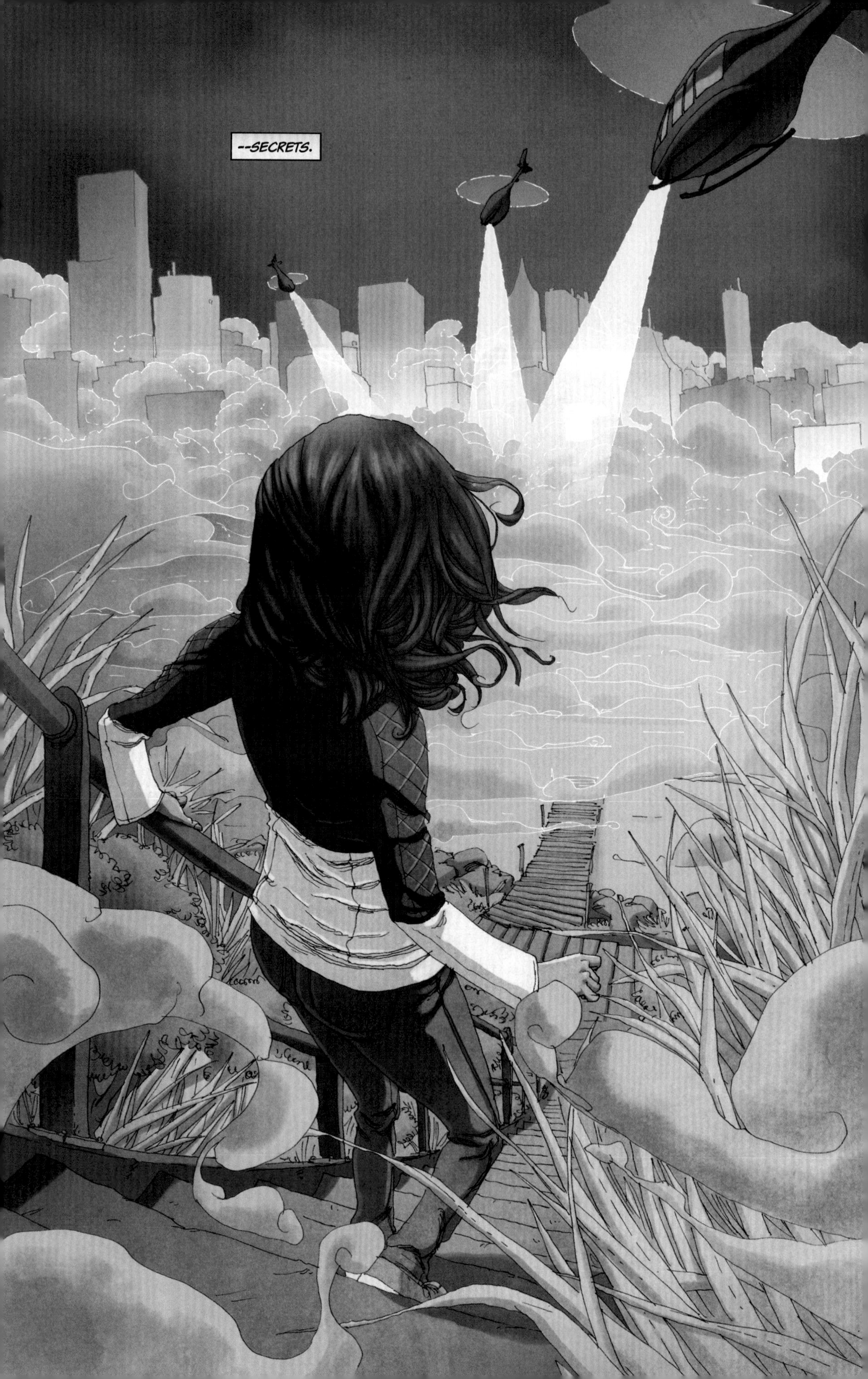
--SECRETS.

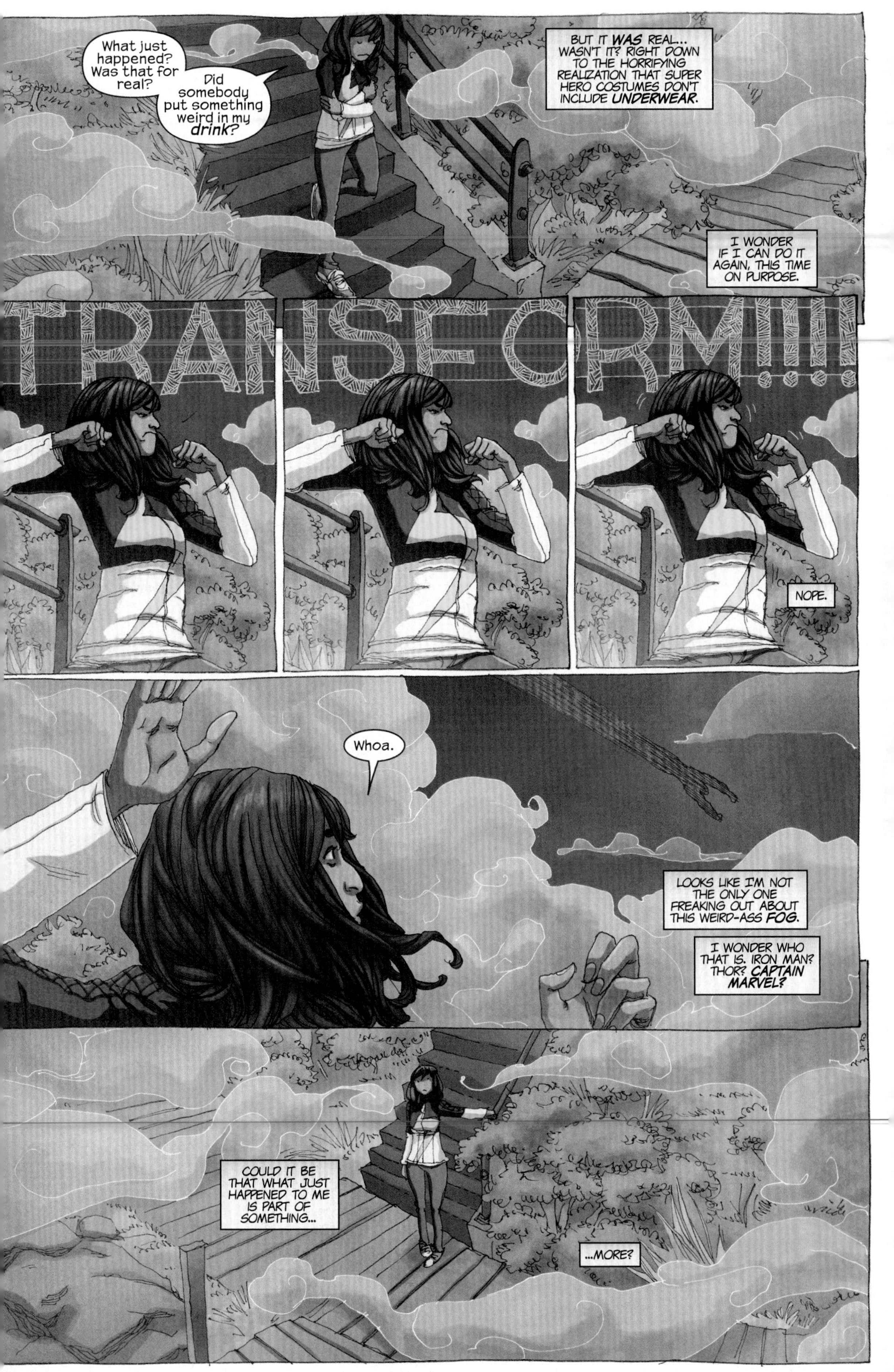
What just happened? Was that for real?
Did somebody put something weird in my drink?
BUT IT WAS REAL... WASN'T IT? RIGHT DOWN TO THE HORRIFYING REALIZATION THAT SUPER HERO COSTUMES DON'T INCLUDE UNDERWEAR.
I WONDER IF I CAN DO IT AGAIN, THIS TIME ON PURPOSE.
TRANSFORM!!!!
NOPE.
Whoa.
LOOKS LIKE I'M NOT THE ONLY ONE FREAKING OUT ABOUT THIS WEIRD-ASS FOG.
I WONDER WHO THAT IS. IRON MAN? THOR? CAPTAIN MARVEL?
COULD IT BE THAT WHAT JUST HAPPENED TO ME IS PART OF SOMETHING...
...MORE?

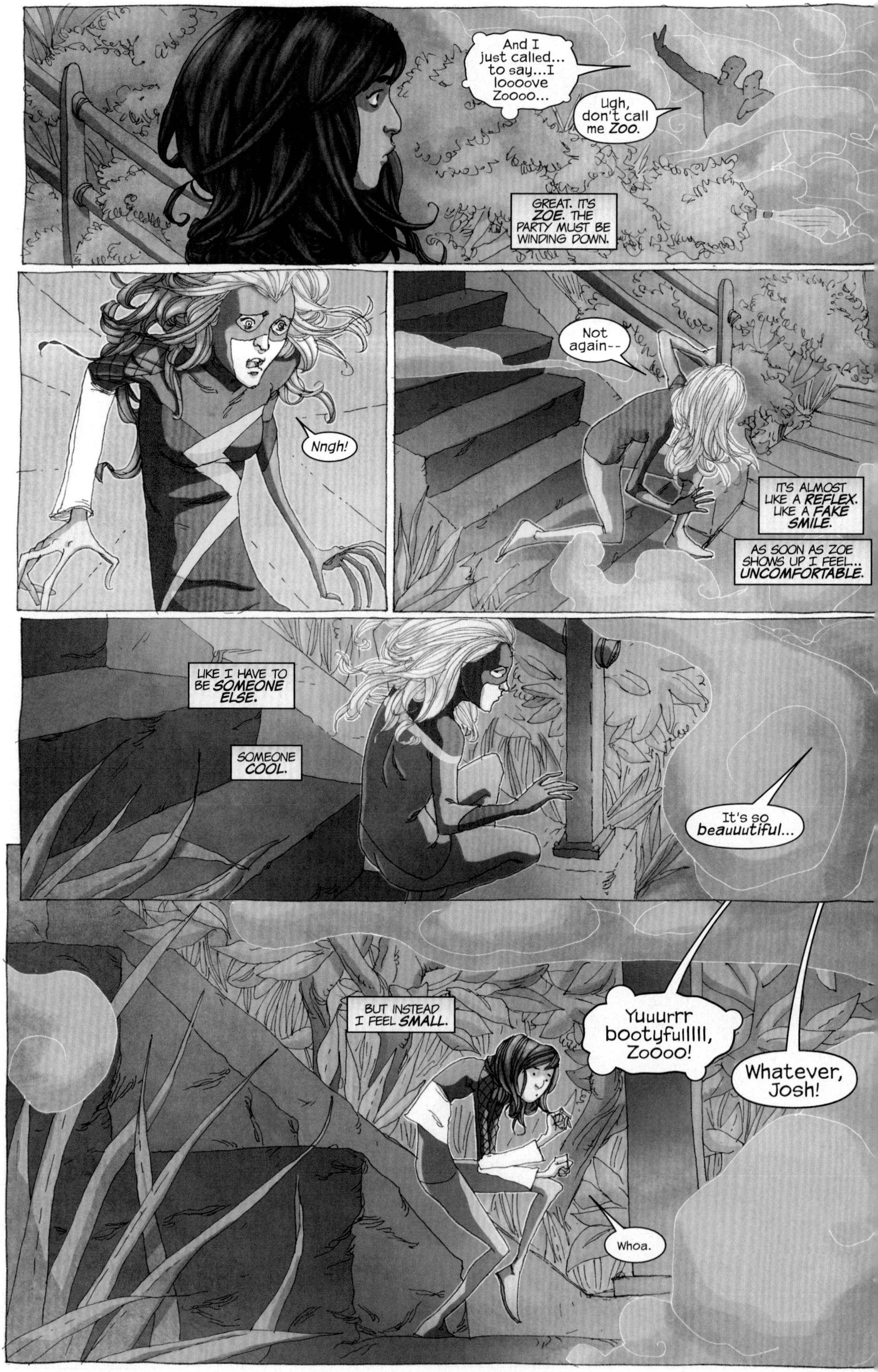
And I just called... to say...I looooove Zoooo...
Ugh, don't call me ZOO.
GREAT. IT'S ZOE. THE PARTY MUST BE WINDING DOWN.
Nngh!
Not again--
IT'S ALMOST LIKE A REFLEX. LIKE A FAKE SMILE.
AS SOON AS ZOE SHOWS UP I FEEL... UNCOMFORTABLE.
LIKE I HAVE TO BE SOMEONE ELSE.
SOMEONE COOL.
It's so beauuutiful...
BUT INSTEAD I FEEL SMALL.
Yuuurrr bootyfullllll, Zoooo!
Whatever, Josh!
Whoa.

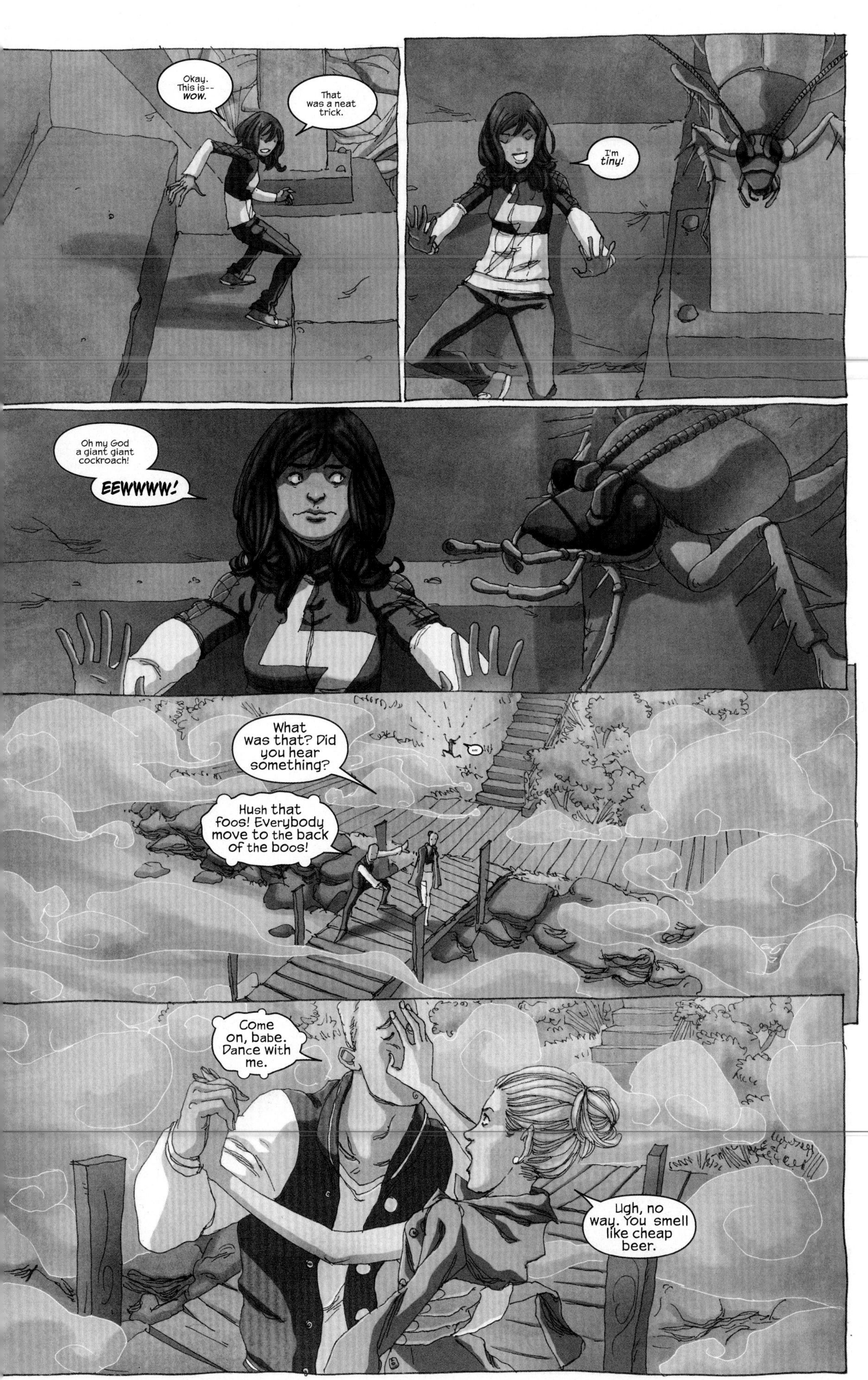
Okay. This is-- WOW.
That was a neat trick.
I'm tiny!
Oh my God a giant giant cockroach!
EEWWWW!
What was that? Did you hear something?
Hush that foos! Everybody move to the back of the boos!
Come on, babe. Dance with me.
Ugh, no way. You smell like cheap beer.

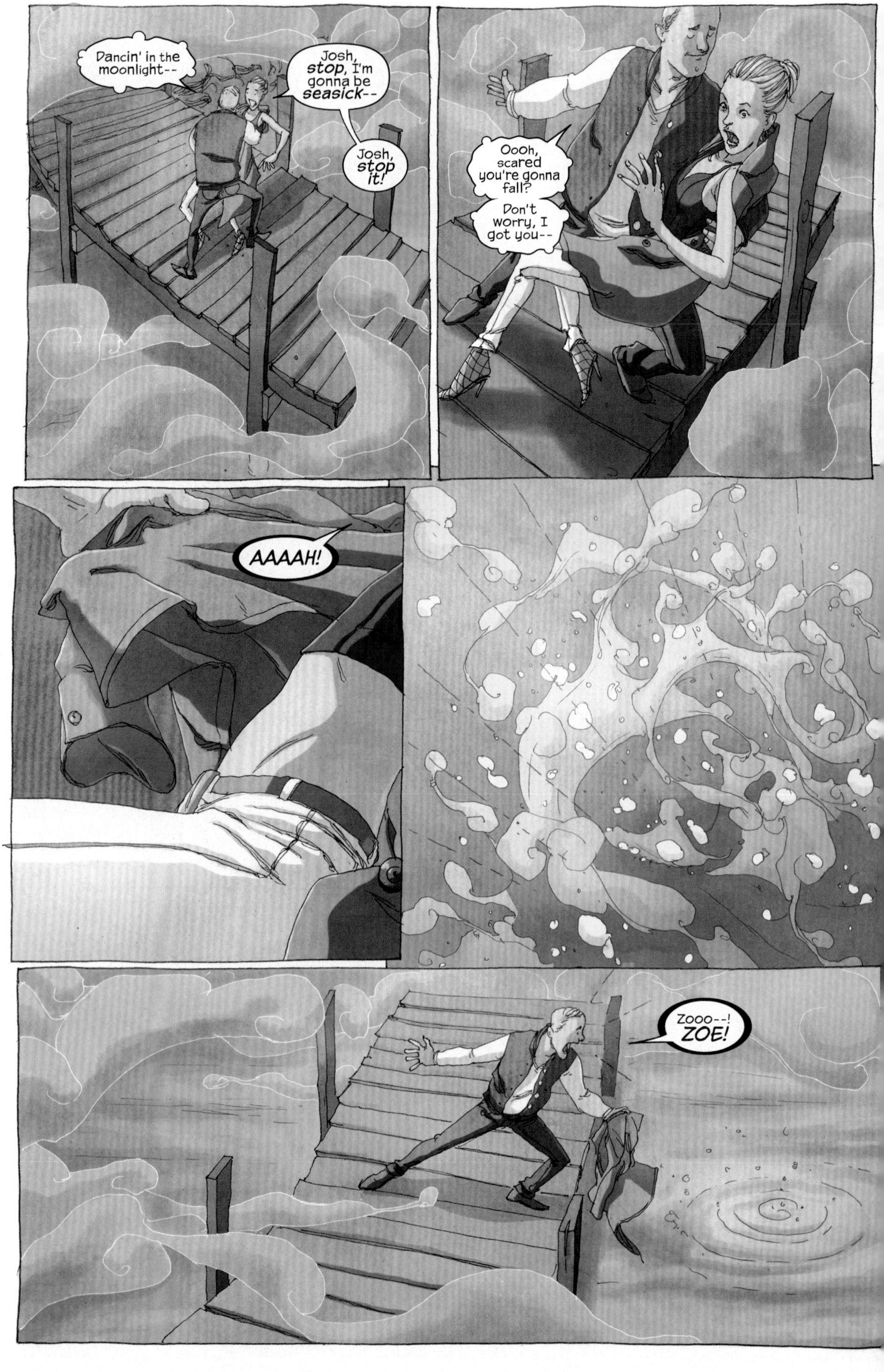
Dancin' in the moonlight--
Josh, stop, I'm gonna be seasick--
Josh, stop it!
Oooh, scared you're gonna fall?
Don't worry, I got you--
AAAAH!
Zooo--! ZOE!

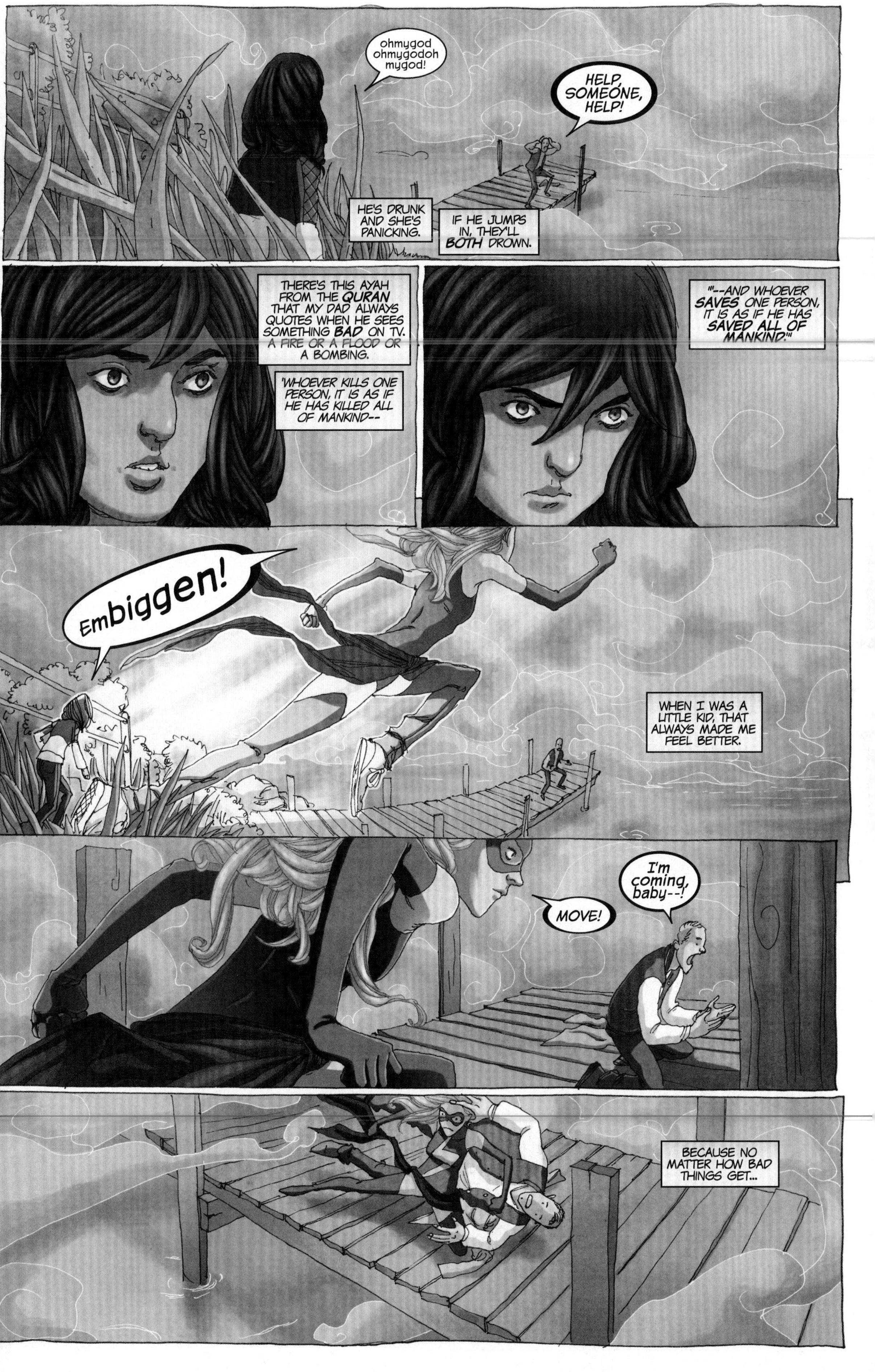
ohmygod ohmygodoh mygod!
HELP, SOMEONE, HELP!
HE'S DRUNK AND SHE'S PANICKING.
IF HE JUMPS IN, THEY'LL BOTH DROWN.
THERE'S THIS AYAH FROM THE QURAN THAT MY DAD ALWAYS QUOTES WHEN HE SEES SOMETHING BAD ON TV. A FIRE OR A FLOOD OR A BOMBING.
'WHOEVER KILLS ONE PERSON, IT IS AS IF HE HAS KILLED ALL OF MANKIND--
'"--AND WHOEVER SAVES ONE PERSON, IT IS AS IF HE HAS SAVED ALL OF MANKIND.'"
Embiggen!
WHEN I WAS A LITTLE KID, THAT ALWAYS MADE ME FEEL BETTER.
I'm coming, baby--!
MOVE!
BECAUSE NO MATTER HOW BAD THINGS GET...

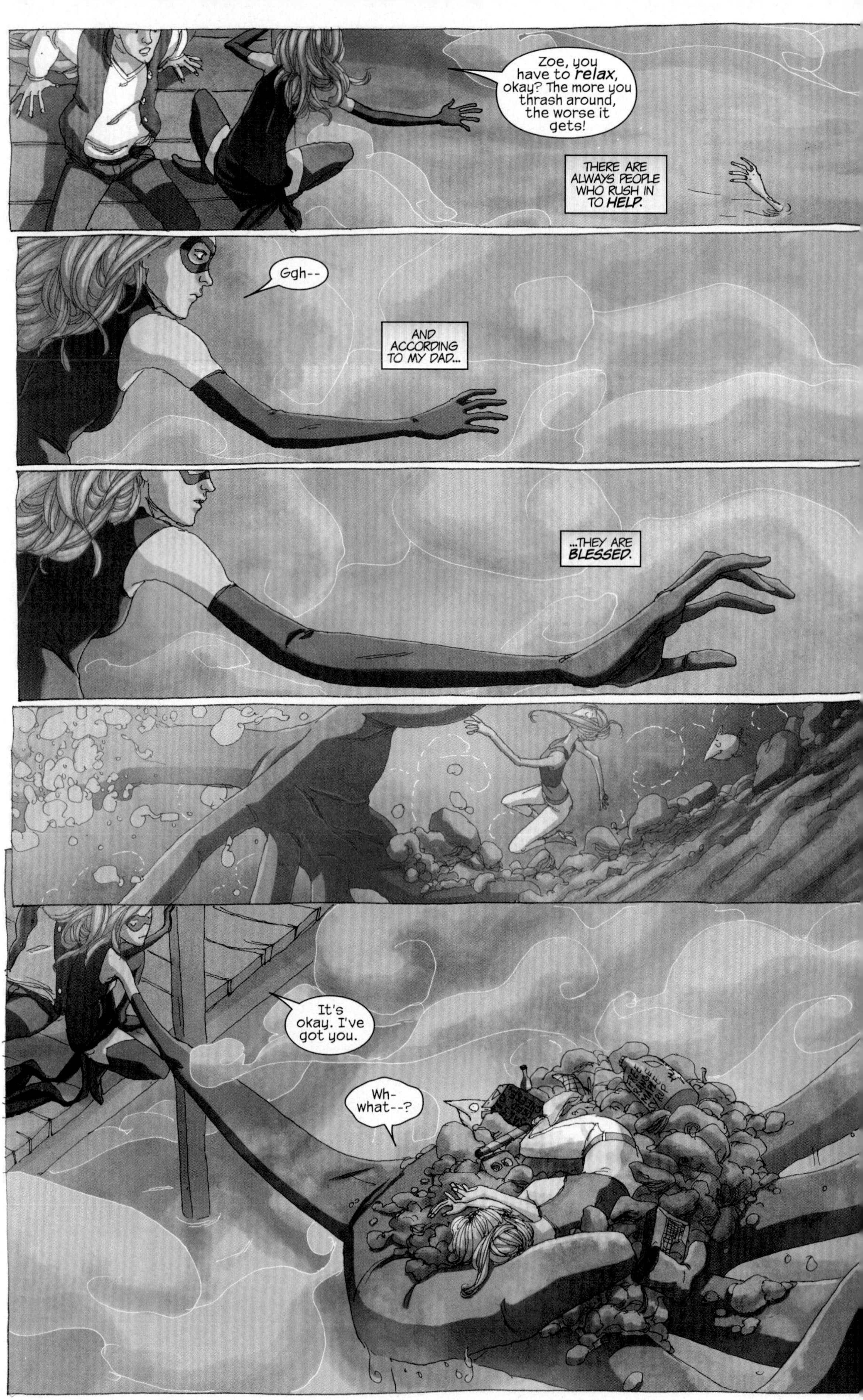
Zoe, you have to relax, okay? The more you thrash around, the worse it gets!
THERE ARE ALWAYS PEOPLE WHO RUSH IN TO HELP.
Ggh--
AND ACCORDING TO MY DAD...
...THEY ARE BLESSED.
It's okay. I've got you.
Wh- what--?

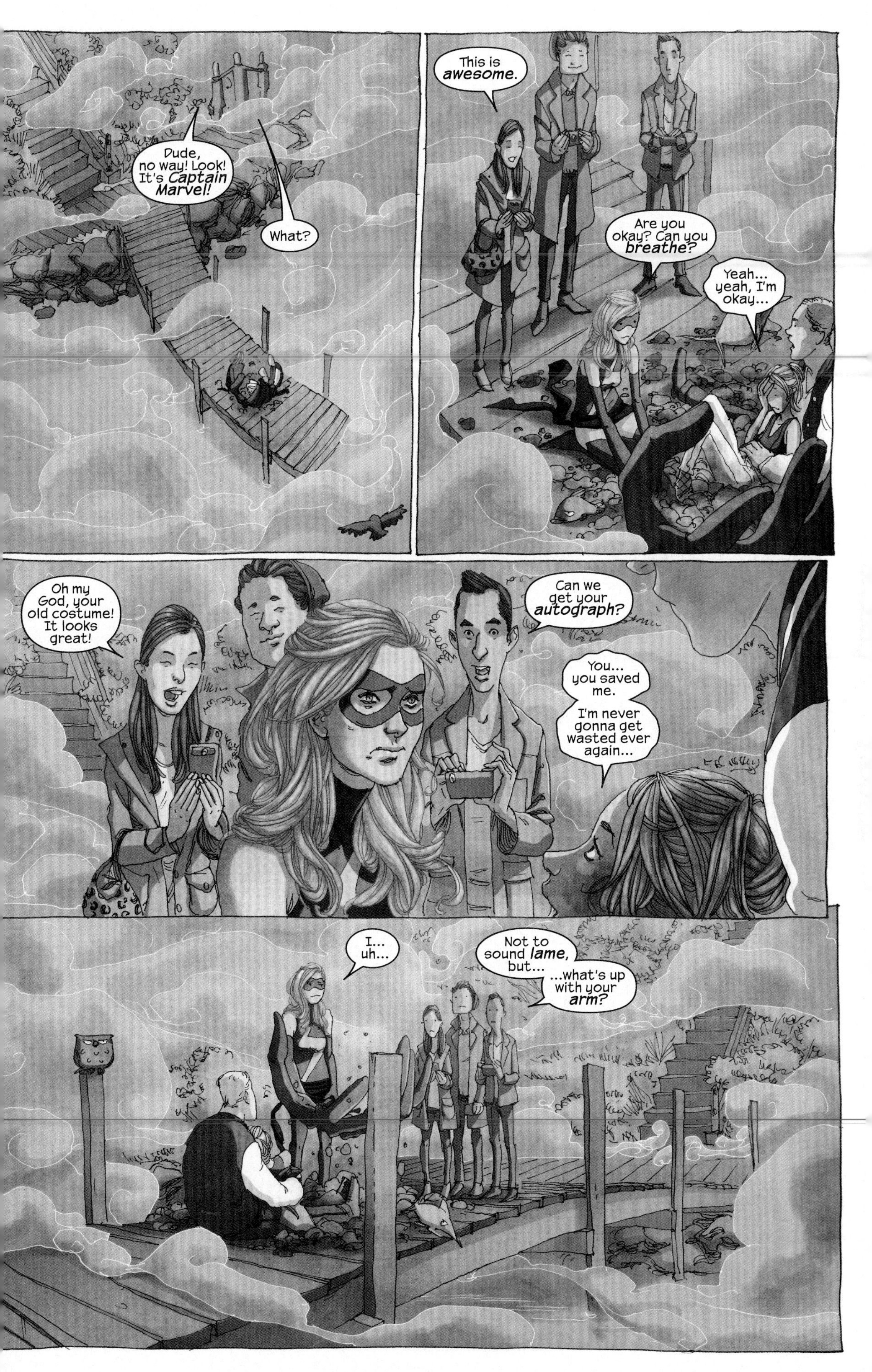
Dude, no way! Look! It's *Captain Marvel!*
What?
This is **awesome**.
Are you okay? Can you **breathe**?
Yeah... yeah, I'm okay...
Oh my God, your old costume! It looks great!
Can we get your **autograph**?
You... you saved me.
I'm never gonna get wasted ever again...
I... uh...
Not to sound **lame**, but...
...what's up with your **arm**?

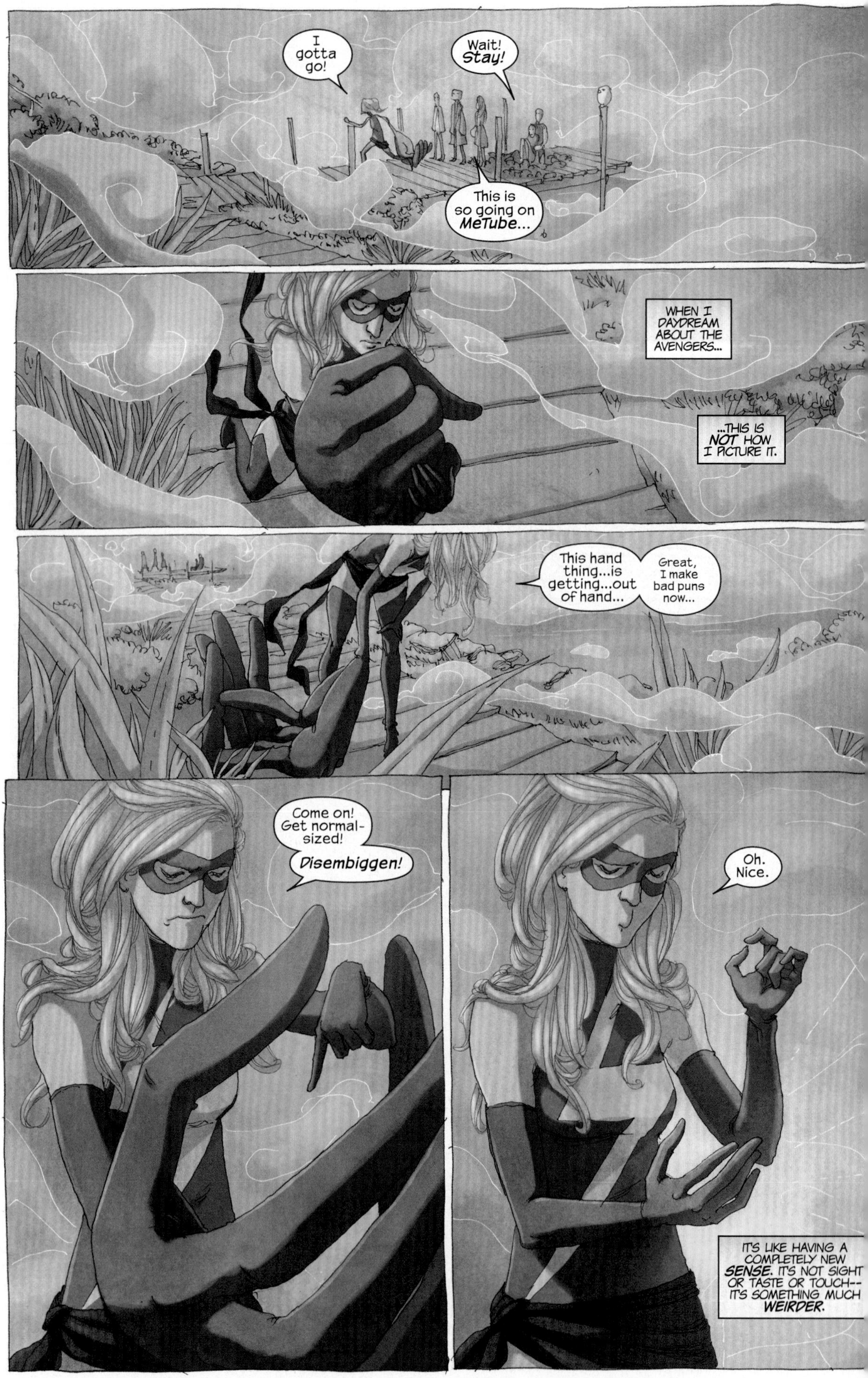
I gotta go!
Wait! Stay!
This is so going on MeTube...
WHEN I DAYDREAM ABOUT THE AVENGERS...
...THIS IS NOT HOW I PICTURE IT.
This hand thing...is getting...out of hand...
Great, I make bad puns now...
Come on! Get normal-sized!
Disembiggen!
Oh. Nice.
IT'S LIKE HAVING A COMPLETELY NEW SENSE. IT'S NOT SIGHT OR TASTE OR TOUCH--IT'S SOMETHING MUCH WEIRDER.

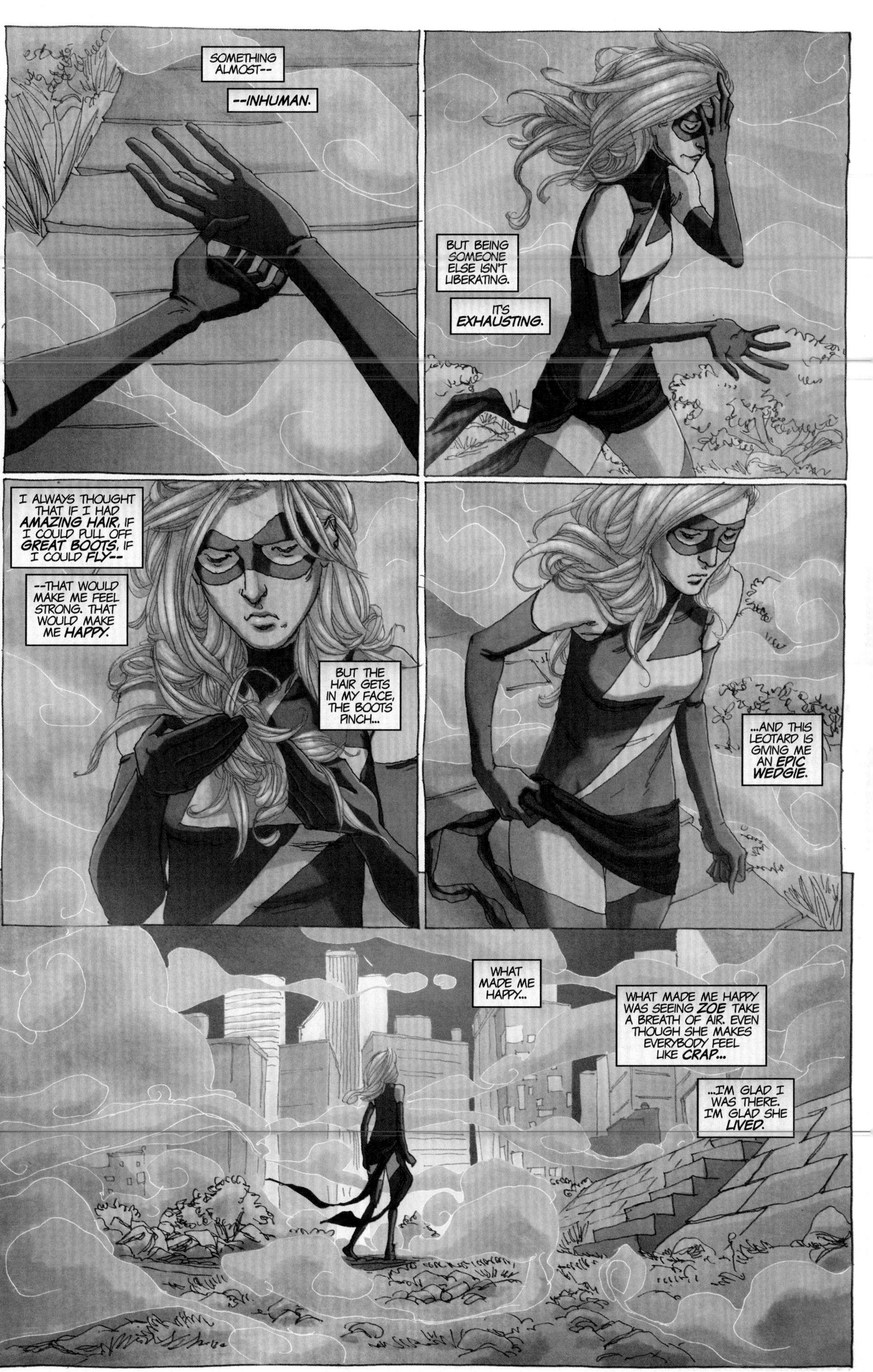
SOMETHING ALMOST--
--INHUMAN.
BUT BEING SOMEONE ELSE ISN'T LIBERATING.
IT'S EXHAUSTING.
I ALWAYS THOUGHT THAT IF I HAD AMAZING HAIR, IF I COULD PULL OFF GREAT BOOTS, IF I COULD FLY--
--THAT WOULD MAKE ME FEEL STRONG. THAT WOULD MAKE ME HAPPY.
BUT THE HAIR GETS IN MY FACE, THE BOOTS PINCH...
...AND THIS LEOTARD IS GIVING ME AN EPIC WEDGIE.
WHAT MADE ME HAPPY...
WHAT MADE ME HAPPY WAS SEEING ZOE TAKE A BREATH OF AIR. EVEN THOUGH SHE MAKES EVERYBODY FEEL LIKE CRAP...
...I'M GLAD I WAS THERE. I'M GLAD SHE LIVED.

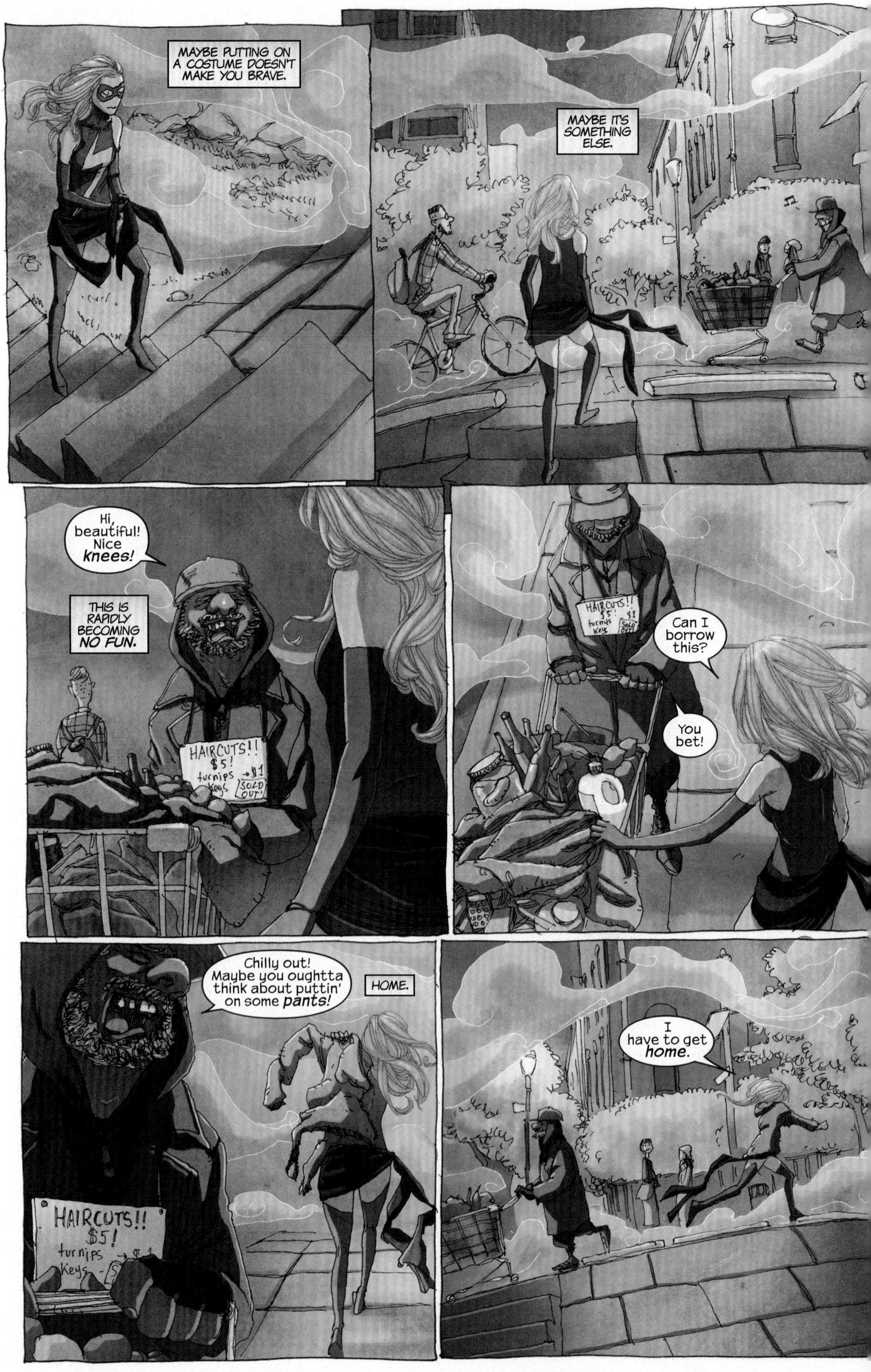
MAYBE PUTTING ON A COSTUME DOESN'T MAKE YOU BRAVE.
MAYBE IT'S SOMETHING ELSE.
Hi, beautiful! Nice knees!
THIS IS RAPIDLY BECOMING NO FUN.
HAIRCUTS!! $5! turnips → $1 Keys SOLD OUT!
Can I borrow this?
You bet!
Chilly out! Maybe you oughtta think about puttin' on some pants!
HOME.
I have to get home.

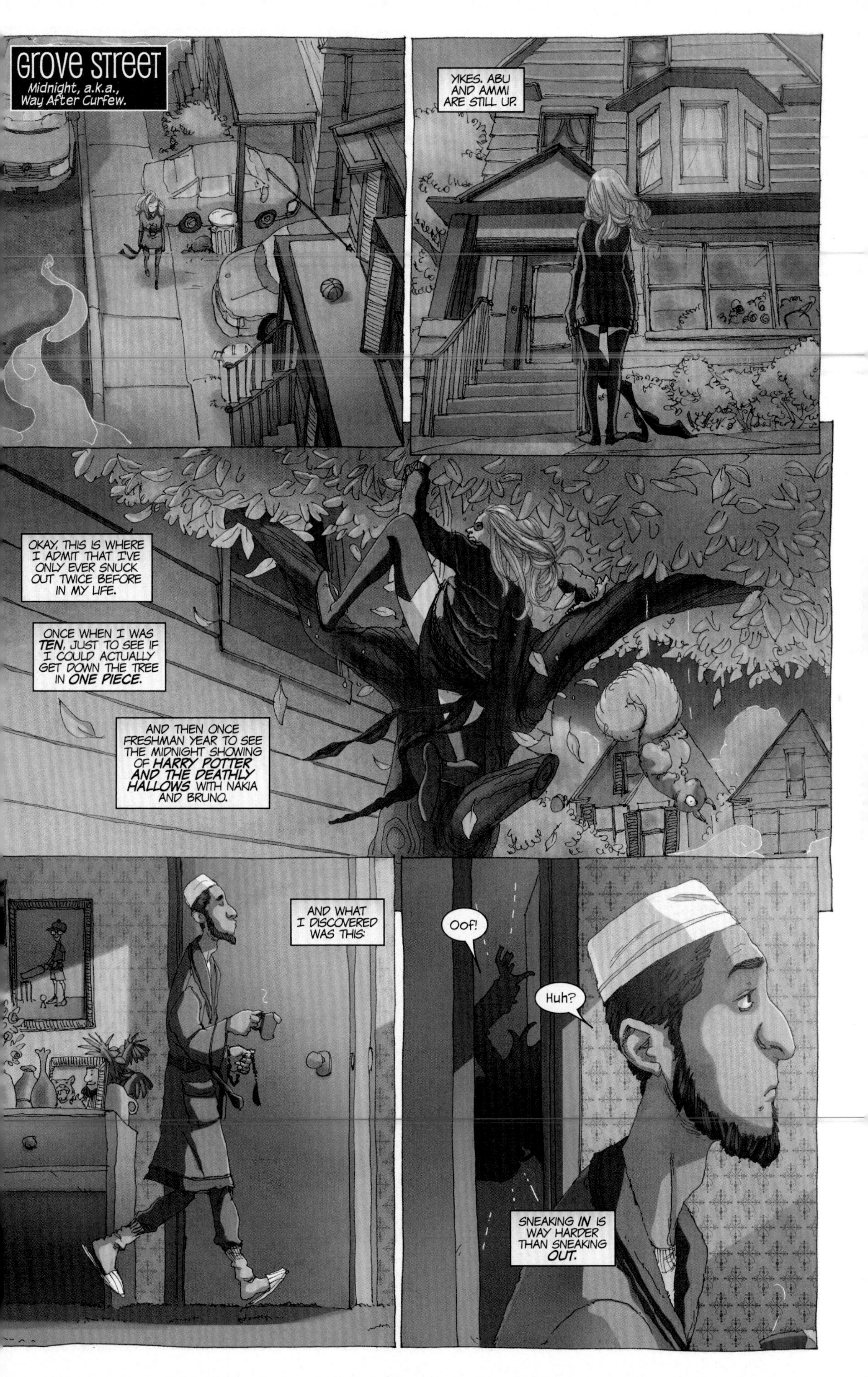
Grove Street
Midnight, a.k.a., Way After Curfew.
YIKES. ABU AND AMMI ARE STILL UP.
OKAY, THIS IS WHERE I ADMIT THAT I'VE ONLY EVER SNUCK OUT TWICE BEFORE IN MY LIFE.
ONCE WHEN I WAS TEN, JUST TO SEE IF I COULD ACTUALLY GET DOWN THE TREE IN ONE PIECE.
AND THEN ONCE FRESHMAN YEAR TO SEE THE MIDNIGHT SHOWING OF HARRY POTTER AND THE DEATHLY HALLOWS WITH NAKIA AND BRUNO.
AND WHAT I DISCOVERED WAS THIS:
Oof!
Huh?
SNEAKING IN IS WAY HARDER THAN SNEAKING OUT.

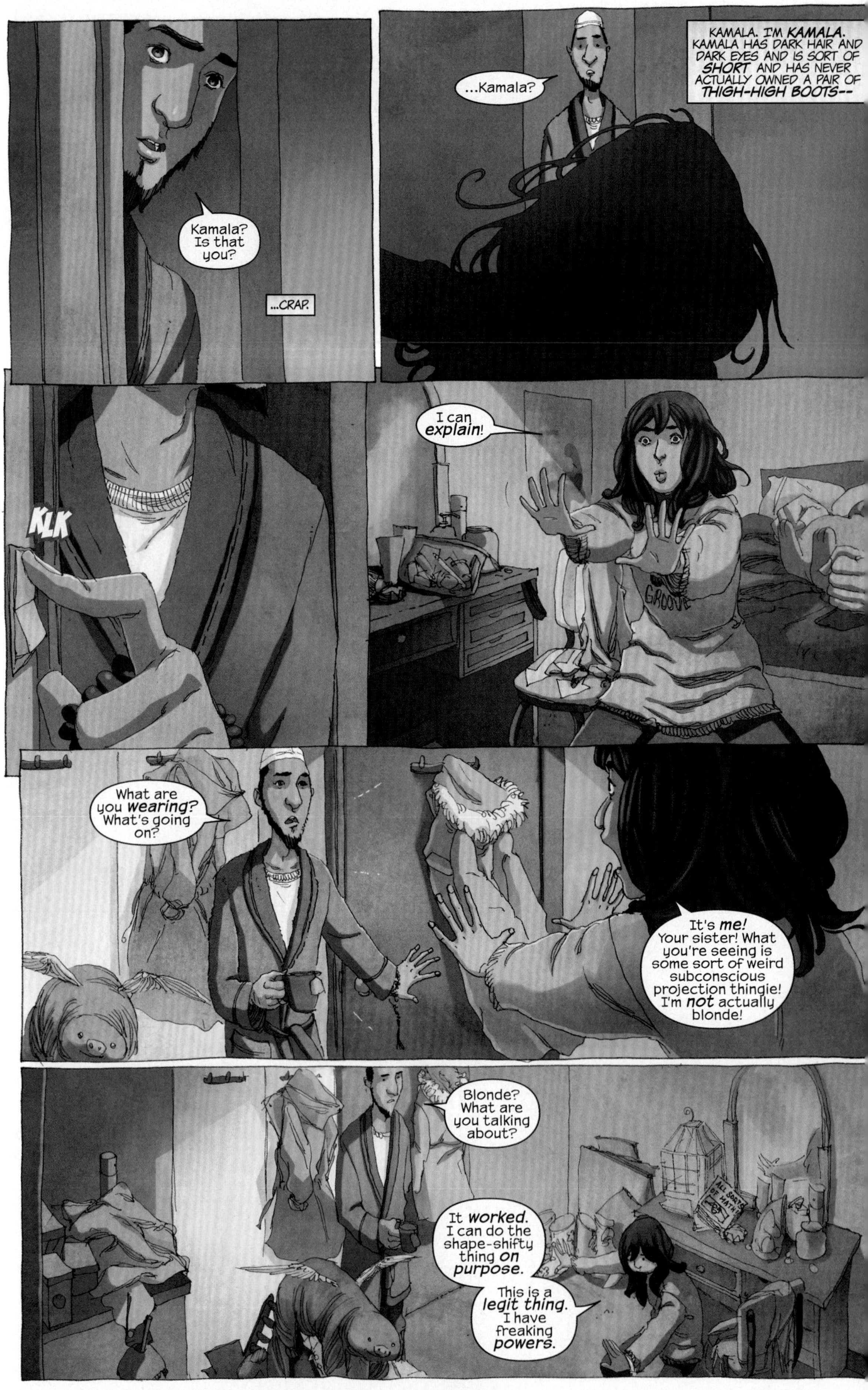
Kamala? Is that you?
...CRAP.
...Kamala?
KAMALA. I'M KAMALA. KAMALA HAS DARK HAIR AND DARK EYES AND IS SORT OF SHORT AND HAS NEVER ACTUALLY OWNED A PAIR OF THIGH-HIGH BOOTS--
KLK
I can explain!
GROOVE
What are you wearing? What's going on?
It's me! Your sister! What you're seeing is some sort of weird subconscious projection thingie! I'm not actually blonde!
Blonde? What are you talking about?
It worked. I can do the shape-shifty thing on purpose.
This is a legit thing. I have freaking powers.
ALL SORTS OF MATH

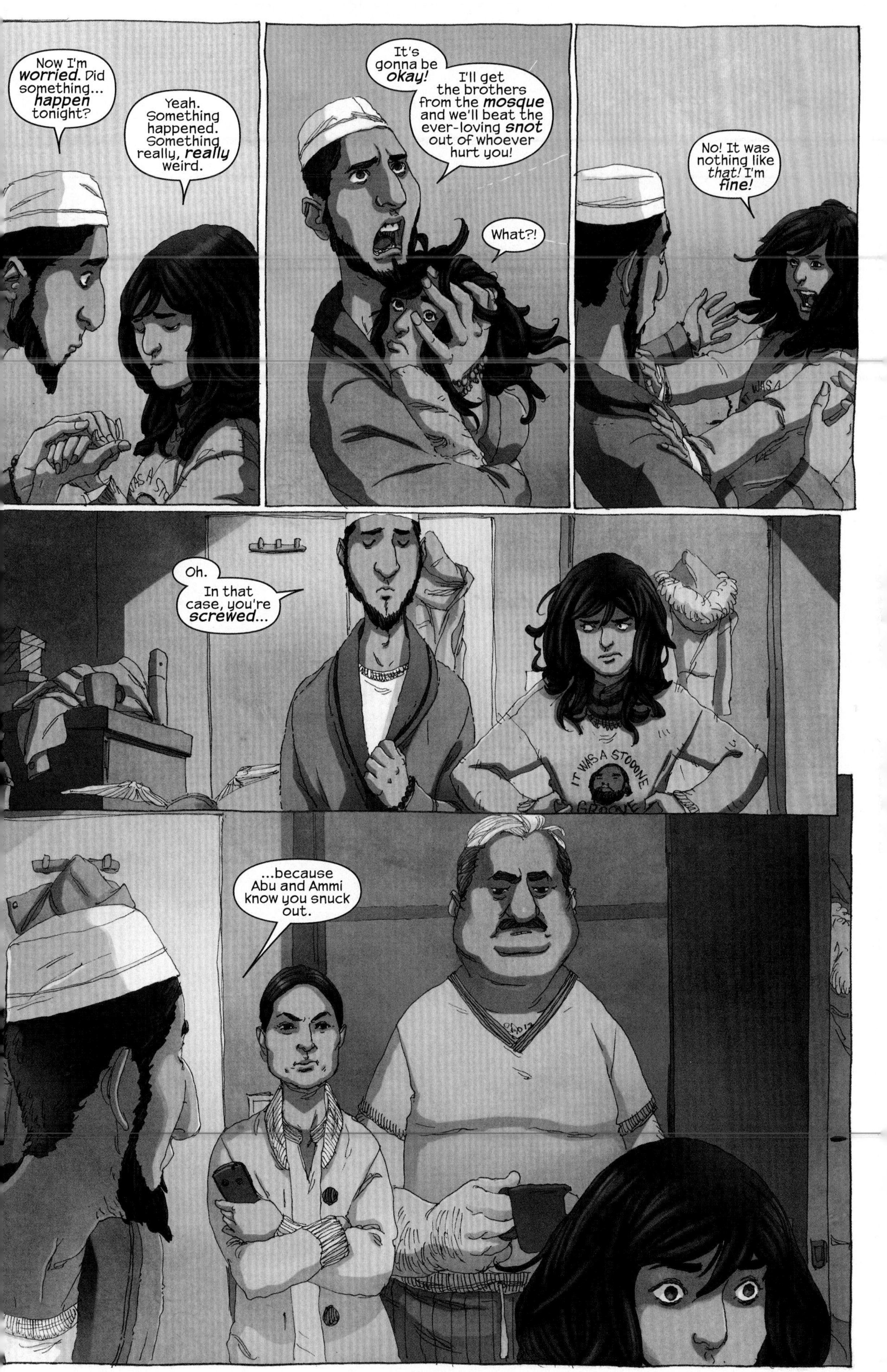
Now I'm *worried*. Did something... *happen* tonight?
Yeah. Something happened. Something really, *really* weird.
It's gonna be *okay!*
I'll get the brothers from the *mosque* and we'll beat the ever-loving *snot* out of whoever hurt you!
What?!
No! It was nothing like *that!* I'm *fine!*
Oh.
In that case, you're *screwed*...
IT WAS A STOONE GROOVE
...because Abu and Ammi know you snuck out.

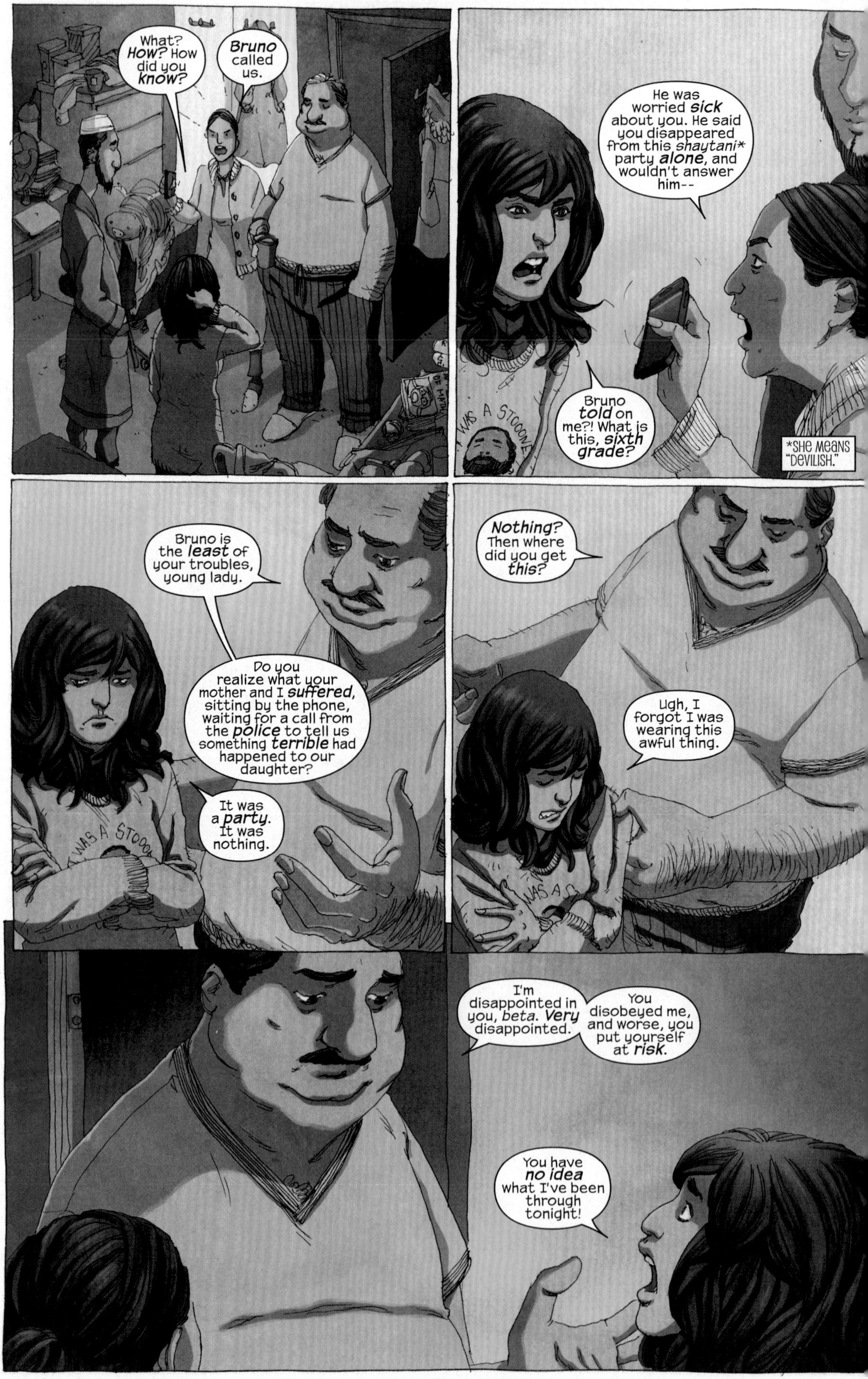
What? HOW? How did you KNOW?
Bruno called us.
He was worried sick about you. He said you disappeared from this shaytani* party alone, and wouldn't answer him--
Bruno told on me?! What is this, sixth grade?
*SHE MEANS "DEVILISH."
Bruno is the least of your troubles, young lady.
Do you realize what your mother and I suffered, sitting by the phone, waiting for a call from the police to tell us something terrible had happened to our daughter?
It was a party. It was nothing.
Nothing? Then where did you get this?
Ugh, I forgot I was wearing this awful thing.
I'm disappointed in you, beta. Very disappointed.
You disobeyed me, and worse, you put yourself at risk.
You have no idea what I've been through tonight!

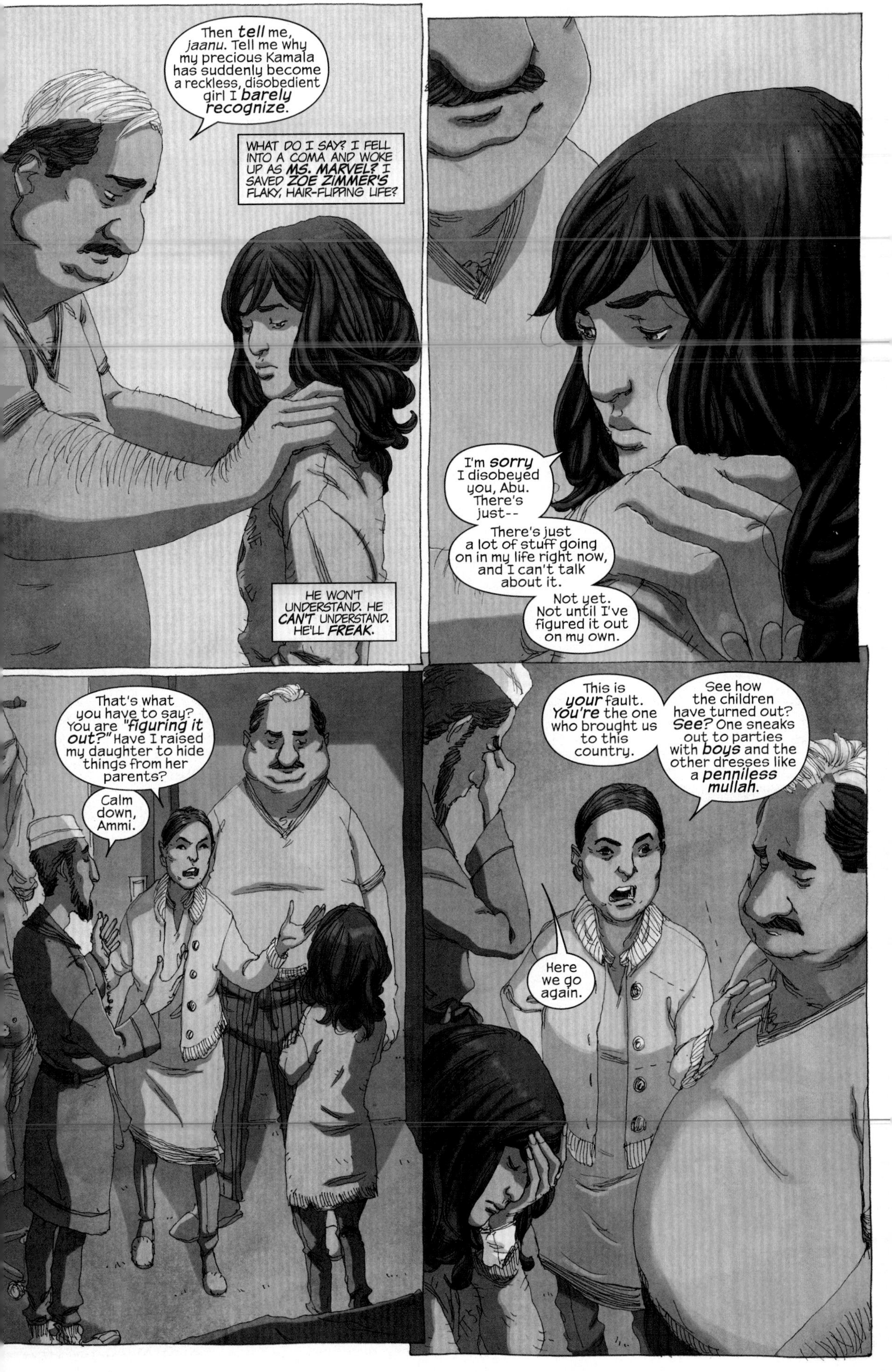
Then tell me, jaanu. Tell me why my precious Kamala has suddenly become a reckless, disobedient girl I barely recognize.
WHAT DO I SAY? I FELL INTO A COMA AND WOKE UP AS MS. MARVEL? I SAVED ZOE ZIMMER'S FLAKY, HAIR-FLIPPING LIFE?
HE WON'T UNDERSTAND. HE CAN'T UNDERSTAND. HE'LL FREAK.
I'm sorry I disobeyed you, Abu. There's just--
There's just a lot of stuff going on in my life right now, and I can't talk about it.
Not yet. Not until I've figured it out on my own.
That's what you have to say? You are "figuring it out?" Have I raised my daughter to hide things from her parents?
Calm down, Ammi.
This is your fault. You're the one who brought us to this country.
See how the children have turned out? See? One sneaks out to parties with boys and the other dresses like a penniless mullah.
Here we go again.

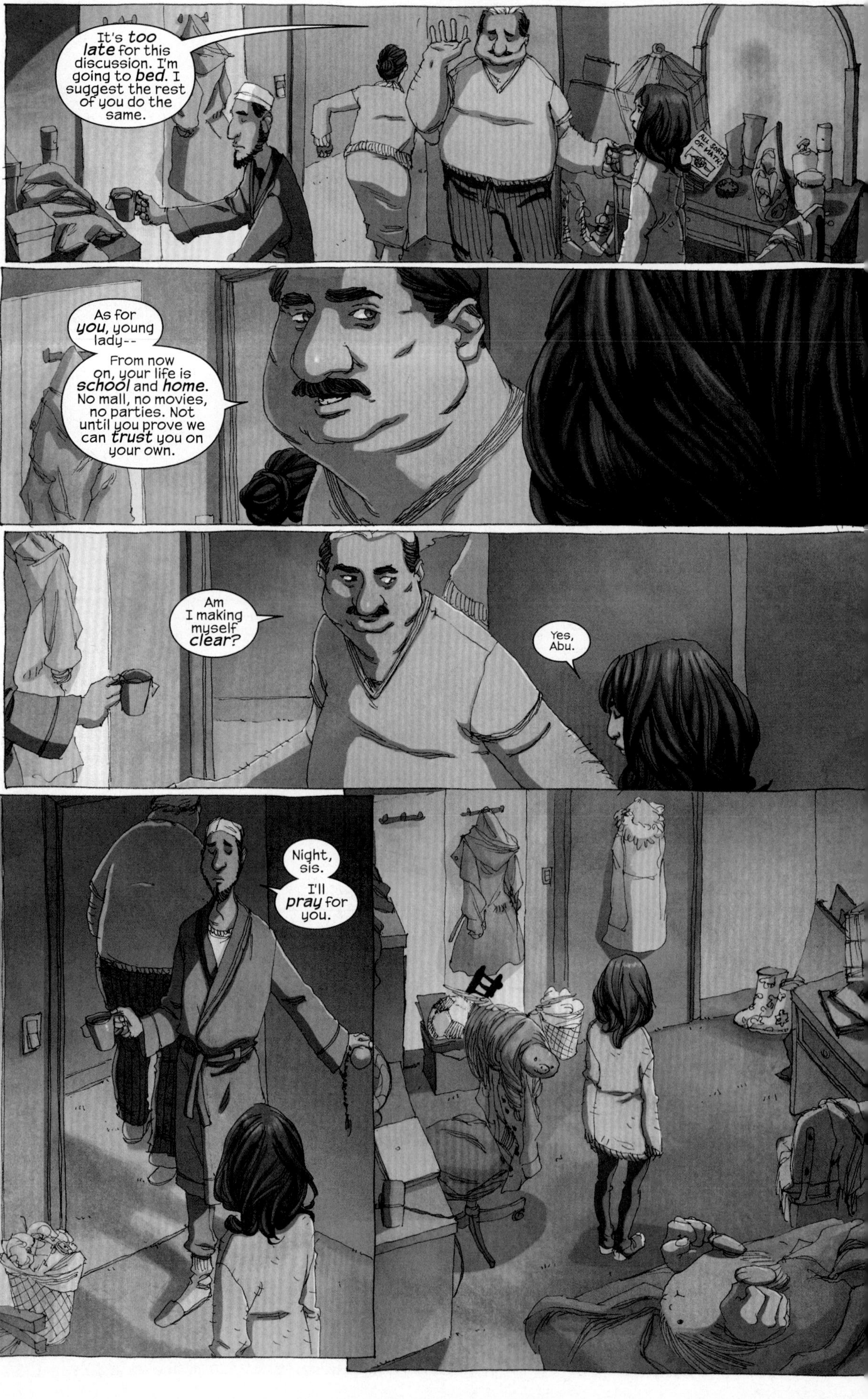
It's *too late* for this discussion. I'm going to *bed*. I suggest the rest of you do the same.
ALL SORTS OF MATH!
As for *you*, young lady--
From now on, your life is *school* and *home*. No mall, no movies, no parties. Not until you prove we can *trust* you on your own.
Am I making myself *clear*?
Yes, Abu.
Night, sis.
I'll *pray* for you.

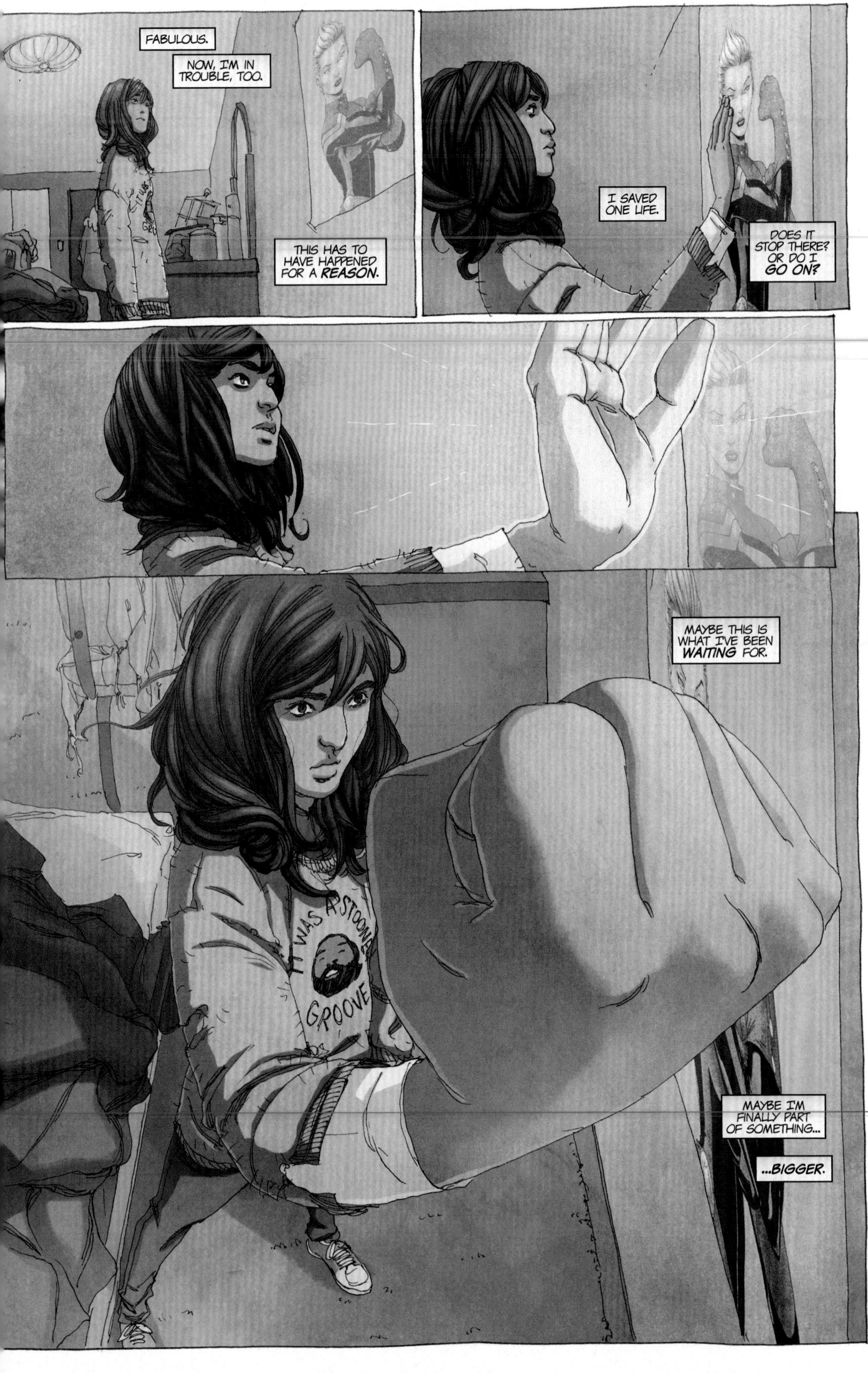
FABULOUS.
NOW, I'M IN TROUBLE, TOO.
THIS HAS TO HAVE HAPPENED FOR A REASON.
I SAVED ONE LIFE.
DOES IT STOP THERE? OR DO I GO ON?
MAYBE THIS IS WHAT I'VE BEEN WAITING FOR.
IT WAS A STOONER GROOVE
MAYBE I'M FINALLY PART OF SOMETHING...
...BIGGER.

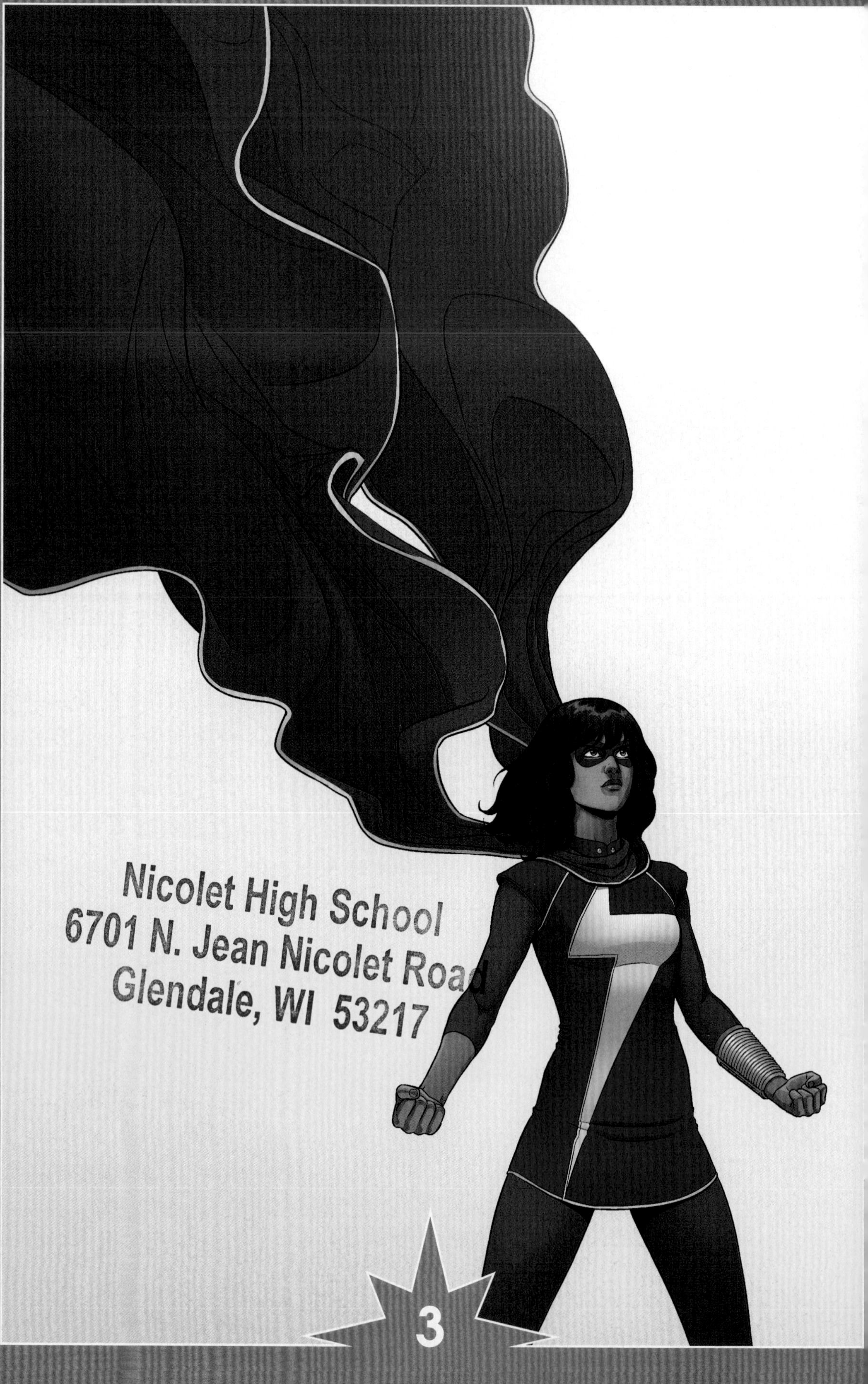
3

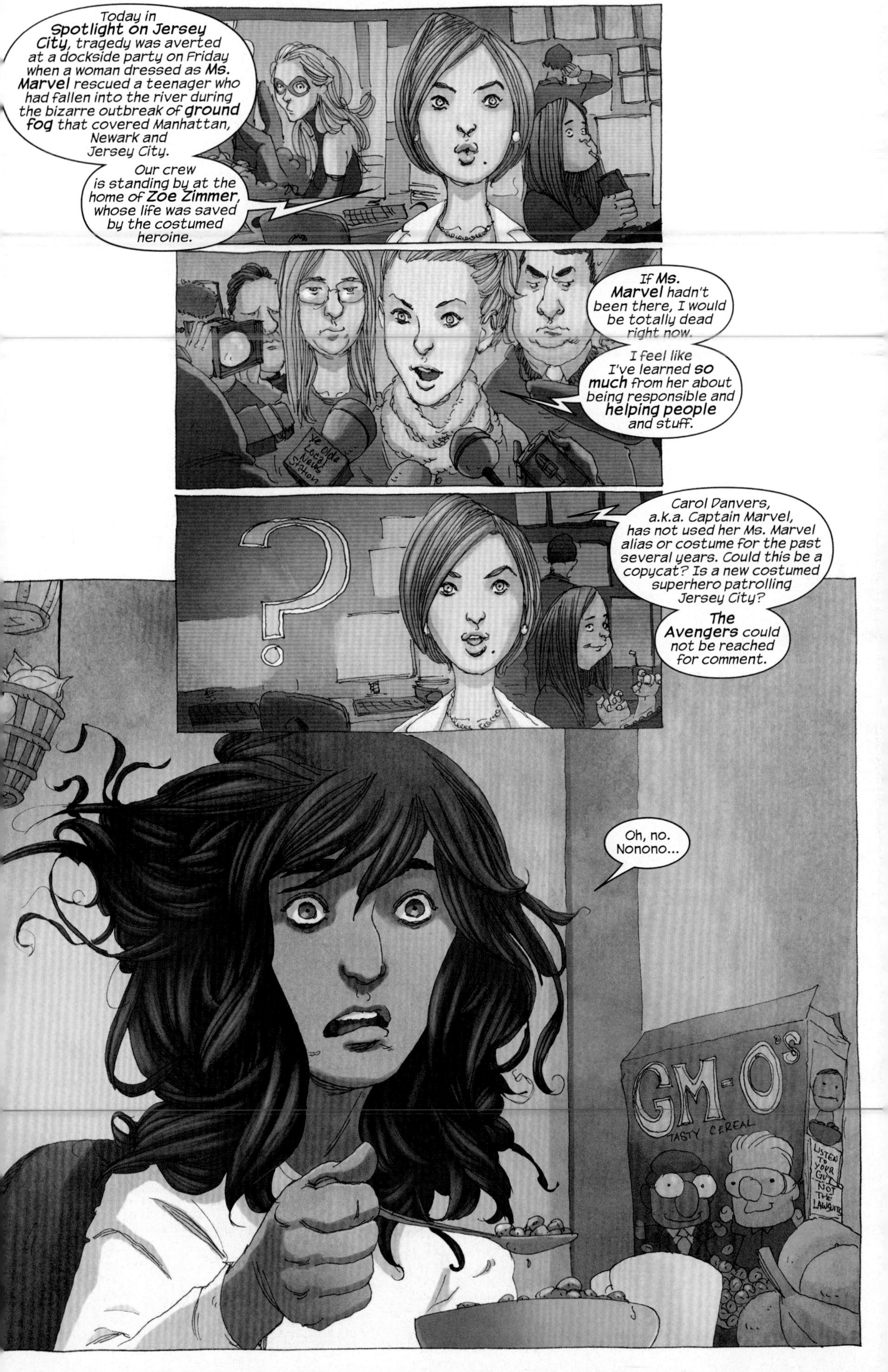
Today in Spotlight on Jersey City, tragedy was averted at a dockside party on Friday when a woman dressed as Ms. Marvel rescued a teenager who had fallen into the river during the bizarre outbreak of ground fog that covered Manhattan, Newark and Jersey City.
Our crew is standing by at the home of Zoe Zimmer, whose life was saved by the costumed heroine.
If Ms. Marvel hadn't been there, I would be totally dead right now.
I feel like I've learned so much from her about being responsible and helping people and stuff.
Ye Olde Local News Station
Carol Danvers, a.k.a. Captain Marvel, has not used her Ms. Marvel alias or costume for the past several years. Could this be a copycat? Is a new costumed superhero patrolling Jersey City?
The Avengers could not be reached for comment.
Oh, no. Nonono...
GM-O's
TASTY CEREAL
LISTEN TO YOUR GUT NOT THE LAWSUITS

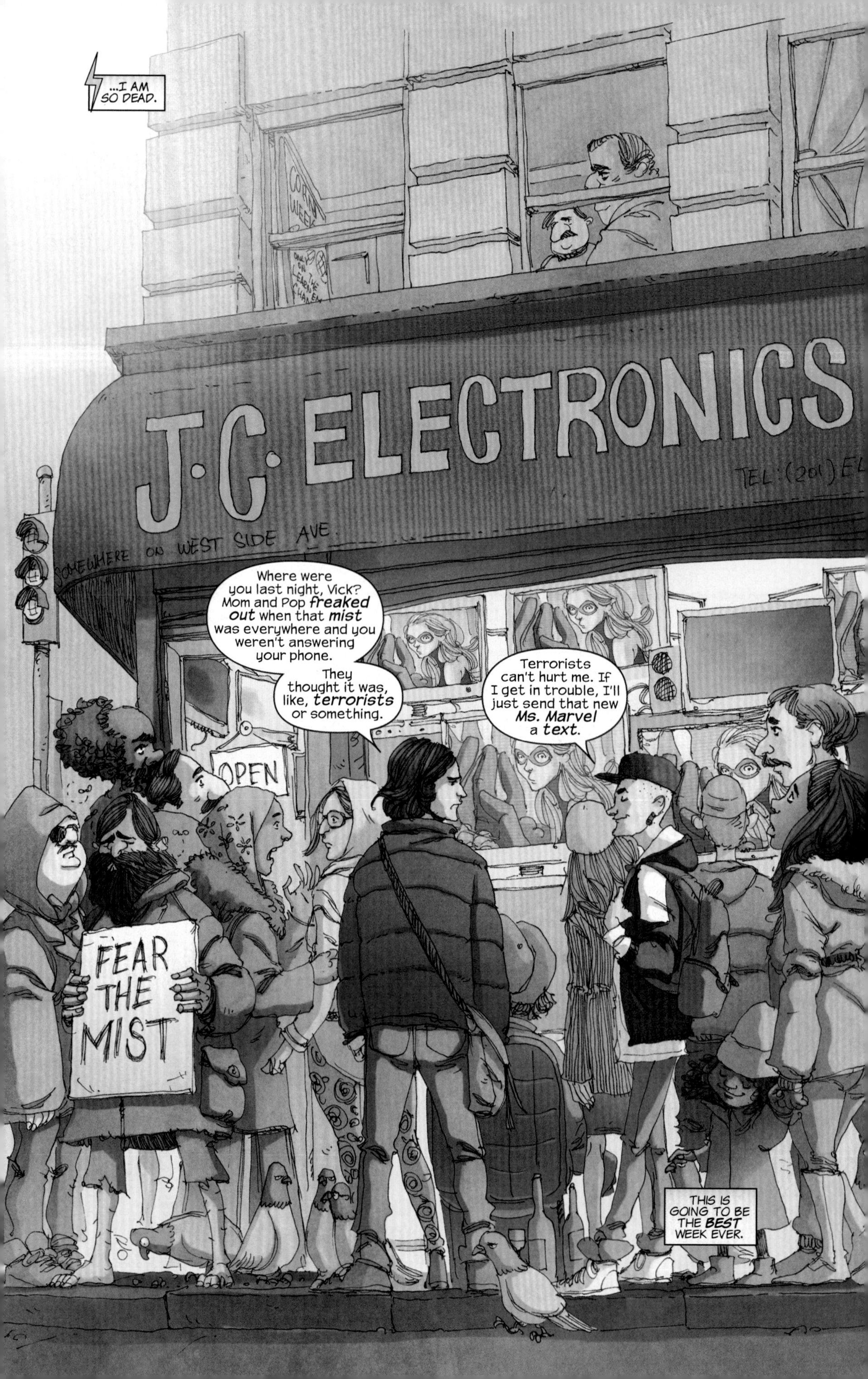
...I AM SO DEAD.
J·C· ELECTRONICS
TEL:(201) EL
SOMEWHERE ON WEST SIDE AVE
OPEN
Where were you last night, Vick? Mom and Pop freaked out when that mist was everywhere and you weren't answering your phone.
They thought it was, like, terrorists or something.
Terrorists can't hurt me. If I get in trouble, I'll just send that new Ms. Marvel a text.
FEAR THE MIST
THIS IS GOING TO BE THE BEST WEEK EVER.

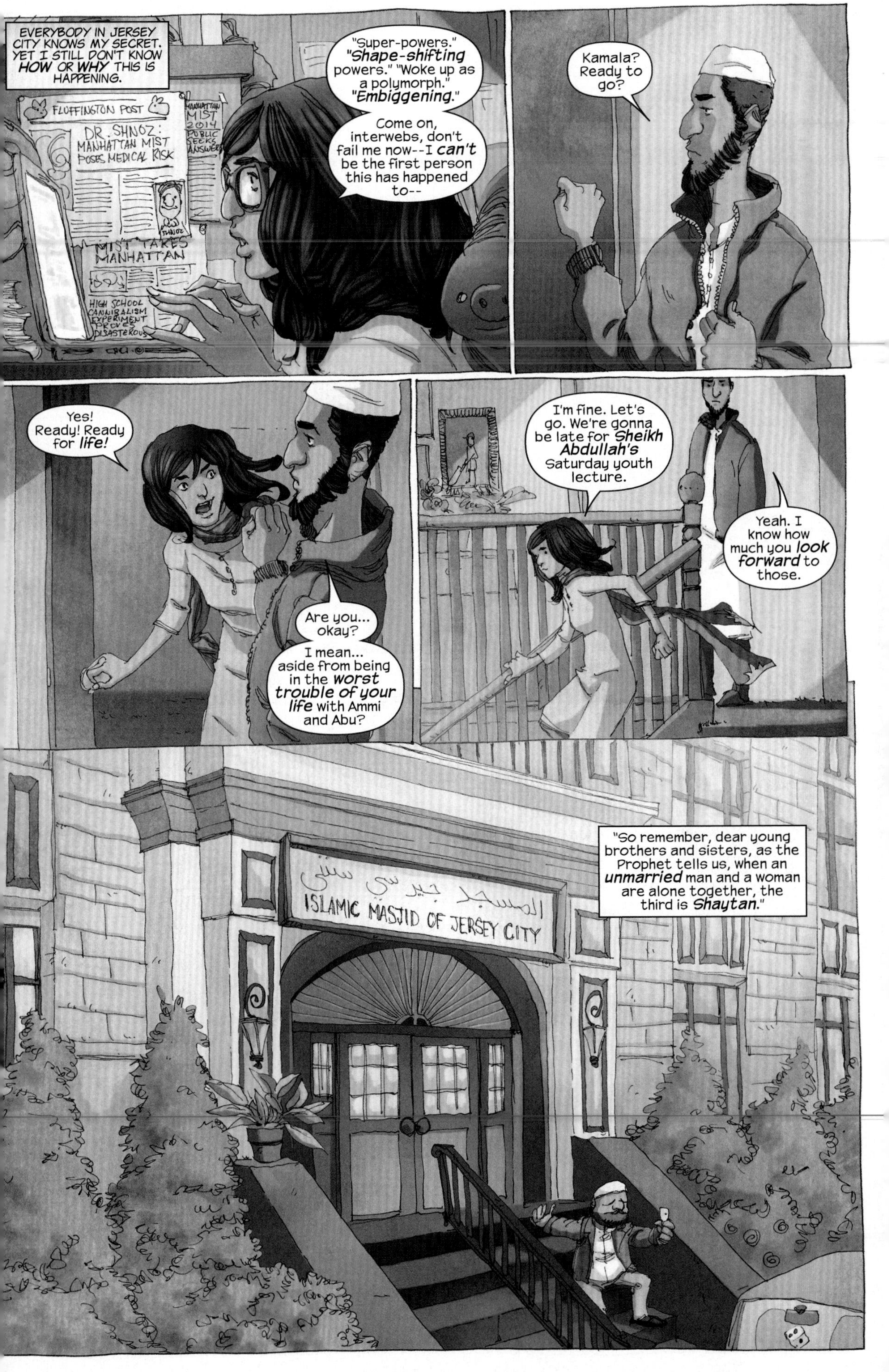
EVERYBODY IN JERSEY CITY KNOWS MY SECRET. YET I STILL DON'T KNOW **HOW** OR **WHY** THIS IS HAPPENING.
FLUFFINGTON POST
DR. SHNOZ: MANHATTAN MIST POSES MEDICAL RISK
MANHATTAN MIST 2014 PUBLIC SEEKS ANSWERS
MIST TAKES MANHATTAN
HIGH SCHOOL CANNIBALISM EXPERIMENT PROVES DISASTEROUS
"Super-powers." "*Shape-shifting* powers." "Woke up as a polymorph." "*Embiggening*."
Come on, interwebs, don't fail me now--I ***can't*** be the first person this has happened to--
Kamala? Ready to go?
Yes! Ready! Ready for *life!*
Are you... okay?
I mean... aside from being in the ***worst trouble of your life*** with Ammi and Abu?
I'm fine. Let's go. We're gonna be late for ***Sheikh Abdullah's*** Saturday youth lecture.
Yeah. I know how much you ***look forward*** to those.
ISLAMIC MASJID OF JERSEY CITY
"So remember, dear young brothers and sisters, as the Prophet tells us, when an ***unmarried*** man and a woman are alone together, the third is ***Shaytan***."

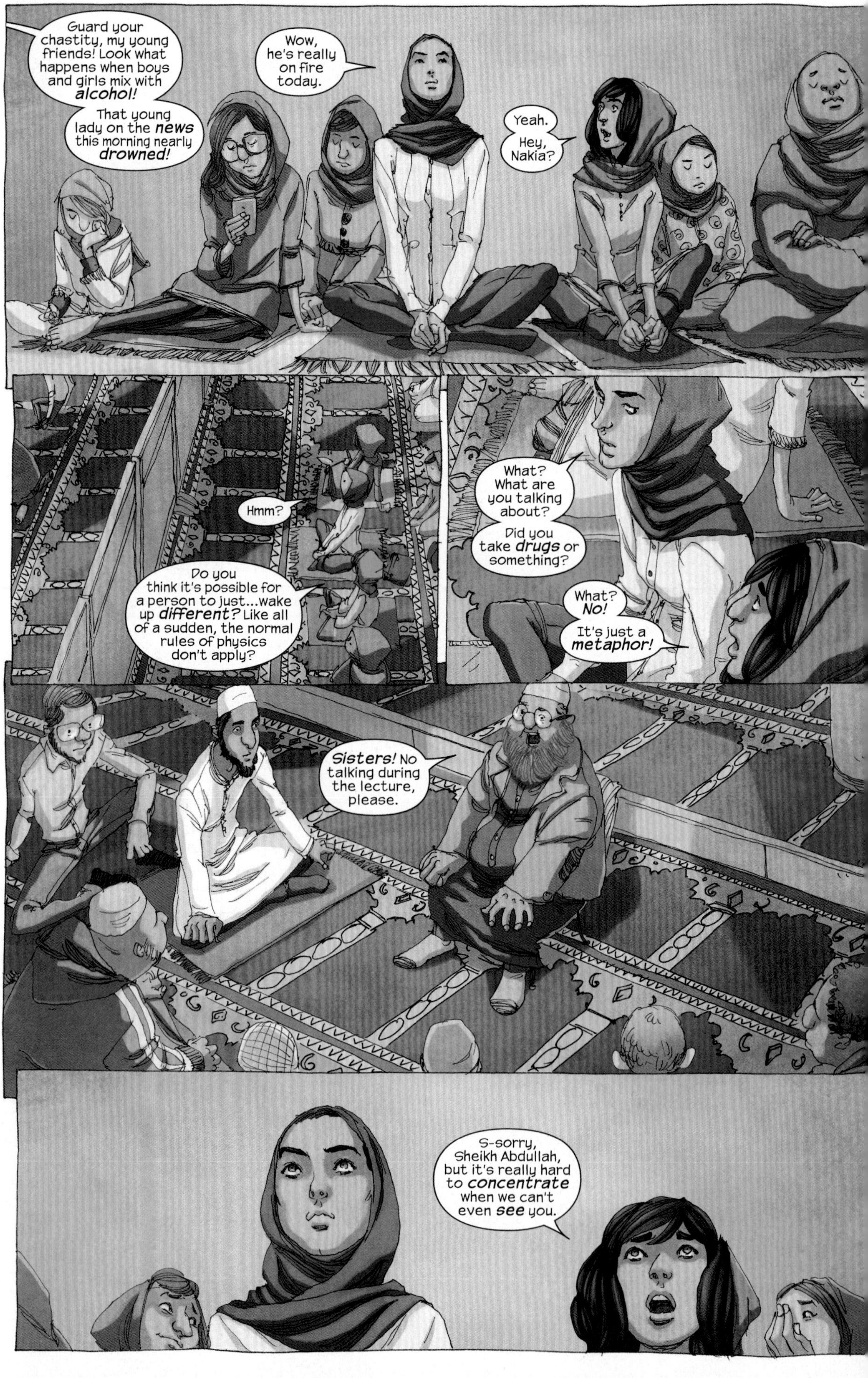
Guard your chastity, my young friends! Look what happens when boys and girls mix with *alcohol!*
That young lady on the *news* this morning nearly *drowned!*
Wow, he's really on fire today.
Yeah.
Hey, Nakia?
Hmm?
Do you think it's possible for a person to just...wake up *different?* Like all of a sudden, the normal rules of physics don't apply?
What? What are you talking about?
Did you take *drugs* or something?
What? *No!*
It's just a *metaphor!*
Sisters! No talking during the lecture, please.
S-sorry, Sheikh Abdullah, but it's really hard to *concentrate* when we can't even *see* you.

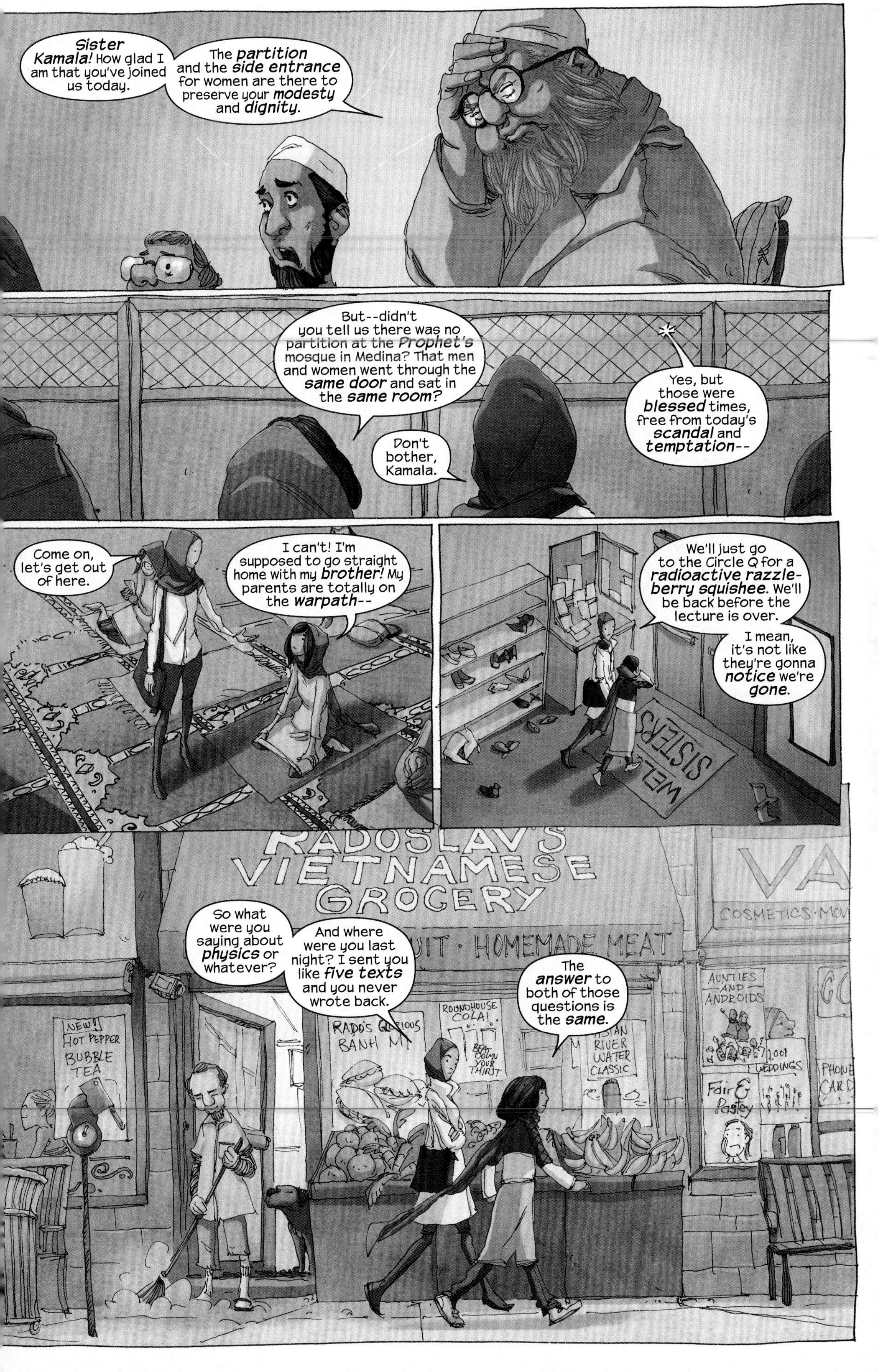

Sister Kamala! How glad I am that you've joined us today.
The partition and the side entrance for women are there to preserve your modesty and dignity.
But--didn't you tell us there was no partition at the Prophet's mosque in Medina? That men and women went through the same door and sat in the same room?
Don't bother, Kamala.
Yes, but those were blessed times, free from today's scandal and temptation--
Come on, let's get out of here.
I can't! I'm supposed to go straight home with my brother! My parents are totally on the warpath--
We'll just go to the Circle Q for a radioactive razzleberry squishee. We'll be back before the lecture is over.
I mean, it's not like they're gonna notice we're gone.
WEL SISTERS
RADOSLAV'S VIETNAMESE GROCERY
COSMETICS · MOV
UIT · HOMEMADE MEAT
So what were you saying about physics or whatever?
And where were you last night? I sent you like five texts and you never wrote back.
The answer to both of those questions is the same.
NEW! HOT PEPPER BUBBLE TEA
RADO'S GLORIOUS BANH MI
ROUNDHOUSE COLA! BEAT DOWN YOUR THIRST
ASIAN RIVER WATER CLASSIC
AUNTIES AND ANDROIDS
1,001 WEDDINGS
Fair & Pastey
PHONE CARD

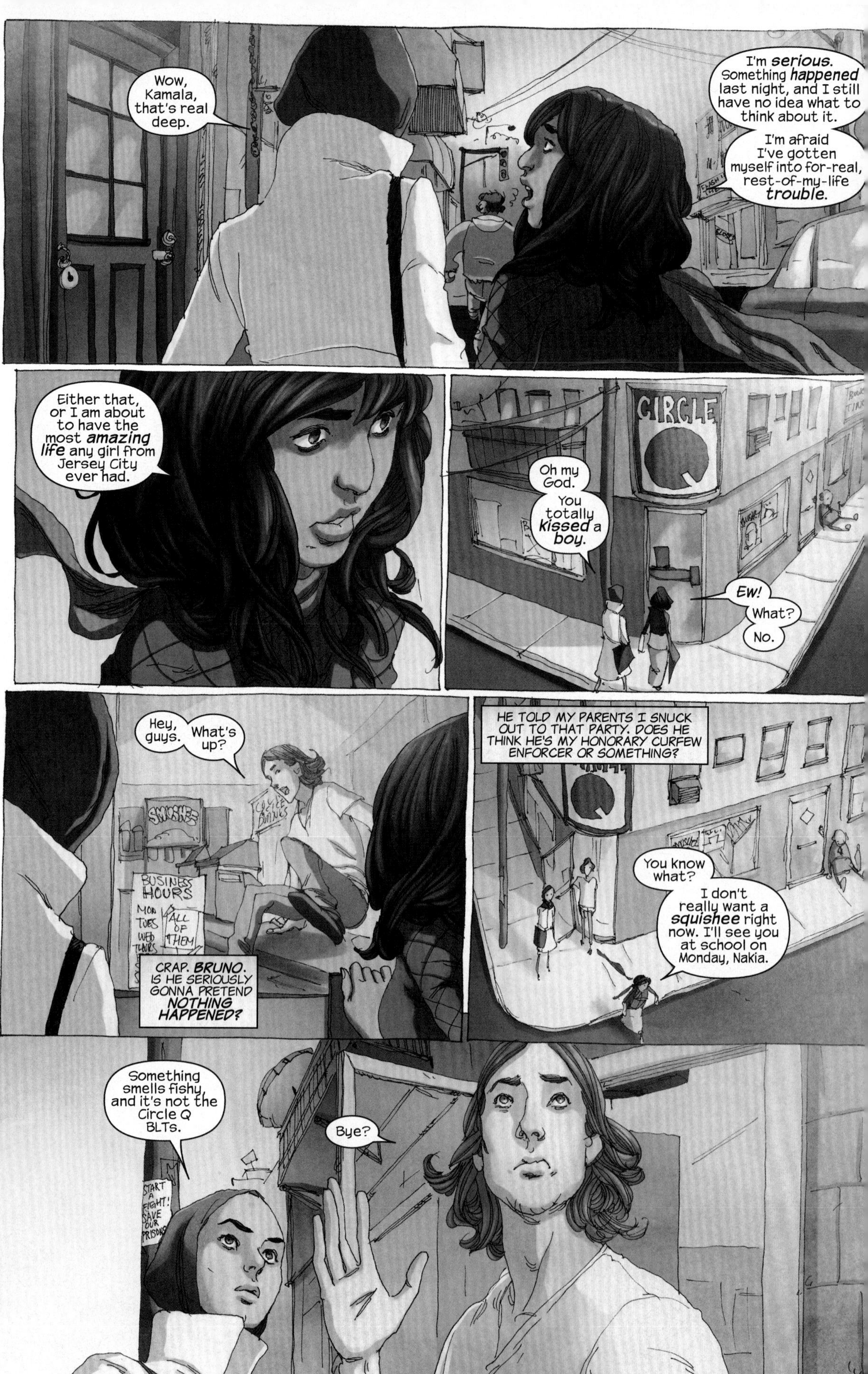
Wow, Kamala, that's real deep.
I'm serious. Something happened last night, and I still have no idea what to think about it.
I'm afraid I've gotten myself into for-real, rest-of-my-life trouble.
Either that, or I am about to have the most amazing life any girl from Jersey City ever had.
CIRCLE
Oh my God.
You totally kissed a boy.
Ew!
What?
No.
Hey, guys.
What's up?
BUSINESS HOURS
MON TUES WED THURS
ALL OF THEM
CRAP. BRUNO. IS HE SERIOUSLY GONNA PRETEND NOTHING HAPPENED?
HE TOLD MY PARENTS I SNUCK OUT TO THAT PARTY. DOES HE THINK HE'S MY HONORARY CURFEW ENFORCER OR SOMETHING?
You know what?
I don't really want a squishee right now. I'll see you at school on Monday, Nakia.
Something smells fishy, and it's not the Circle Q BLTs.
Bye?
START A FIGHT! SAVE OUR PRISONS

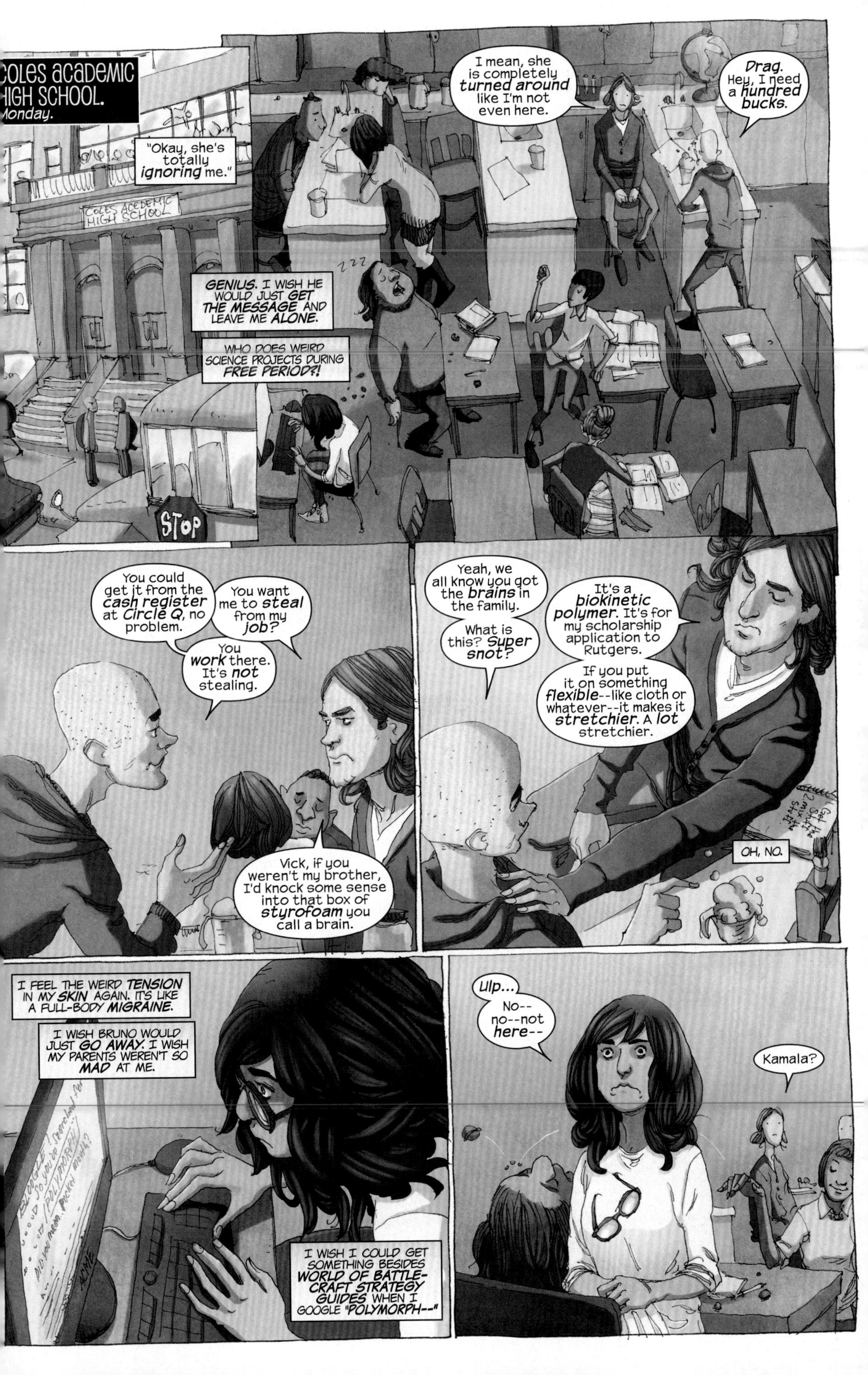
COLES ACADEMIC HIGH SCHOOL. Monday.
"Okay, she's totally ignoring me."
COLES ACADEMIC HIGH SCHOOL
I mean, she is completely turned around like I'm not even here.
Drag. Hey, I need a hundred bucks.
GENIUS. I WISH HE WOULD JUST GET THE MESSAGE AND LEAVE ME ALONE.
WHO DOES WEIRD SCIENCE PROJECTS DURING FREE PERIOD?!
STOP
You could get it from the cash register at Circle Q, no problem.
You want me to steal from my job?
You work there. It's not stealing.
Vick, if you weren't my brother, I'd knock some sense into that box of styrofoam you call a brain.
Yeah, we all know you got the brains in the family.
What is this? Super snot?
It's a biokinetic polymer. It's for my scholarship application to Rutgers.
If you put it on something flexible--like cloth or whatever--it makes it stretchier. A lot stretchier.
OH, NO.
I FEEL THE WEIRD TENSION IN MY SKIN AGAIN. IT'S LIKE A FULL-BODY MIGRAINE.
I WISH BRUNO WOULD JUST GO AWAY. I WISH MY PARENTS WEREN'T SO MAD AT ME.
I WISH I COULD GET SOMETHING BESIDES WORLD OF BATTLECRAFT STRATEGY GUIDES WHEN I GOOGLE "POLYMORPH--"
Ulp...
No-- no--not here--
Kamala?

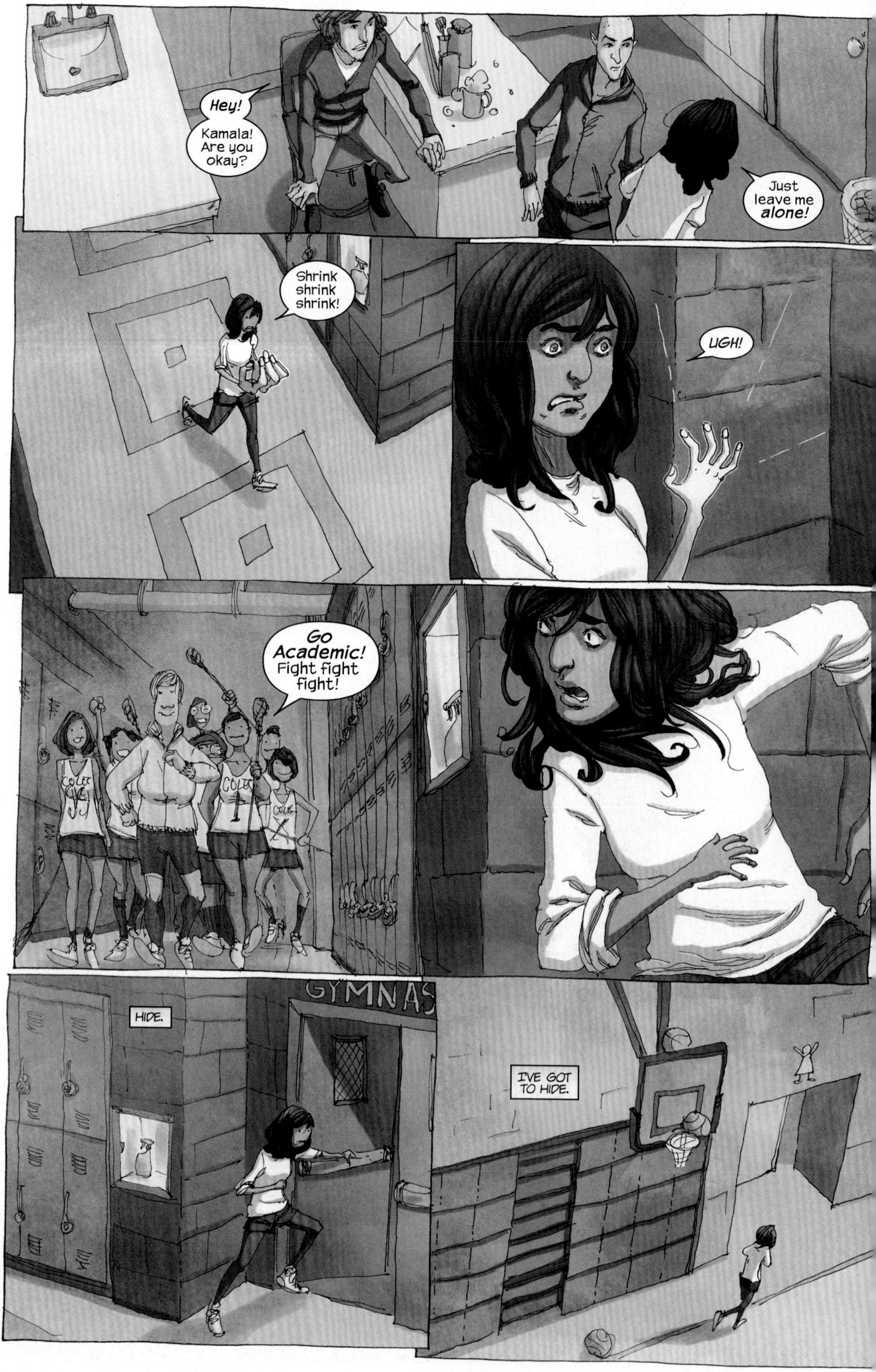

Hey! Kamala! Are you okay?
Just leave me alone!
Shrink shrink shrink!
UGH!
Go Academic! Fight fight fight!
GYMNAS
HIDE.
I'VE GOT TO HIDE.

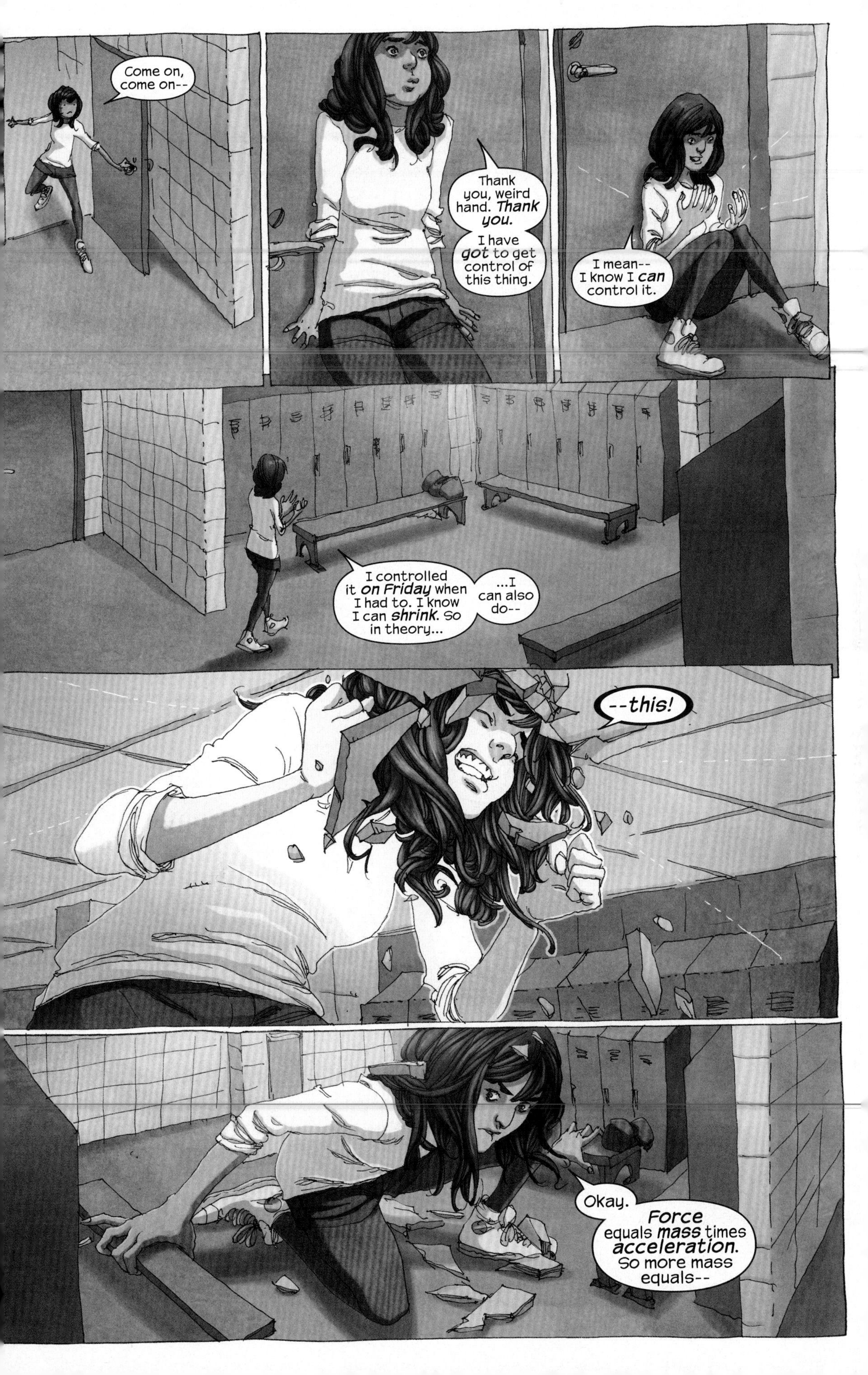
Come on, come on--
Thank you, weird hand. *Thank you.*
I have *got* to get control of this thing.
I mean-- I know I *can* control it.
I controlled it *on Friday* when I had to. I know I can *shrink*. So in theory...
...I can also do--
--this!
Okay.
Force equals *mass* times *acceleration*. So more mass equals--

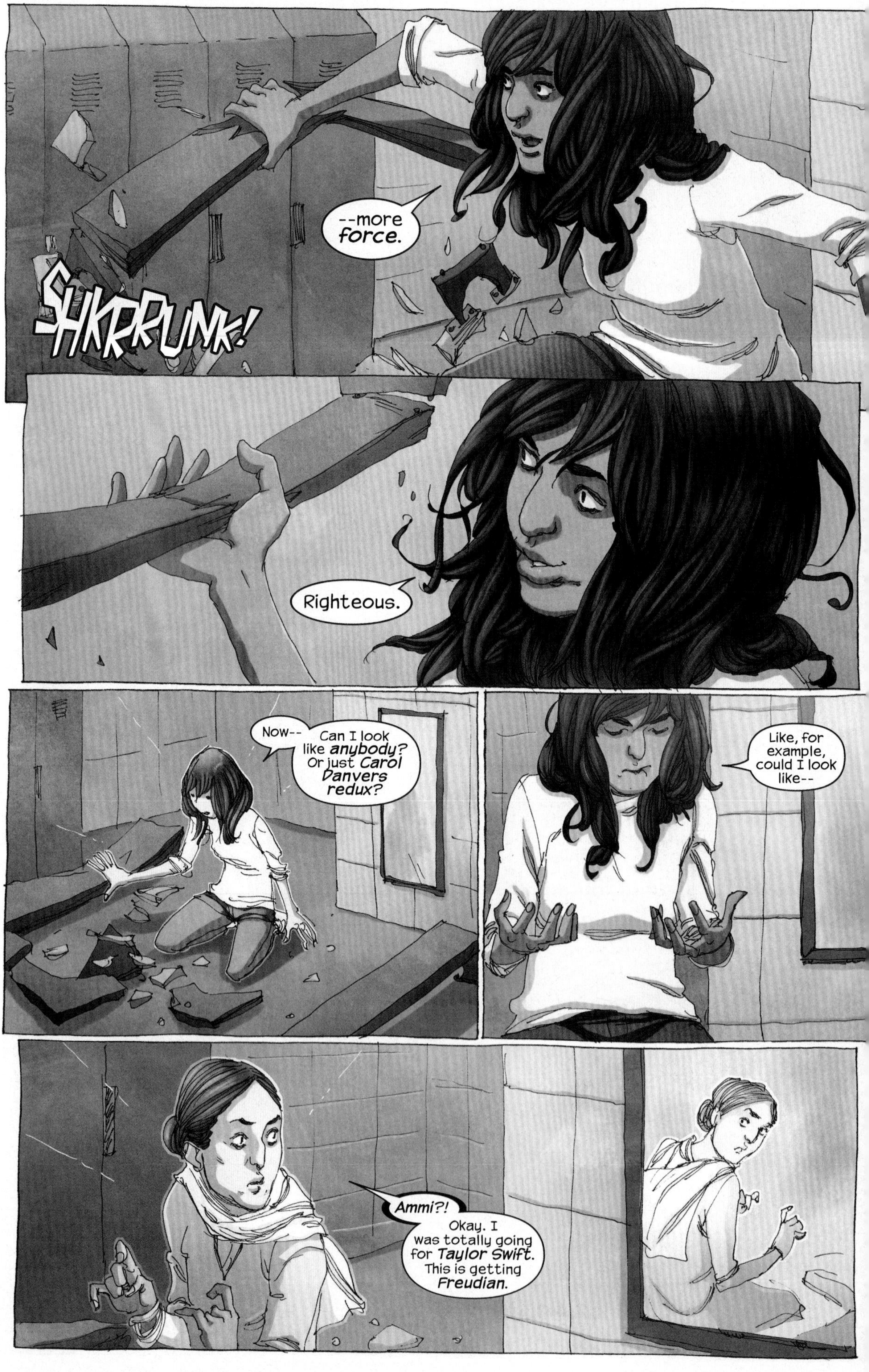

--more force.
SHKRRUNK!
Righteous.
Now--
Can I look like anybody? Or just Carol Danvers redux?
Like, for example, could I look like--
Ammi?!
Okay. I was totally going for Taylor Swift. This is getting Freudian.

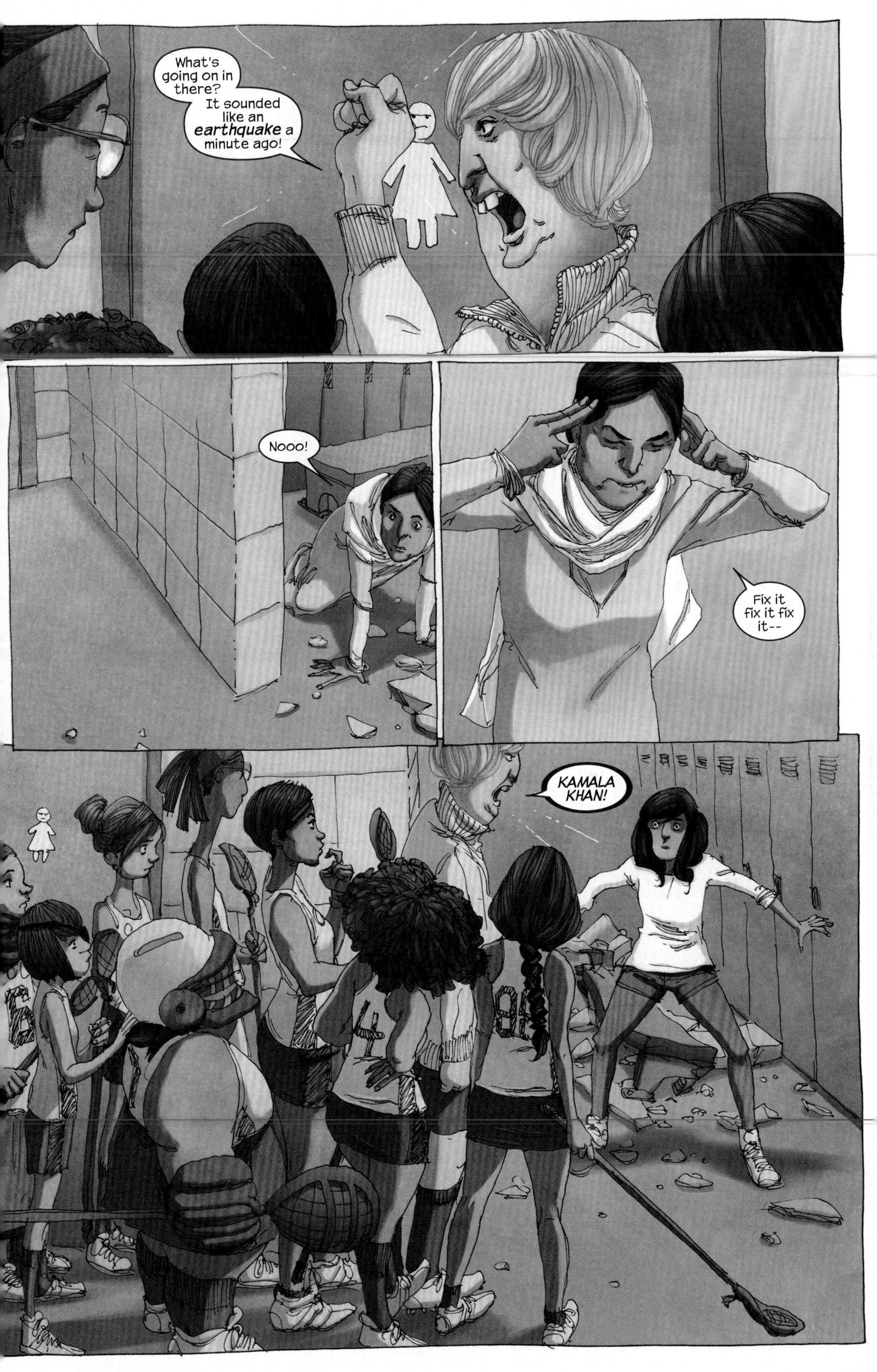
What's going on in there? It sounded like an earthquake a minute ago!
Nooo!
Fix it fix it fix it--
KAMALA KHAN!

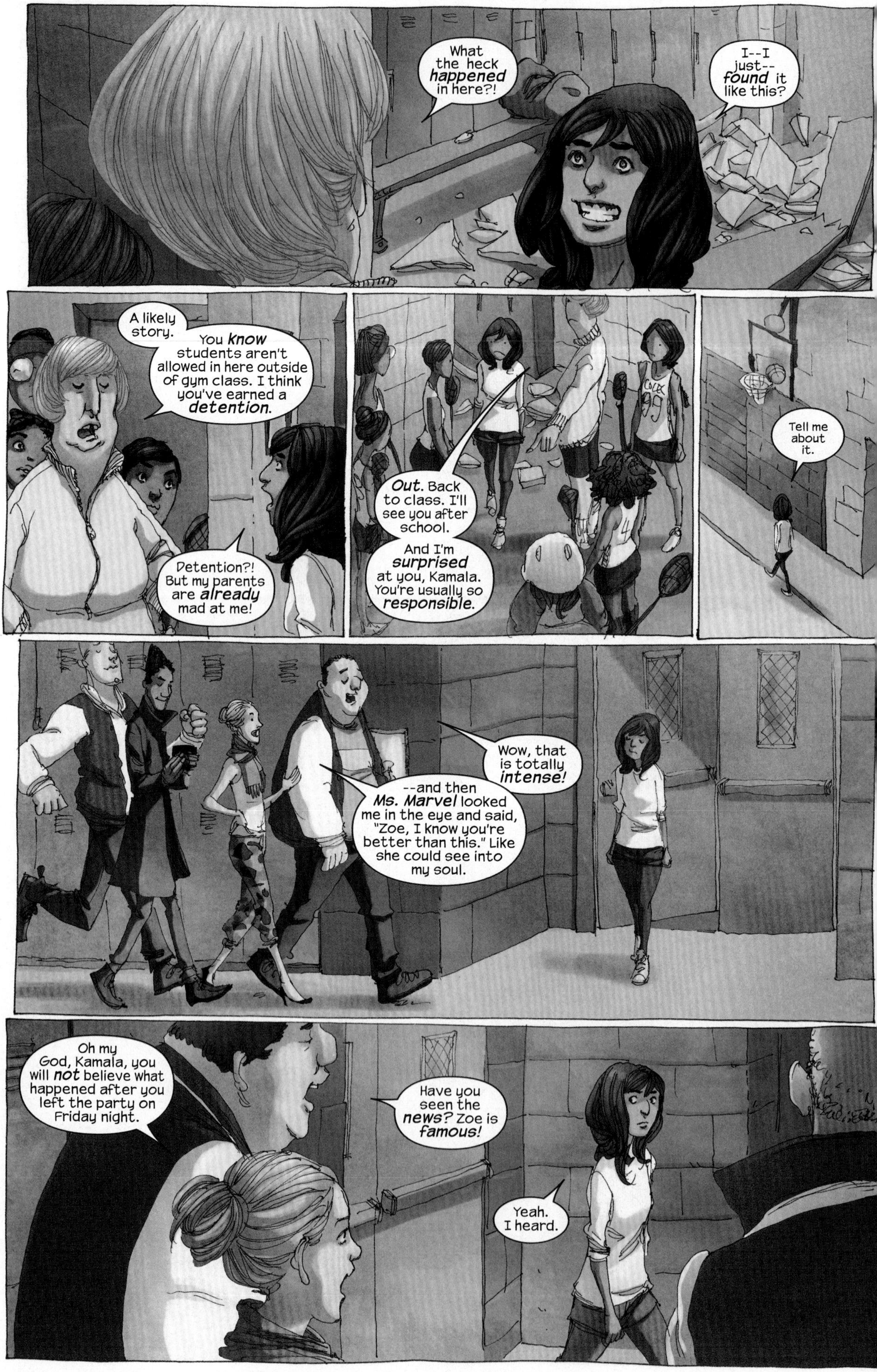

What the heck happened in here?!
I--I just--found it like this?
A likely story.
You know students aren't allowed in here outside of gym class. I think you've earned a detention.
Detention?! But my parents are already mad at me!
Out. Back to class. I'll see you after school.
And I'm surprised at you, Kamala. You're usually so responsible.
Tell me about it.
Wow, that is totally intense!
--and then Ms. Marvel looked me in the eye and said, "Zoe, I know you're better than this." Like she could see into my soul.
Oh my God, Kamala, you will not believe what happened after you left the party on Friday night.
Have you seen the news? Zoe is famous!
Yeah. I heard.

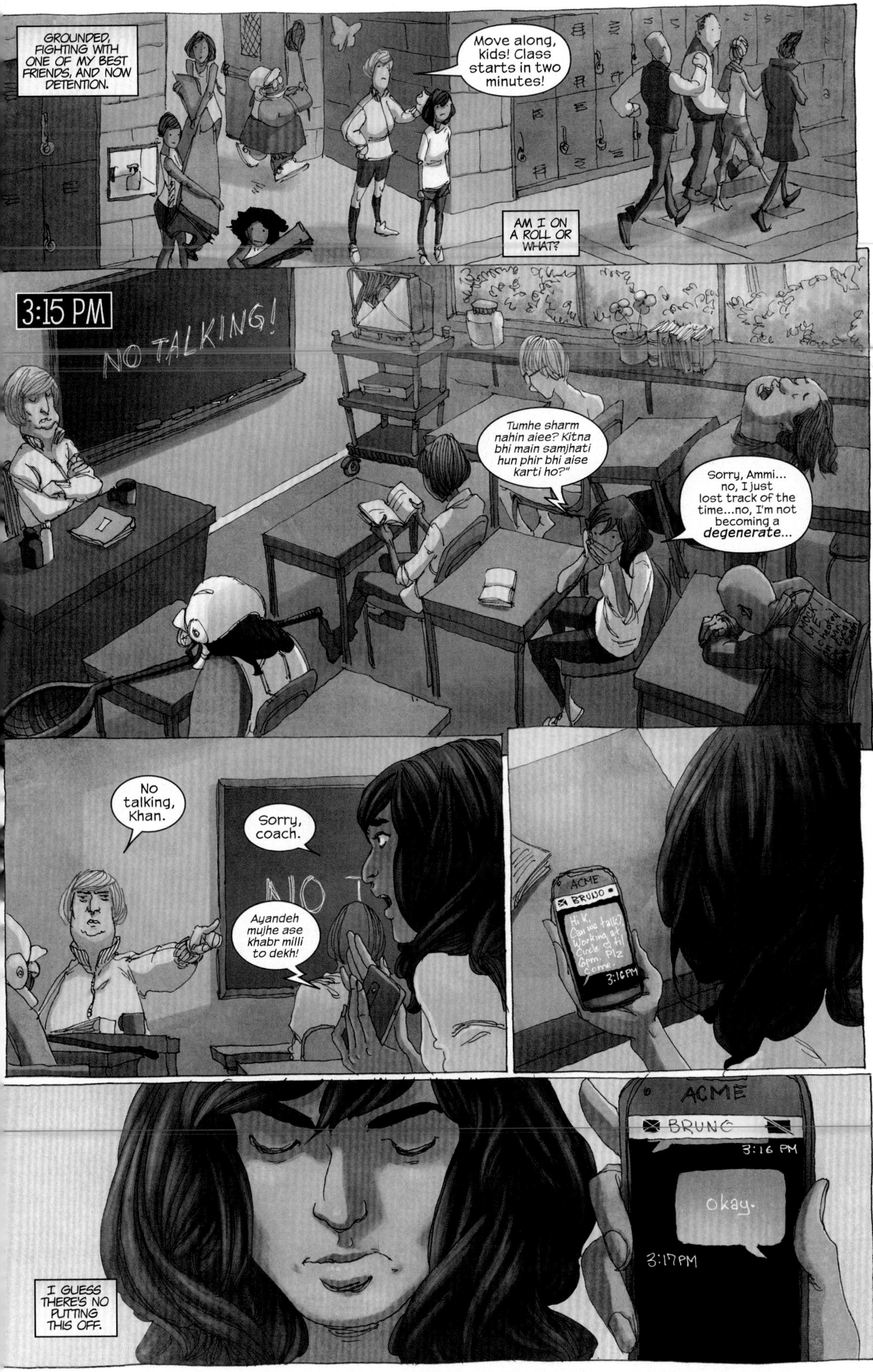
GROUNDED, FIGHTING WITH ONE OF MY BEST FRIENDS, AND NOW DETENTION.
Move along, kids! Class starts in two minutes!
AM I ON A ROLL OR WHAT?
3:15 PM
NO TALKING!
Tumhe sharm nahin aiee? Kitna bhi main samjhati hun phir bhi aise karti ho?"
Sorry, Ammi... no, I just lost track of the time...no, I'm not becoming a degenerate...
No talking, Khan.
Sorry, coach.
Ayandeh mujhe ase khabr milli to dekh!
ACME
BRUNO
3:16 PM
ACME
BRUNO
3:16 PM
okay.
3:17PM
I GUESS THERE'S NO PUTTING THIS OFF.

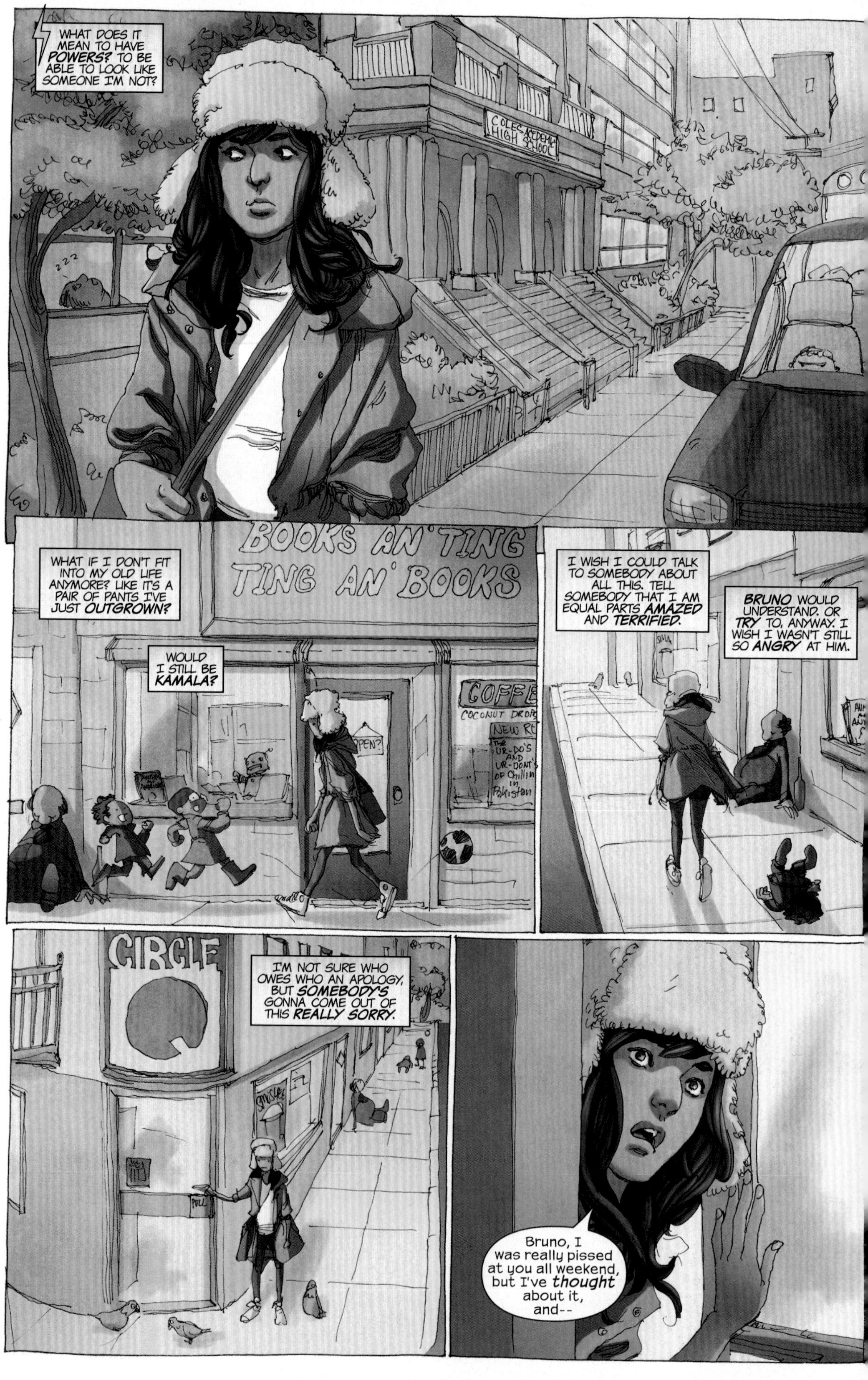
WHAT DOES IT MEAN TO HAVE POWERS? TO BE ABLE TO LOOK LIKE SOMEONE I'M NOT?
COLES ACADEMIC HIGH SCHOOL
BOOKS AN' TING
TING AN' BOOKS
WHAT IF I DON'T FIT INTO MY OLD LIFE ANYMORE? LIKE IT'S A PAIR OF PANTS I'VE JUST OUTGROWN?
WOULD I STILL BE KAMALA?
COFFEE
COCONUT DROPS
OPEN?
THE UR-DO'S AND UR-DONT'S OF Chillin in Pakistan
I WISH I COULD TALK TO SOMEBODY ABOUT ALL THIS. TELL SOMEBODY THAT I AM EQUAL PARTS AMAZED AND TERRIFIED.
BRUNO WOULD UNDERSTAND. OR TRY TO, ANYWAY. I WISH I WASN'T STILL SO ANGRY AT HIM.
CIRCLE
I'M NOT SURE WHO OWES WHO AN APOLOGY, BUT SOMEBODY'S GONNA COME OUT OF THIS REALLY SORRY.
PULL
Bruno, I was really pissed at you all weekend, but I've thought about it, and--

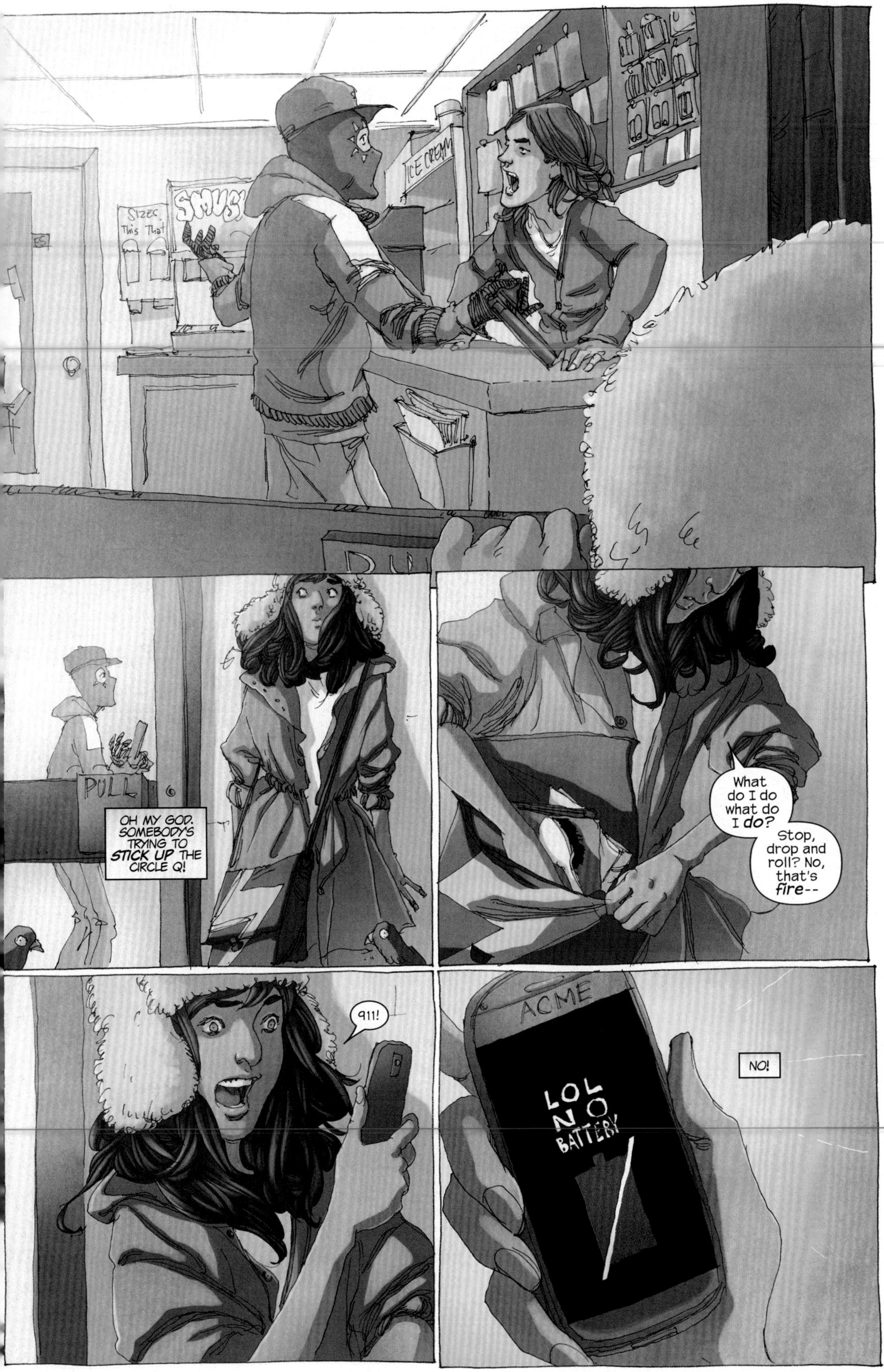
OH MY GOD. SOMEBODY'S TRYING TO STICK UP THE CIRCLE Q!
What do I do what do I do?
Stop, drop and roll? No, that's fire--
911!
ACME
LOL NO BATTERY
NO!

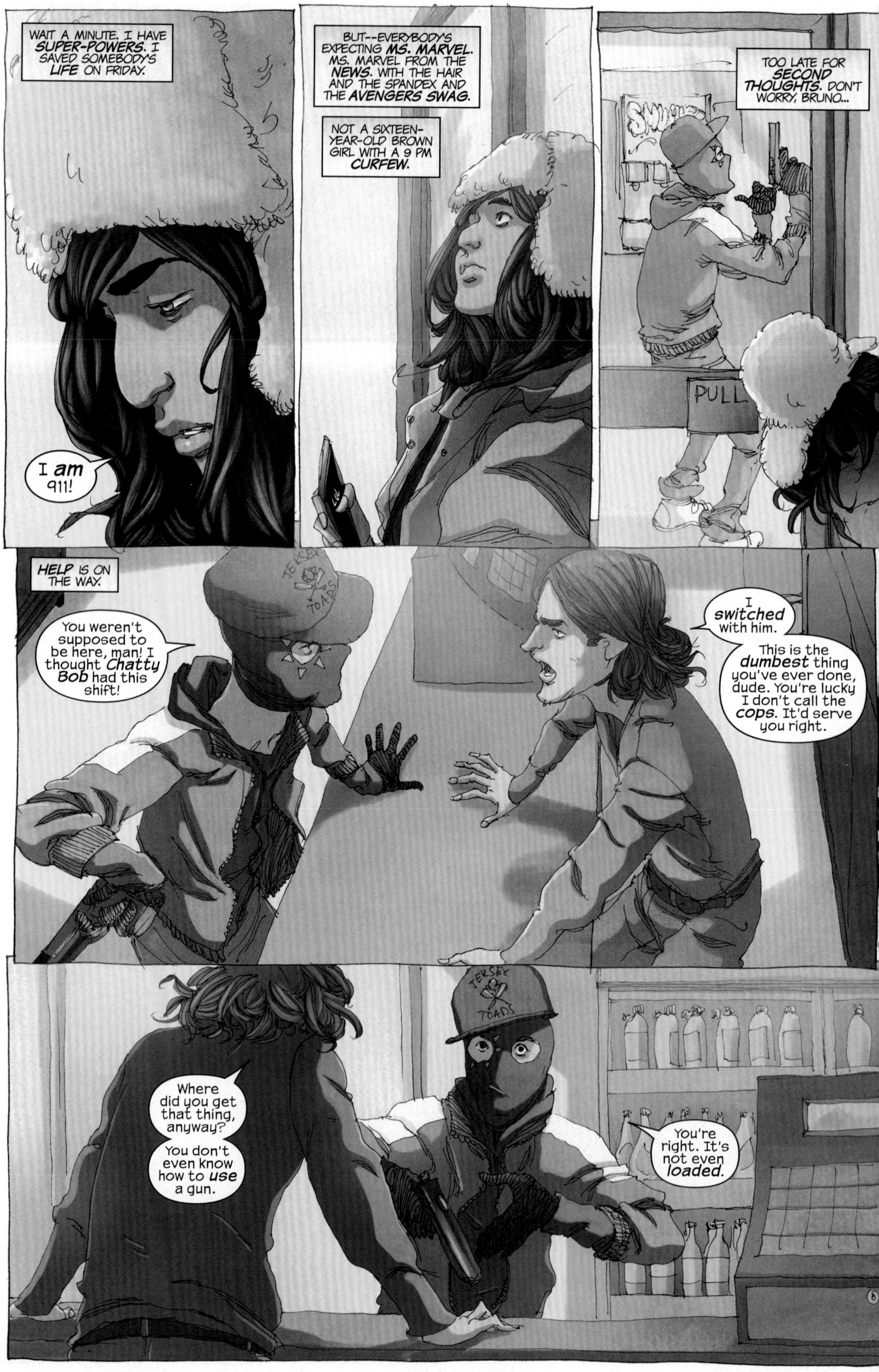
WAIT A MINUTE. I HAVE SUPER-POWERS. I SAVED SOMEBODY'S LIFE ON FRIDAY.
I am 911!
BUT--EVERYBODY'S EXPECTING MS. MARVEL. MS. MARVEL FROM THE NEWS. WITH THE HAIR AND THE SPANDEX AND THE AVENGERS SWAG.
NOT A SIXTEEN-YEAR-OLD BROWN GIRL WITH A 9 PM CURFEW.
TOO LATE FOR SECOND THOUGHTS. DON'T WORRY, BRUNO...
PULL
HELP IS ON THE WAY.
You weren't supposed to be here, man! I thought Chatty Bob had this shift!
I switched with him.
This is the dumbest thing you've ever done, dude. You're lucky I don't call the cops. It'd serve you right.
Where did you get that thing, anyway?
You don't even know how to use a gun.
You're right. It's not even loaded.

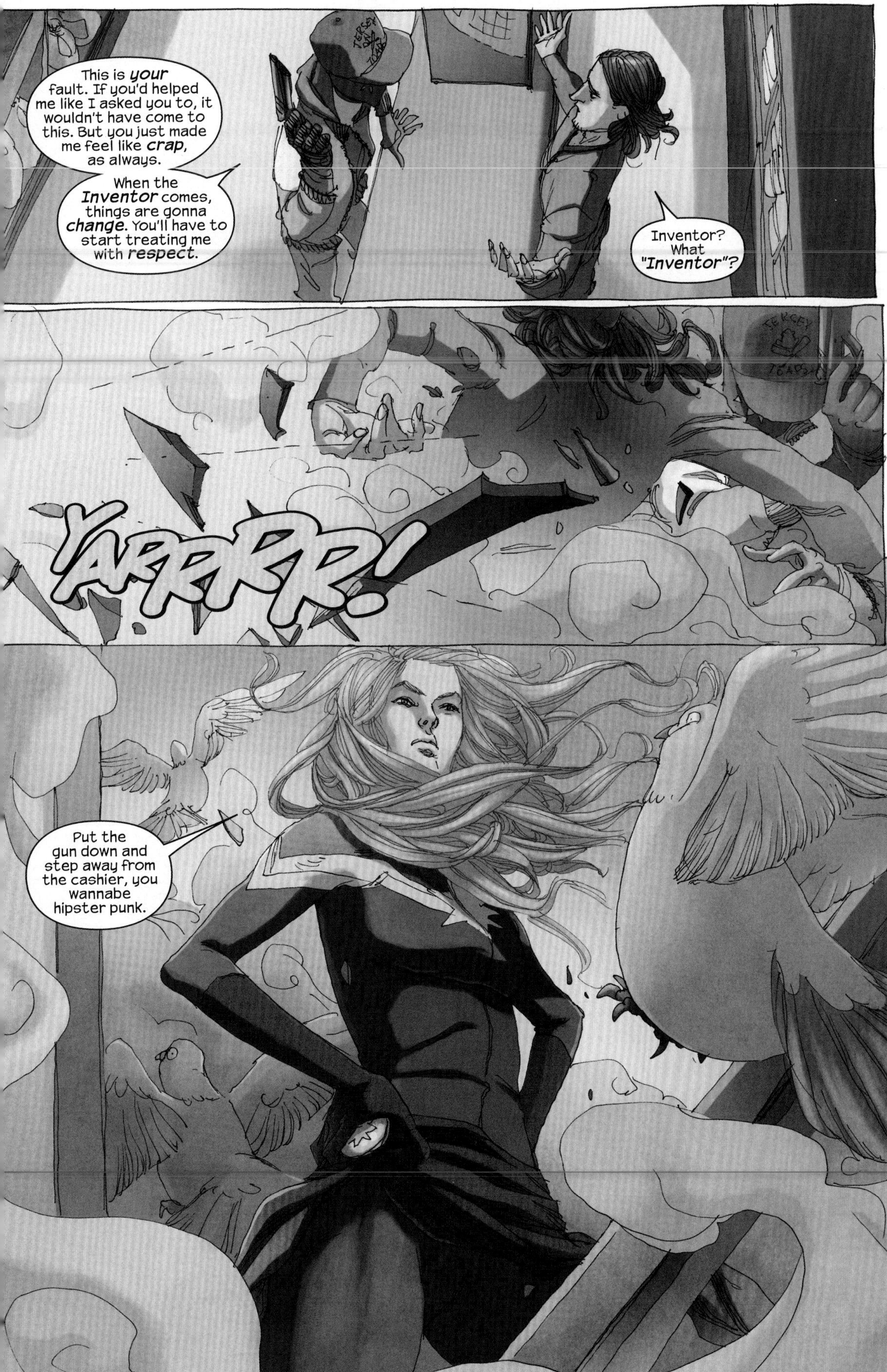
This is your fault. If you'd helped me like I asked you to, it wouldn't have come to this. But you just made me feel like crap, as always.
When the Inventor comes, things are gonna change. You'll have to start treating me with respect.
Inventor? What "Inventor"?
YARRRR!
Put the gun down and step away from the cashier, you wannabe hipster punk.

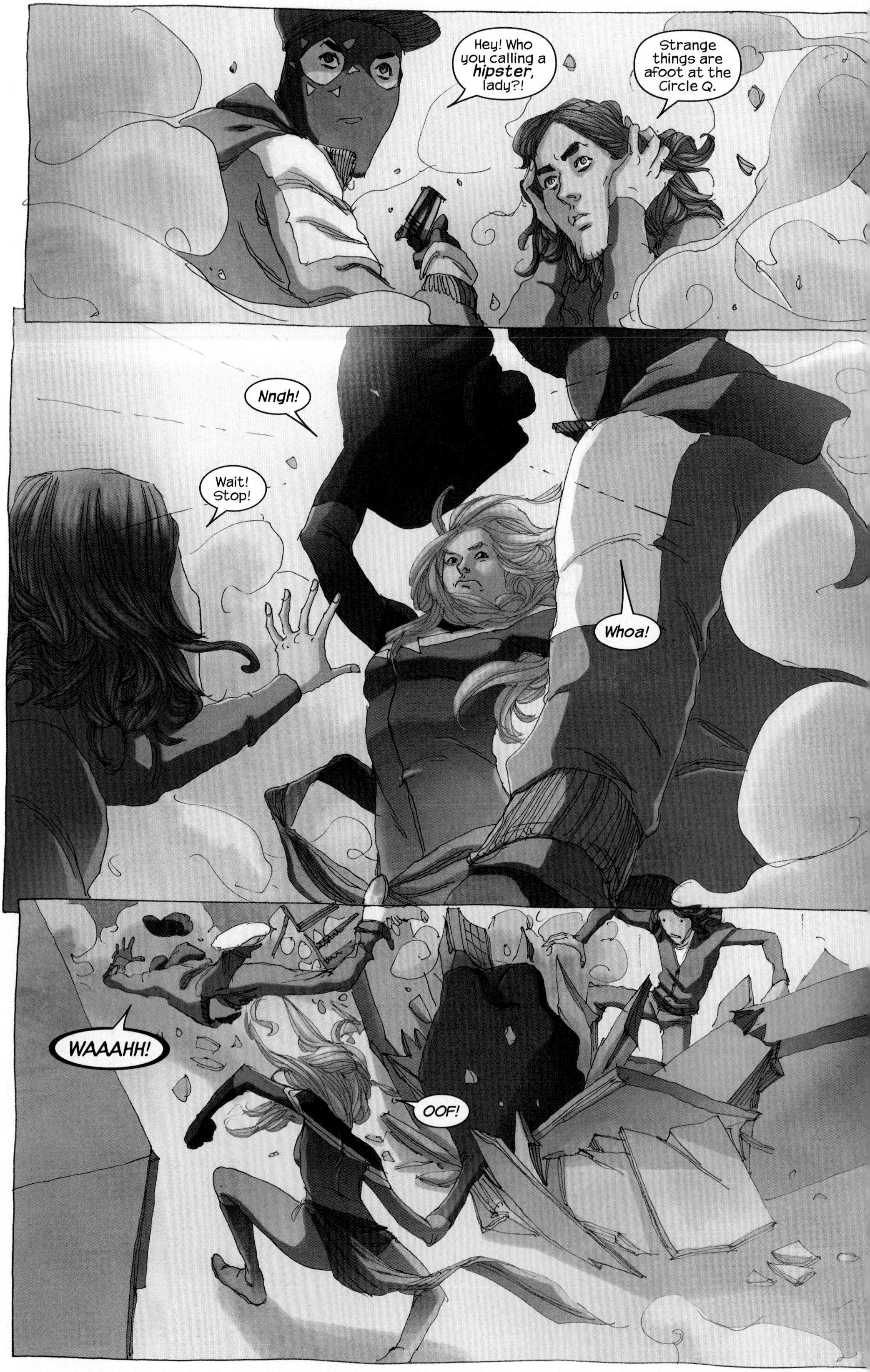
Hey! Who you calling a ***hipster***, lady?!
Strange things are afoot at the Circle Q.
Nngh!
Wait! Stop!
Whoa!
WAAAHH!
OOF!

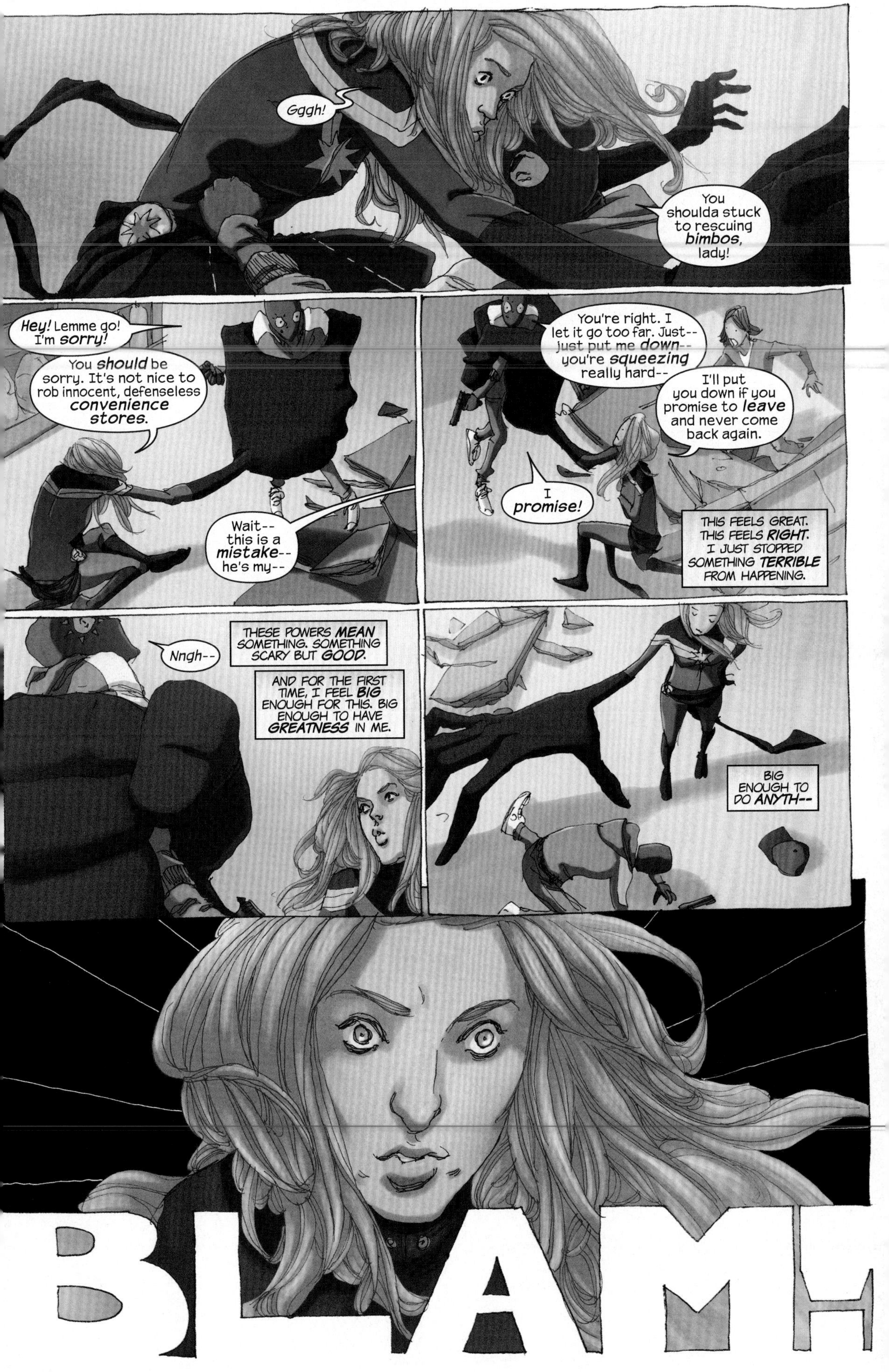
Gggh!
You shoulda stuck to rescuing bimbos, lady!
Hey! Lemme go! I'm sorry!
You should be sorry. It's not nice to rob innocent, defenseless convenience stores.
Wait-- this is a mistake-- he's my--
You're right. I let it go too far. Just-- just put me down-- you're squeezing really hard--
I'll put you down if you promise to leave and never come back again.
I promise!
THIS FEELS GREAT. THIS FEELS RIGHT. I JUST STOPPED SOMETHING TERRIBLE FROM HAPPENING.
Nngh--
THESE POWERS MEAN SOMETHING. SOMETHING SCARY BUT GOOD.
AND FOR THE FIRST TIME, I FEEL BIG ENOUGH FOR THIS. BIG ENOUGH TO HAVE GREATNESS IN ME.
BIG ENOUGH TO DO ANYTH--
BLAMH

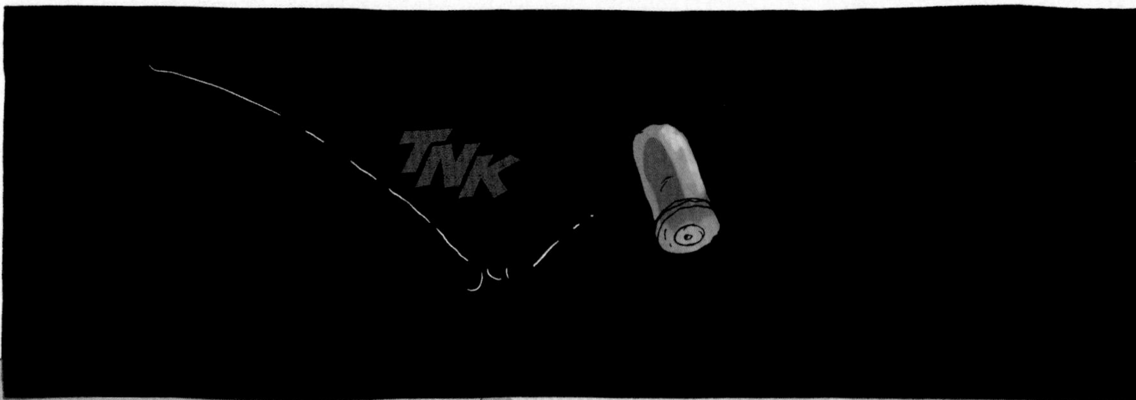
TNK

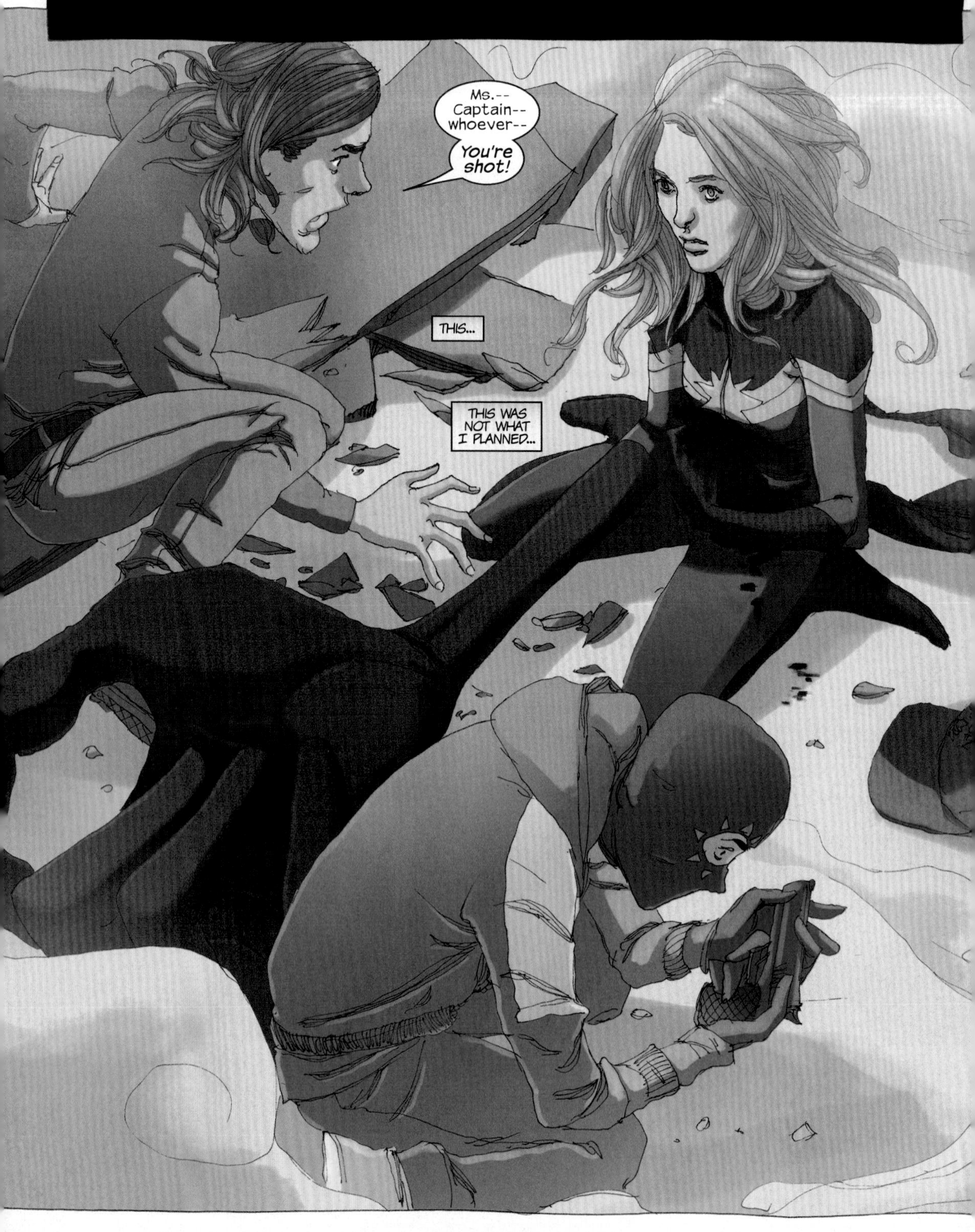
Ms.-- Captain-- whoever--
You're shot!
THIS...
THIS WAS NOT WHAT I PLANNED...

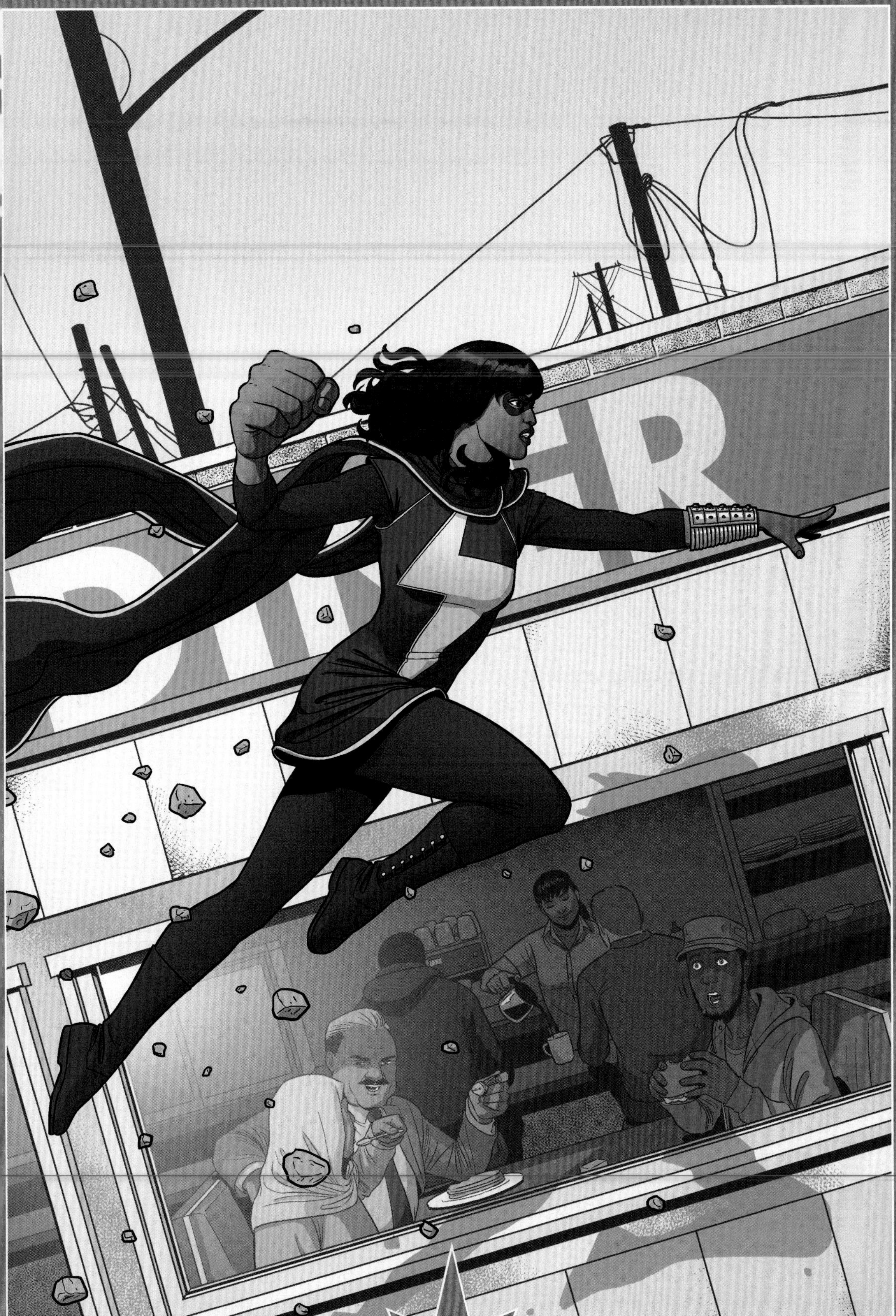
4

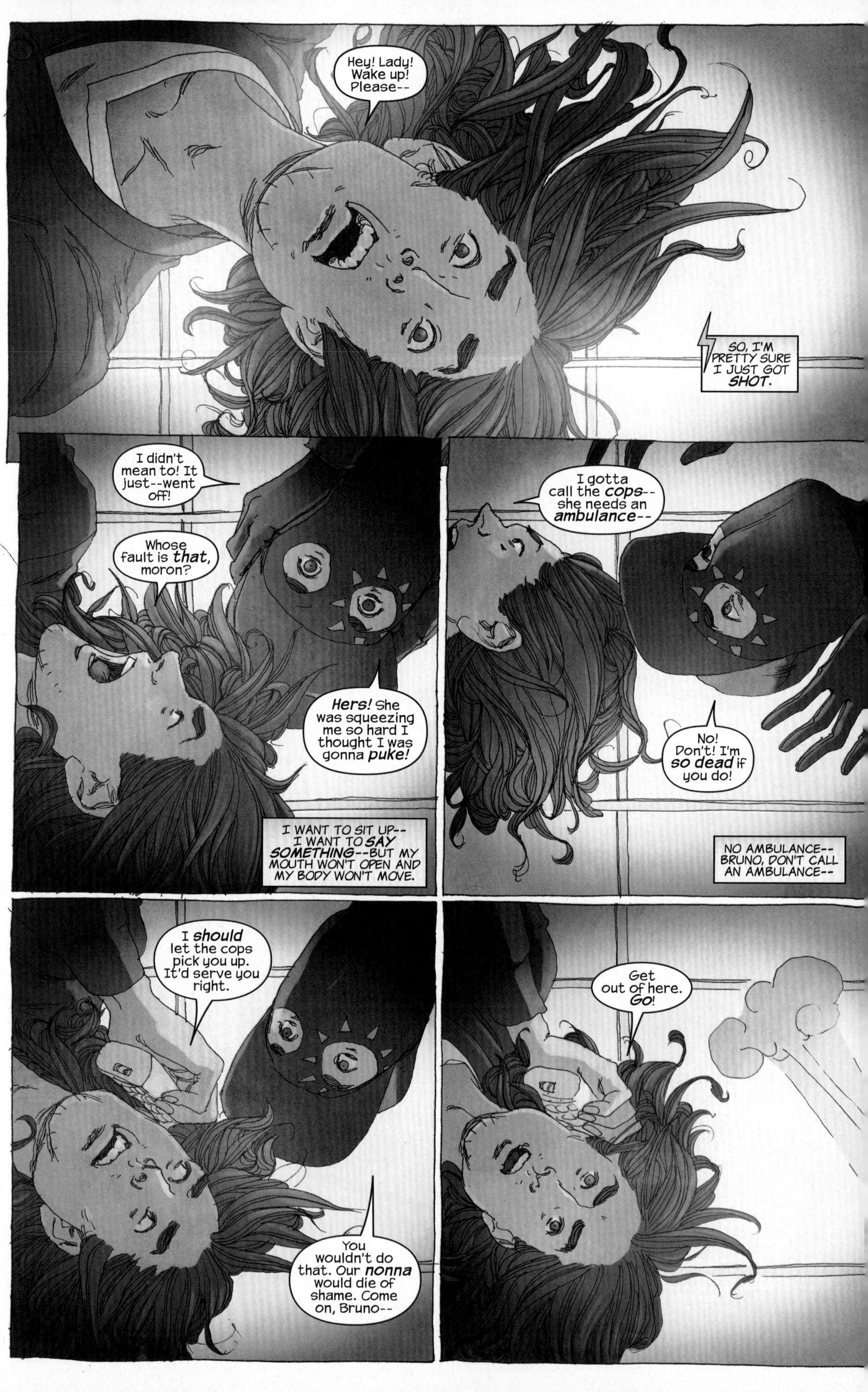
Hey! Lady! Wake up! Please--
SO, I'M PRETTY SURE I JUST GOT SHOT.
I didn't mean to! It just--went off!
Whose fault is that, moron?
Hers! She was squeezing me so hard I thought I was gonna puke!
I WANT TO SIT UP-- I WANT TO SAY SOMETHING--BUT MY MOUTH WON'T OPEN AND MY BODY WON'T MOVE.
I gotta call the cops-- she needs an ambulance--
No! Don't! I'm so dead if you do!
NO AMBULANCE-- BRUNO, DON'T CALL AN AMBULANCE--
I should let the cops pick you up. It'd serve you right.
You wouldn't do that. Our nonna would die of shame. Come on, Bruno--
Get out of here. Go!

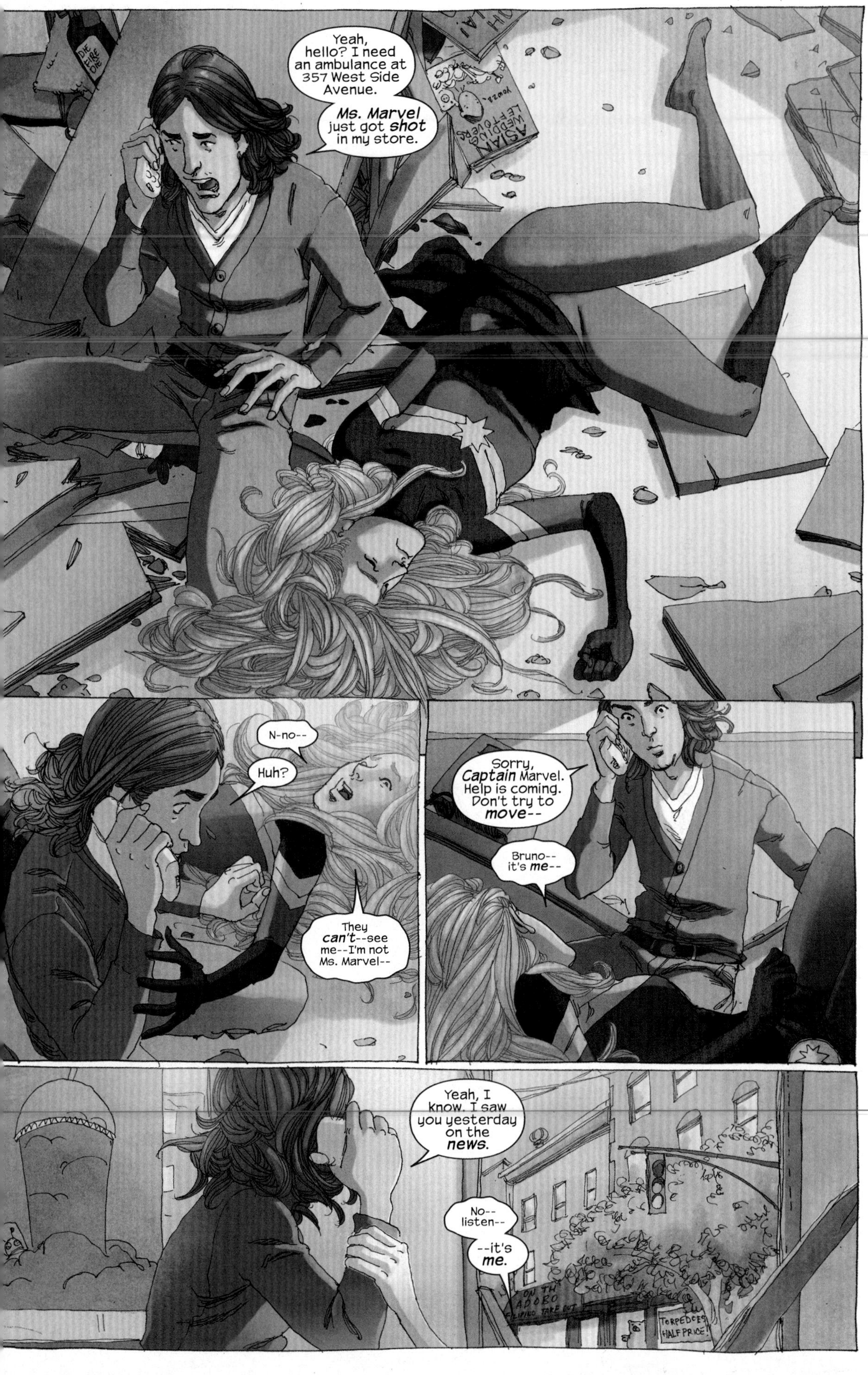
Yeah, hello? I need an ambulance at 357 West Side Avenue.
Ms. Marvel just got shot in my store.
N-no--
Huh?
They can't--see me--I'm not Ms. Marvel--
Sorry, Captain Marvel. Help is coming. Don't try to move--
Bruno-- it's me--
Yeah, I know. I saw you yesterday on the news.
No-- listen--
--it's me.
TORPEDOES HALF PRICE!

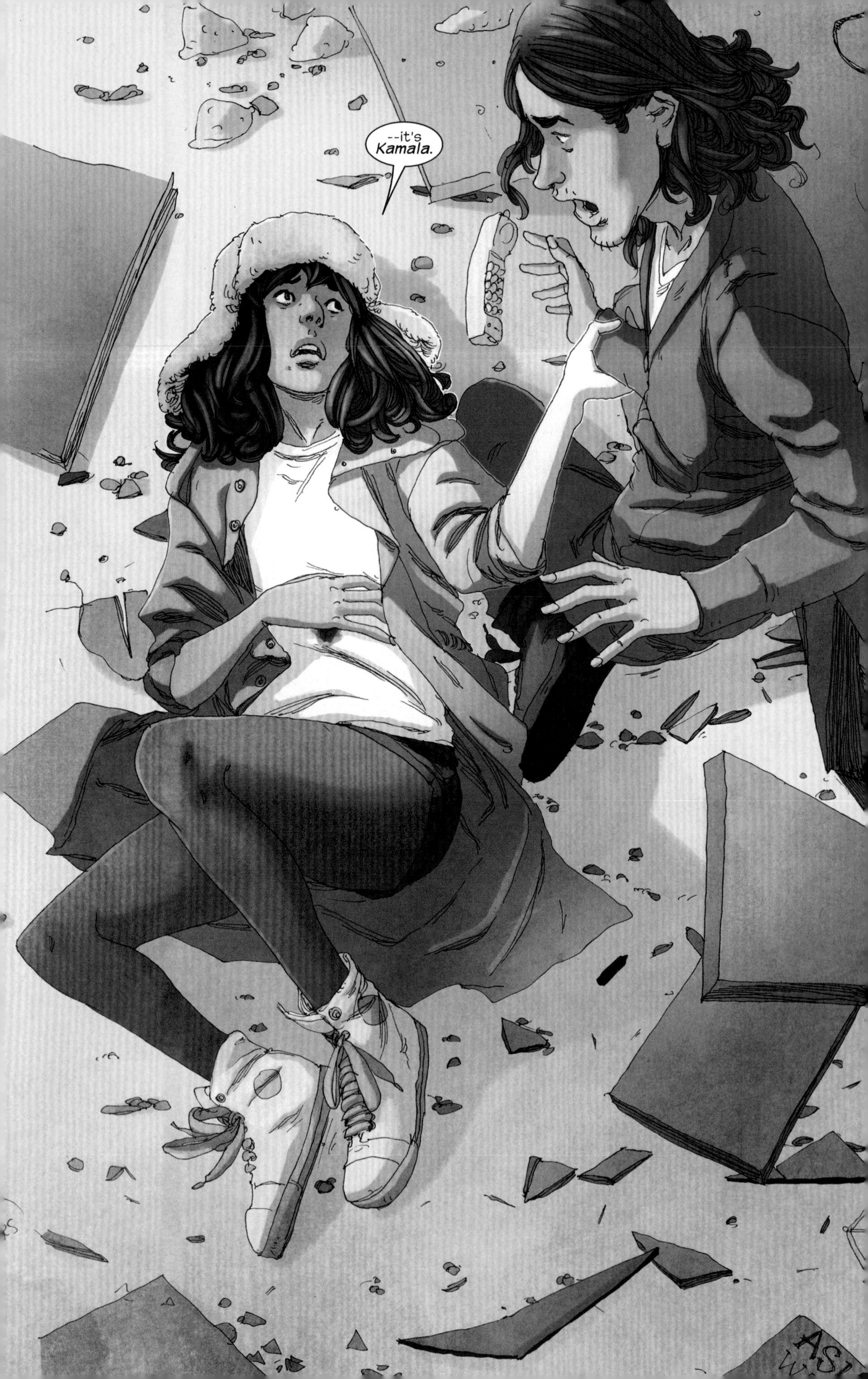
--it's *Kamala.*

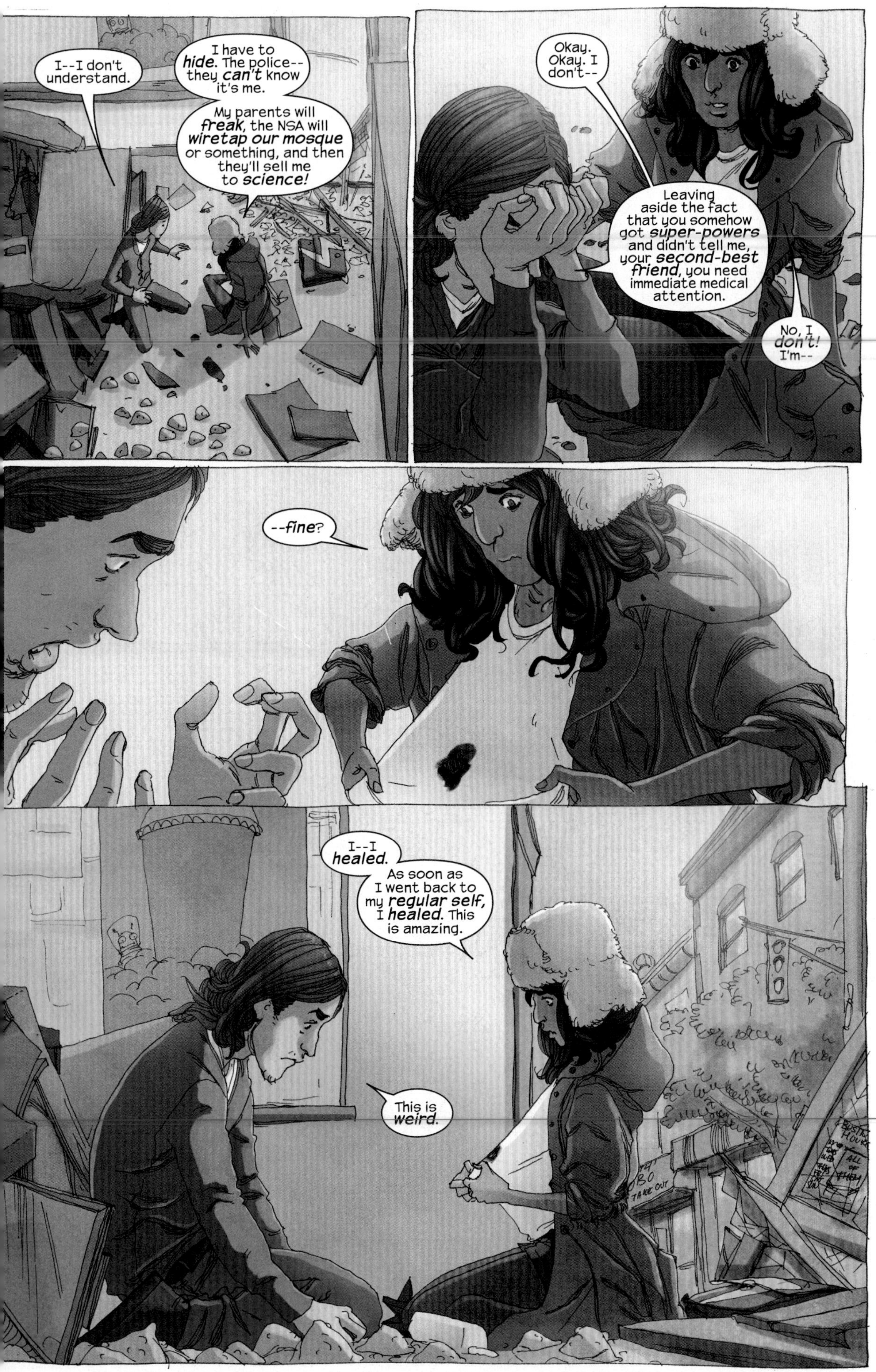
I--I don't understand.
I have to hide. The police--they can't know it's me.
My parents will freak, the NSA will wiretap our mosque or something, and then they'll sell me to science!
Okay. Okay. I don't--
Leaving aside the fact that you somehow got super-powers and didn't tell me, your second-best friend, you need immediate medical attention.
No, I don't! I'm--
--fine?
I--I healed.
As soon as I went back to my regular self, I healed. This is amazing.
This is weird.

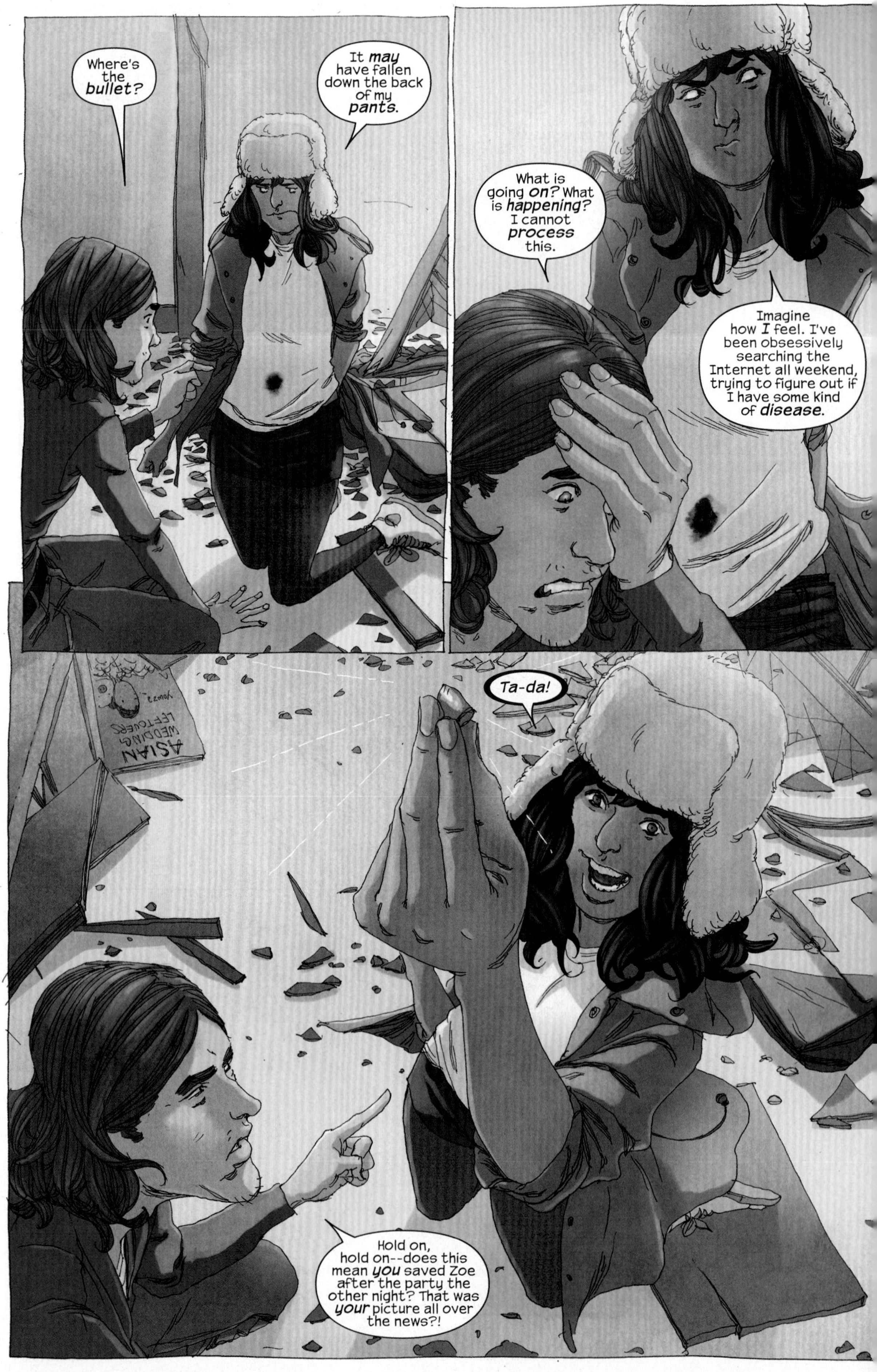
Where's the *bullet?*
It *may* have fallen down the back of my *pants*.
What is going *on?* What is *happening?* I cannot *process* this.
Imagine how *I* feel. I've been obsessively searching the Internet all weekend, trying to figure out if I have some kind of *disease*.
ASIAN WEDDING LEFTOVERS
Ta-da!
Hold on, hold on--does this mean *you* saved Zoe after the party the other night? That was *your* picture all over the news?!

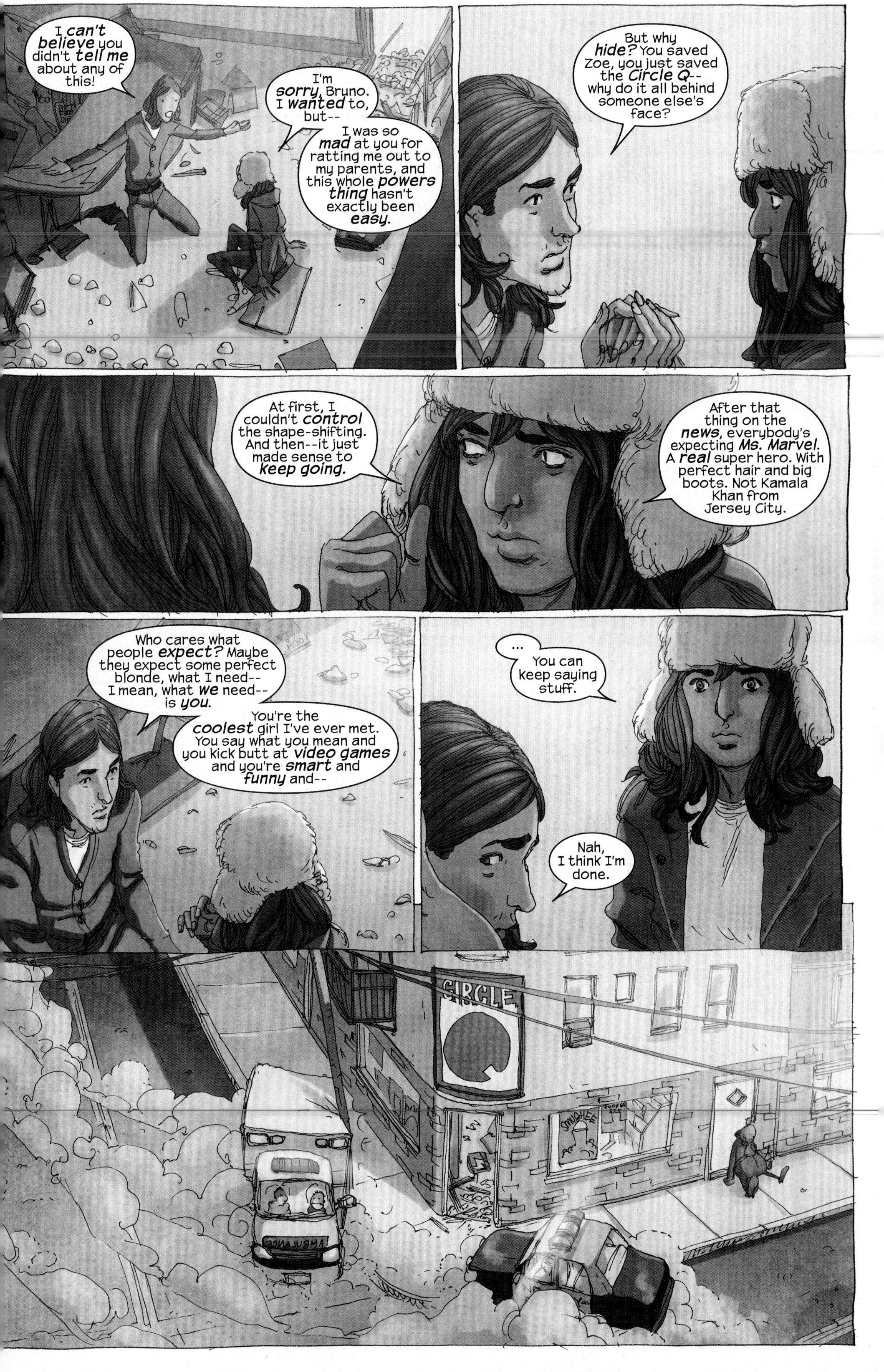
I can't believe you didn't tell me about any of this!
I'm sorry, Bruno. I wanted to, but--
I was so mad at you for ratting me out to my parents, and this whole powers thing hasn't exactly been easy.
But why hide? You saved Zoe, you just saved the Circle Q-- why do it all behind someone else's face?
At first, I couldn't control the shape-shifting. And then--it just made sense to keep going.
After that thing on the news, everybody's expecting Ms. Marvel. A real super hero. With perfect hair and big boots. Not Kamala Khan from Jersey City.
Who cares what people expect? Maybe they expect some perfect blonde, what I need-- I mean, what we need-- is you.
You're the coolest girl I've ever met. You say what you mean and you kick butt at video games and you're smart and funny and--
... You can keep saying stuff.
Nah, I think I'm done.
CIRCLE
AMBULANCE

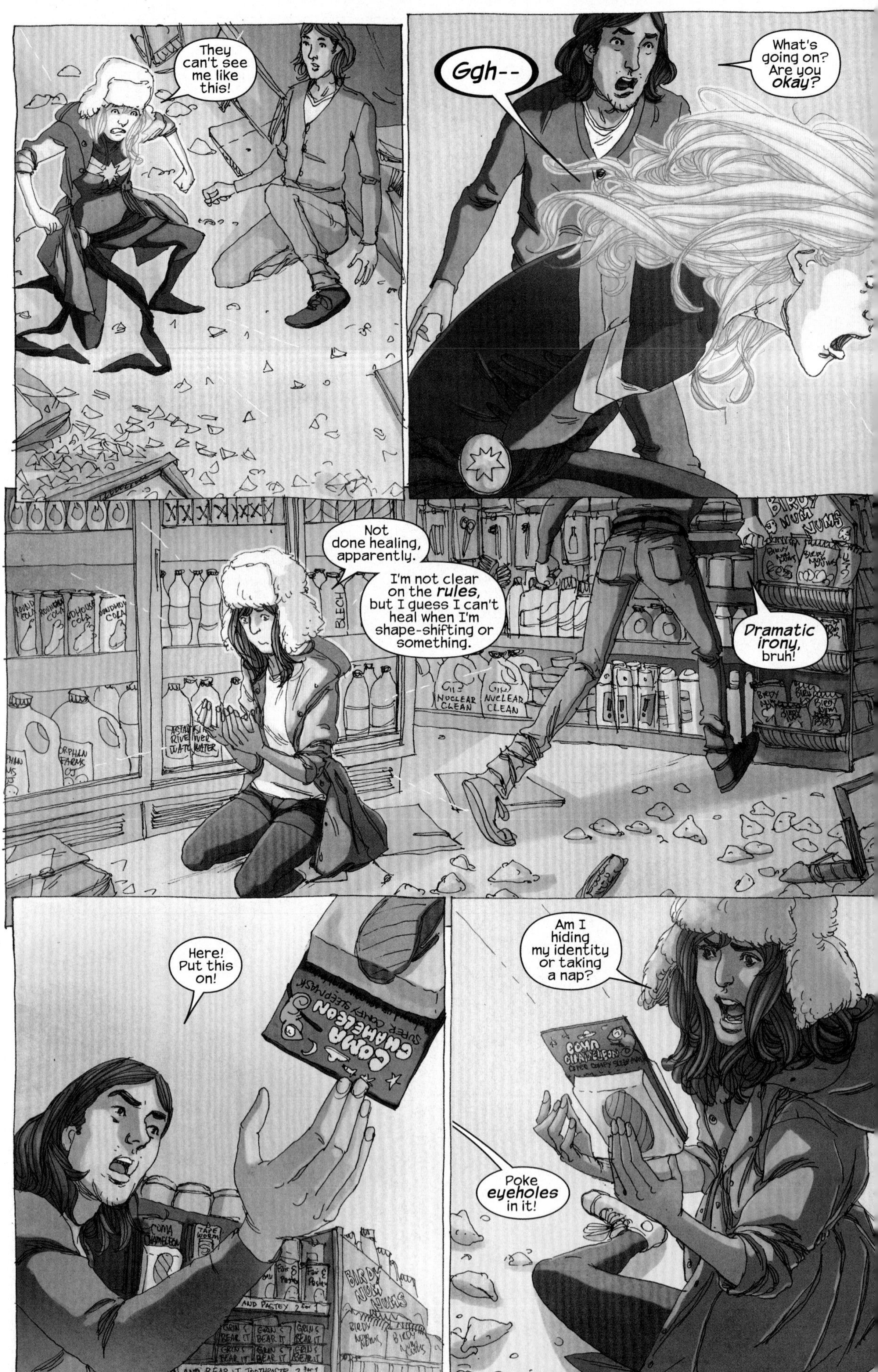
They can't see me like this!
Ggh--
What's going on? Are you okay?
Not done healing, apparently.
I'm not clear on the rules, but I guess I can't heal when I'm shape-shifting or something.
Dramatic irony, bruh!
Here! Put this on!
COMA CHAMELEON
Am I hiding my identity or taking a nap?
Poke eyeholes in it!

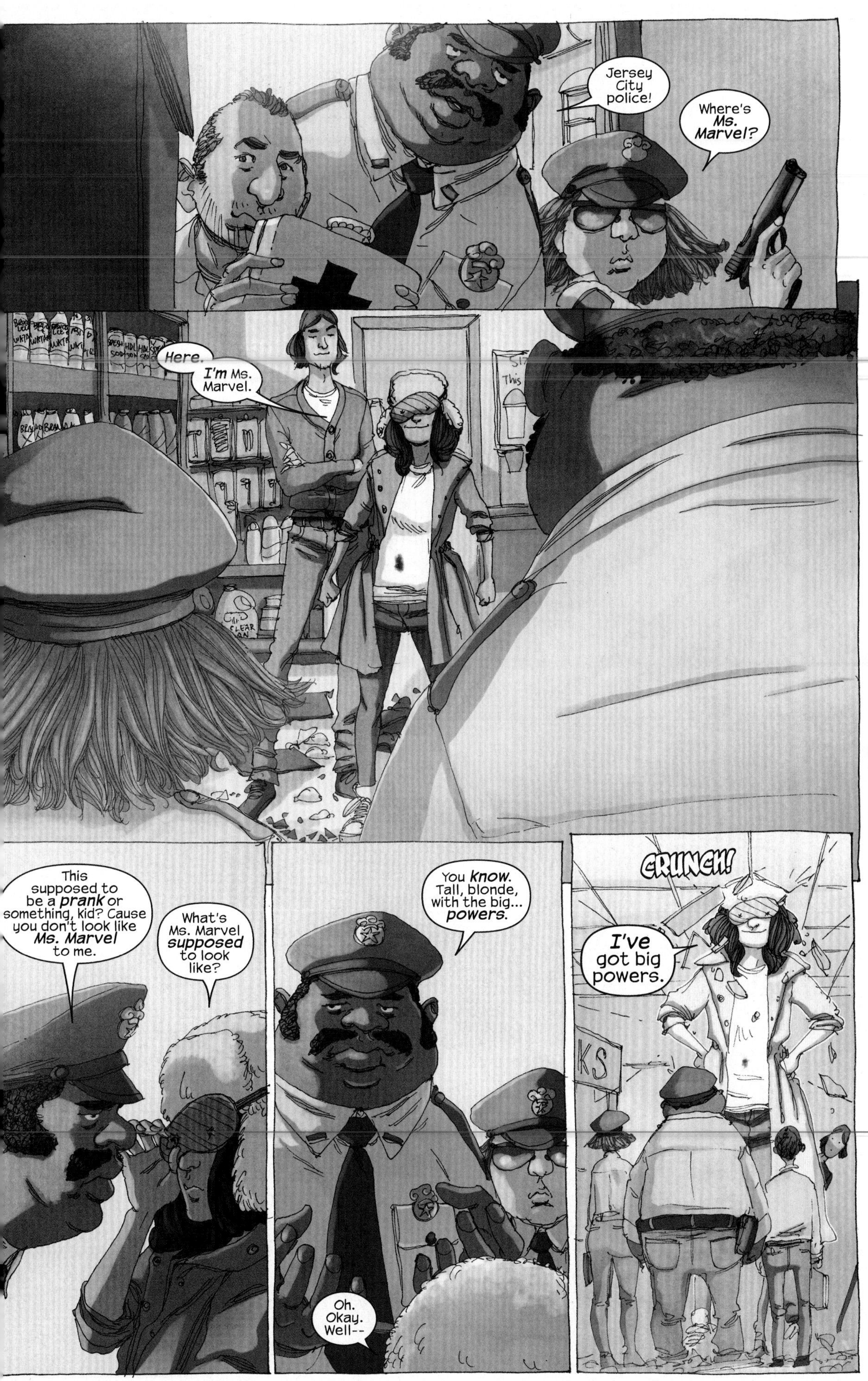
Jersey City police!
Where's Ms. Marvel?
Here.
I'm Ms. Marvel.
This supposed to be a prank or something, kid? Cause you don't look like Ms. Marvel to me.
What's Ms. Marvel supposed to look like?
You know. Tall, blonde, with the big... powers.
Oh. Okay. Well--
CRUNCH!
I've got big powers.

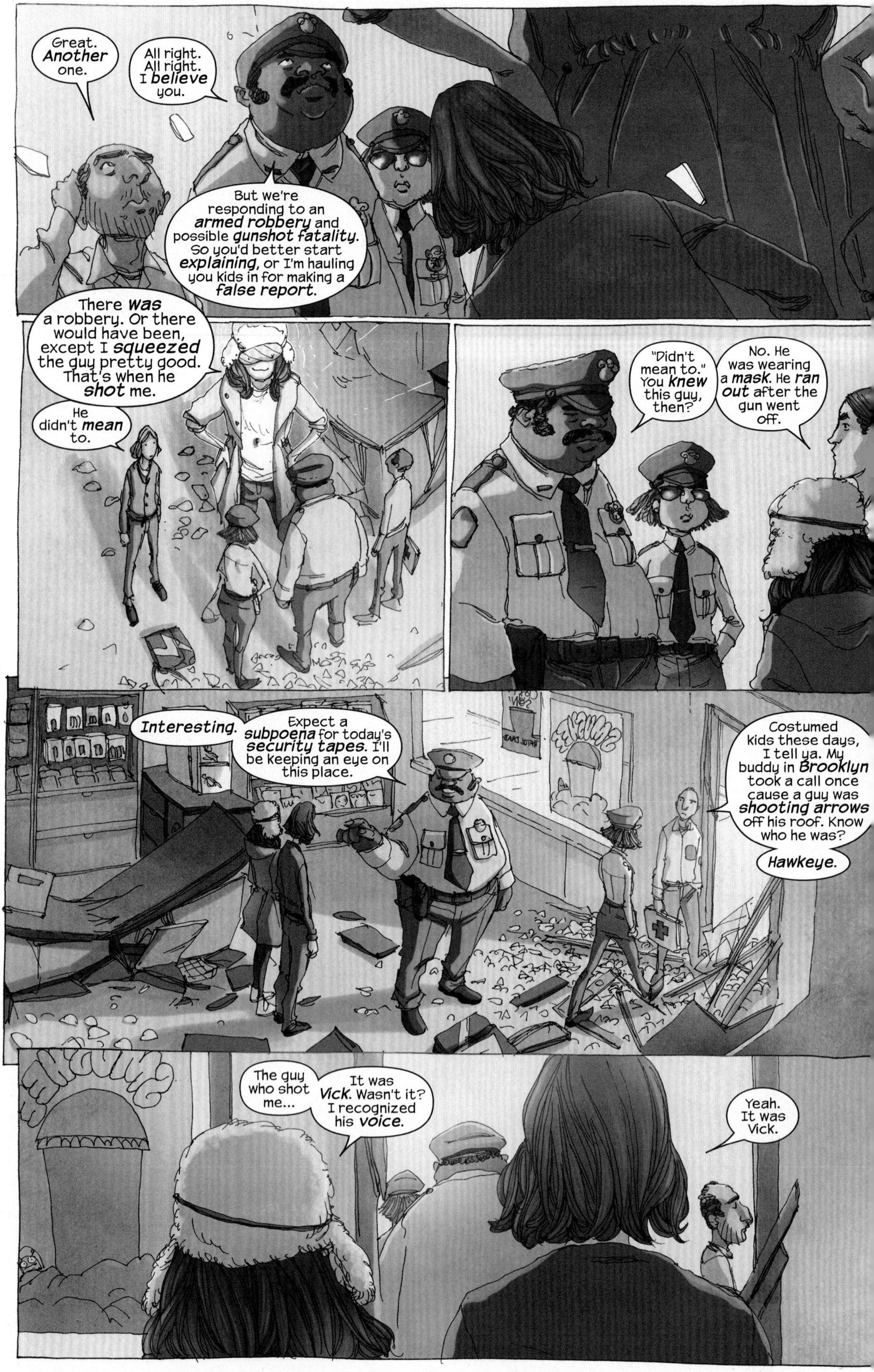
Great. Another one.
All right. All right. I believe you.
But we're responding to an armed robbery and possible gunshot fatality. So you'd better start explaining, or I'm hauling you kids in for making a false report.
There was a robbery. Or there would have been, except I squeezed the guy pretty good. That's when he shot me.
He didn't mean to.
"Didn't mean to." You knew this guy, then?
No. He was wearing a mask. He ran out after the gun went off.
Interesting.
Expect a subpoena for today's security tapes. I'll be keeping an eye on this place.
Costumed kids these days, I tell ya. My buddy in Brooklyn took a call once cause a guy was shooting arrows off his roof. Know who he was?
Hawkeye.
The guy who shot me...
It was Vick. Wasn't it? I recognized his voice.
Yeah. It was Vick.

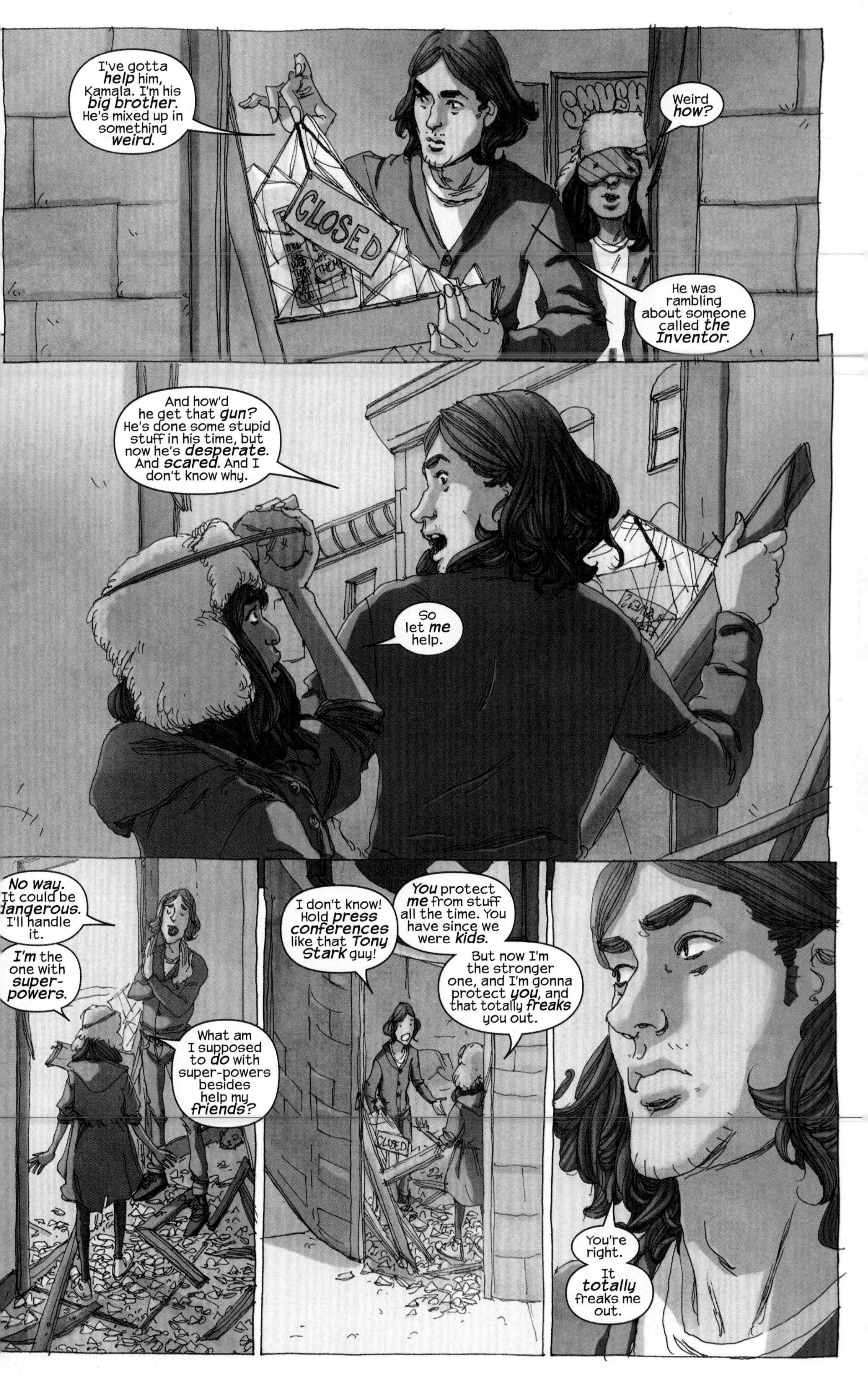

I've gotta help him, Kamala. I'm his big brother. He's mixed up in something weird.
Weird how?
He was rambling about someone called the Inventor.
And how'd he get that gun? He's done some stupid stuff in his time, but now he's desperate. And scared. And I don't know why.
So let me help.
No way. It could be dangerous. I'll handle it.
I'm the one with super-powers.
What am I supposed to do with super-powers besides help my friends?
I don't know! Hold press conferences like that Tony Stark guy!
You protect me from stuff all the time. You have since we were kids.
But now I'm the stronger one, and I'm gonna protect you, and that totally freaks you out.
You're right.
It totally freaks me out.

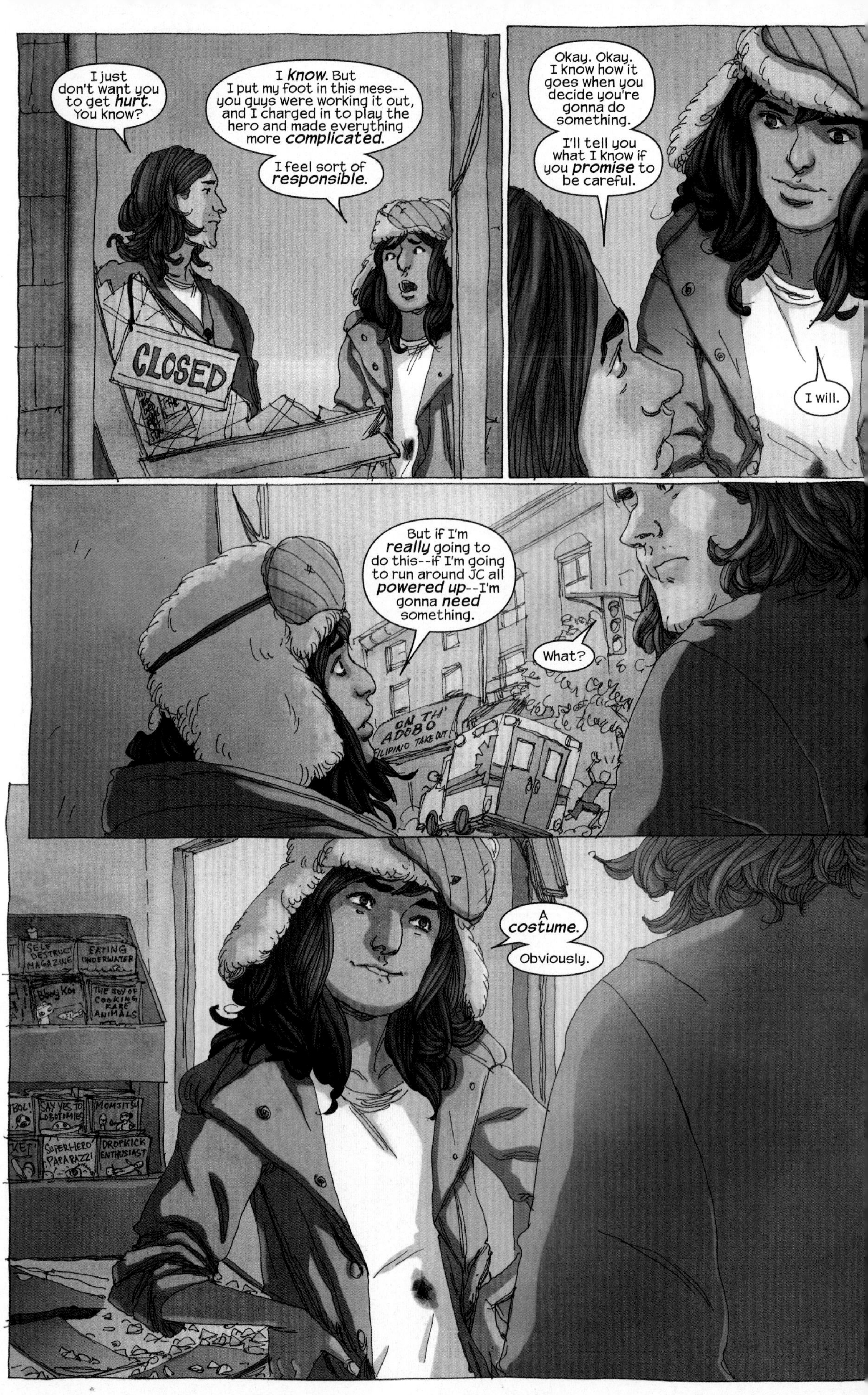
I just don't want you to get hurt. You know?
I know. But I put my foot in this mess--you guys were working it out, and I charged in to play the hero and made everything more complicated.
I feel sort of responsible.
CLOSED
Okay. Okay. I know how it goes when you decide you're gonna do something.
I'll tell you what I know if you promise to be careful.
I will.
But if I'm really going to do this--if I'm going to run around JC all powered up--I'm gonna need something.
What?
ON TH' ADOBO
FILIPINO TAKE OUT
A costume.
Obviously.
SELF DESTRUCT MAGAZINE
EATING UNDERWATER
THE JOY OF COOKING RARE ANIMALS
SAY YES TO LOBOTOMIES
MOMJITSU
SUPERHERO PAPARAZZI
DROPKICK ENTHUSIAST

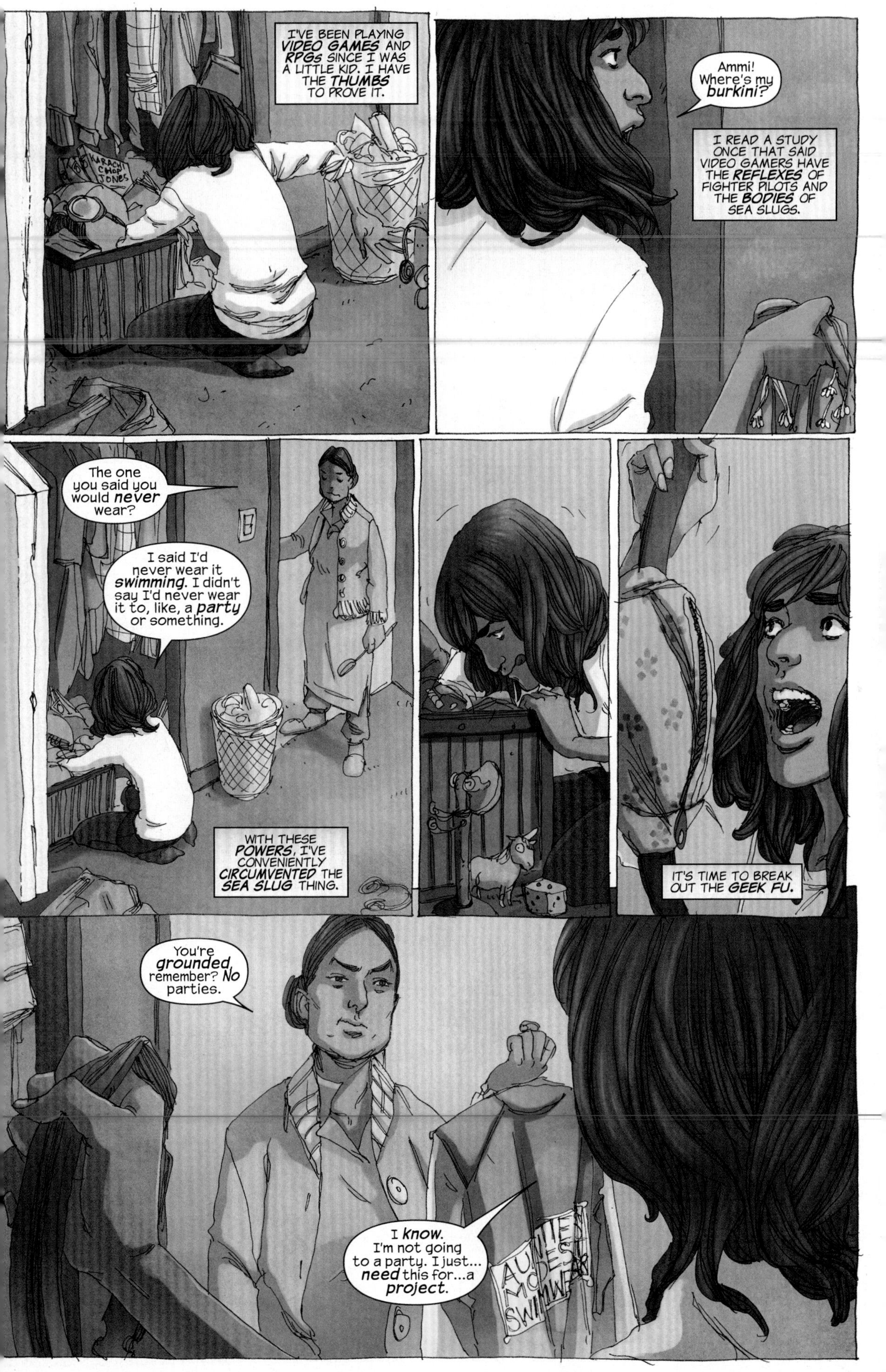
I'VE BEEN PLAYING VIDEO GAMES AND RPGs SINCE I WAS A LITTLE KID. I HAVE THE THUMBS TO PROVE IT.
KARACHI CHOP JONES
Ammi! Where's my burkini?
I READ A STUDY ONCE THAT SAID VIDEO GAMERS HAVE THE REFLEXES OF FIGHTER PILOTS AND THE BODIES OF SEA SLUGS.
The one you said you would never wear?
I said I'd never wear it swimming. I didn't say I'd never wear it to, like, a party or something.
WITH THESE POWERS, I'VE CONVENIENTLY CIRCUMVENTED THE SEA SLUG THING.
IT'S TIME TO BREAK OUT THE GEEK FU.
You're grounded, remember? No parties.
I know. I'm not going to a party. I just... need this for...a project.
AUNTIES MODEST SWIMWEAR

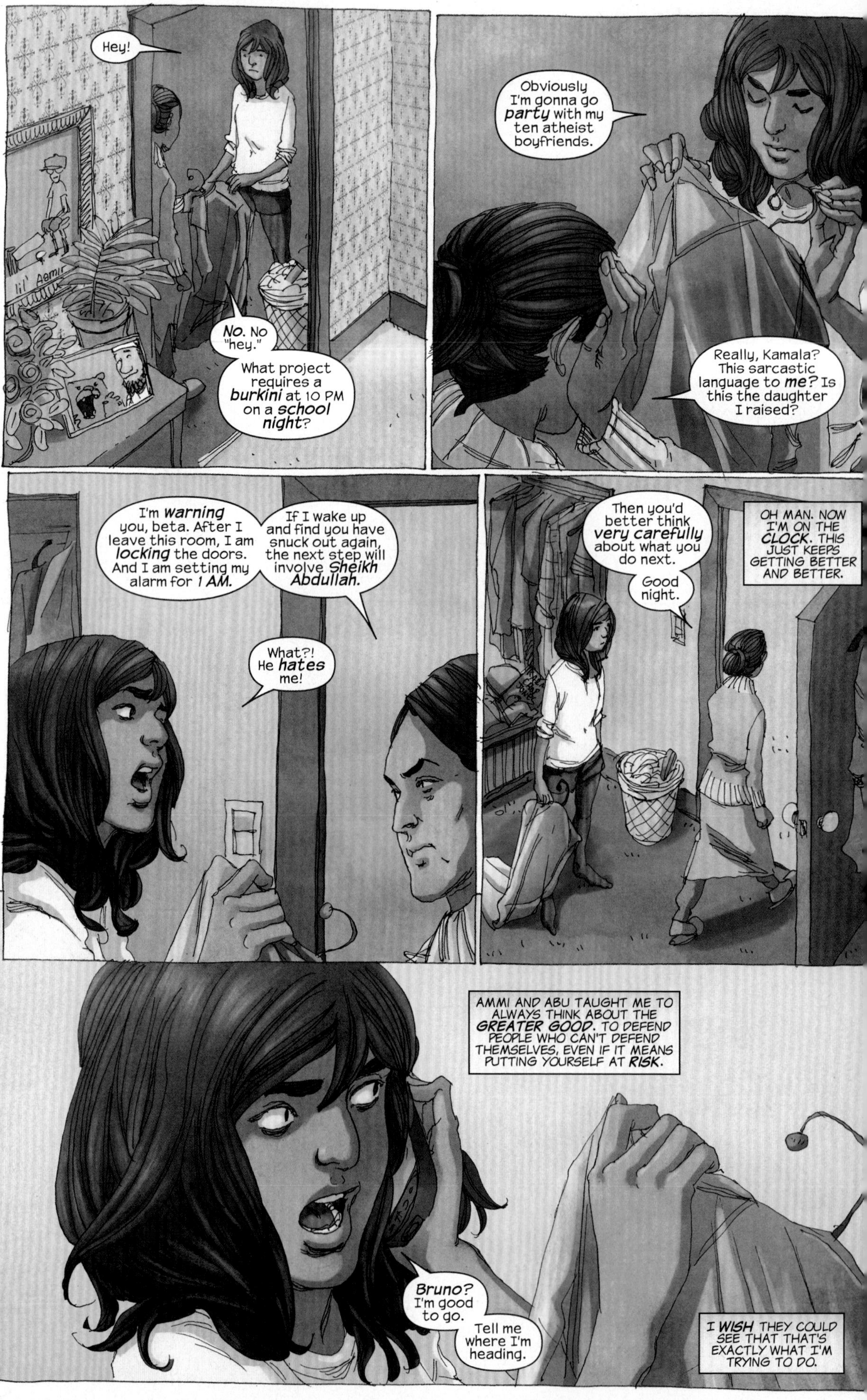
Hey!
Obviously I'm gonna go party with my ten atheist boyfriends.
No. No "hey." What project requires a burkini at 10 PM on a school night?
Really, Kamala? This sarcastic language to me? Is this the daughter I raised?
I'm warning you, beta. After I leave this room, I am locking the doors. And I am setting my alarm for 1 AM.
If I wake up and find you have snuck out again, the next step will involve Sheikh Abdullah.
What?! He hates me!
Then you'd better think very carefully about what you do next.
Good night.
OH MAN. NOW I'M ON THE CLOCK. THIS JUST KEEPS GETTING BETTER AND BETTER.
AMMI AND ABU TAUGHT ME TO ALWAYS THINK ABOUT THE GREATER GOOD. TO DEFEND PEOPLE WHO CAN'T DEFEND THEMSELVES, EVEN IF IT MEANS PUTTING YOURSELF AT RISK.
Bruno? I'm good to go.
Tell me where I'm heading.
I WISH THEY COULD SEE THAT THAT'S EXACTLY WHAT I'M TRYING TO DO.

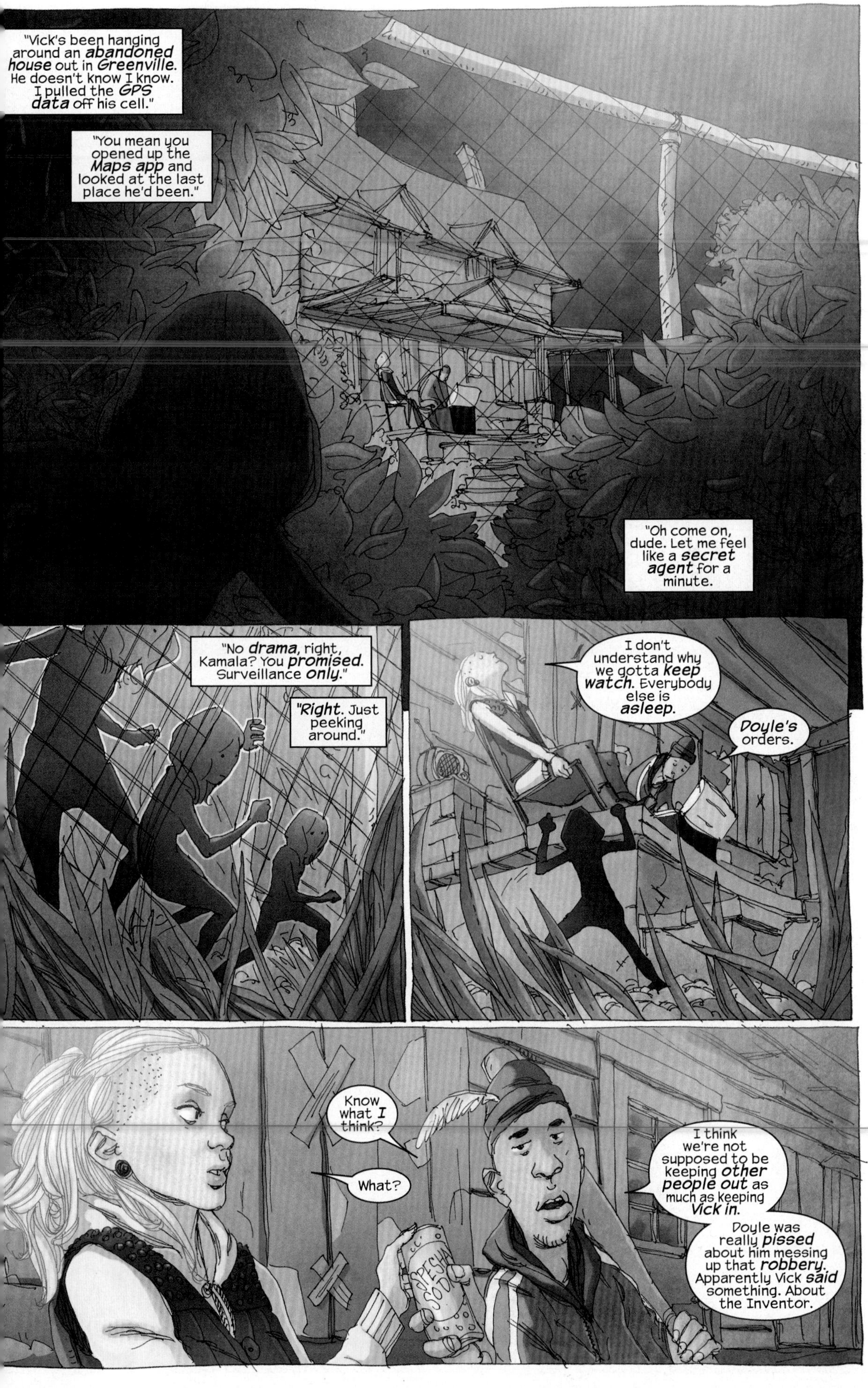
"Vick's been hanging around an abandoned house out in Greenville. He doesn't know I know. I pulled the GPS data off his cell."
"You mean you opened up the Maps app and looked at the last place he'd been."
"Oh come on, dude. Let me feel like a secret agent for a minute.
"No drama, right, Kamala? You promised. Surveillance only."
"Right. Just peeking around."
I don't understand why we gotta keep watch. Everybody else is asleep.
Doyle's orders.
Know what I think?
What?
I think we're not supposed to be keeping other people out as much as keeping Vick in.
Doyle was really pissed about him messing up that robbery. Apparently Vick said something. About the Inventor.

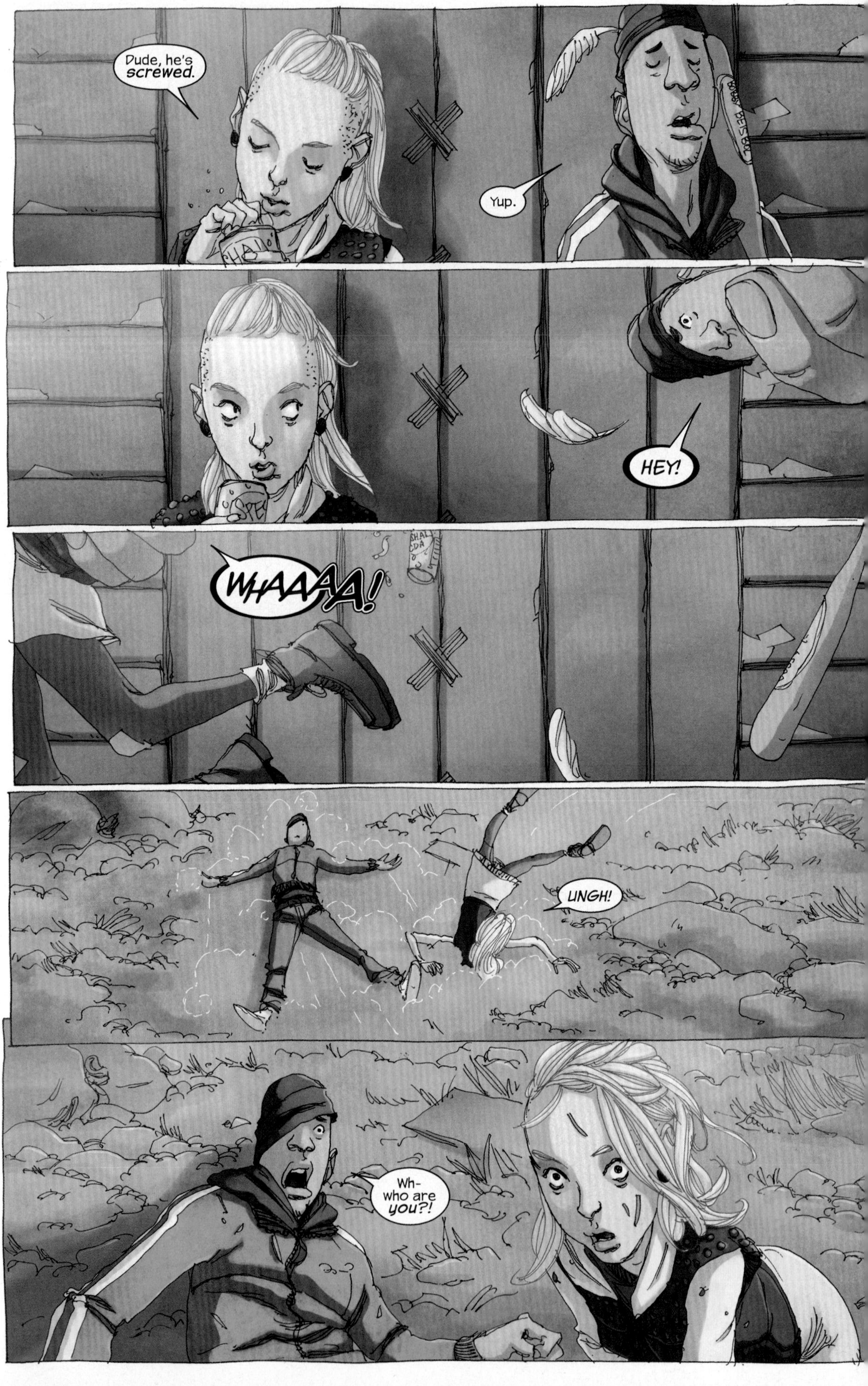
Dude, he's *screwed*.
Yup.
HEY!
WHAAAAA!
UNGH!
Wh- who are *you?!*

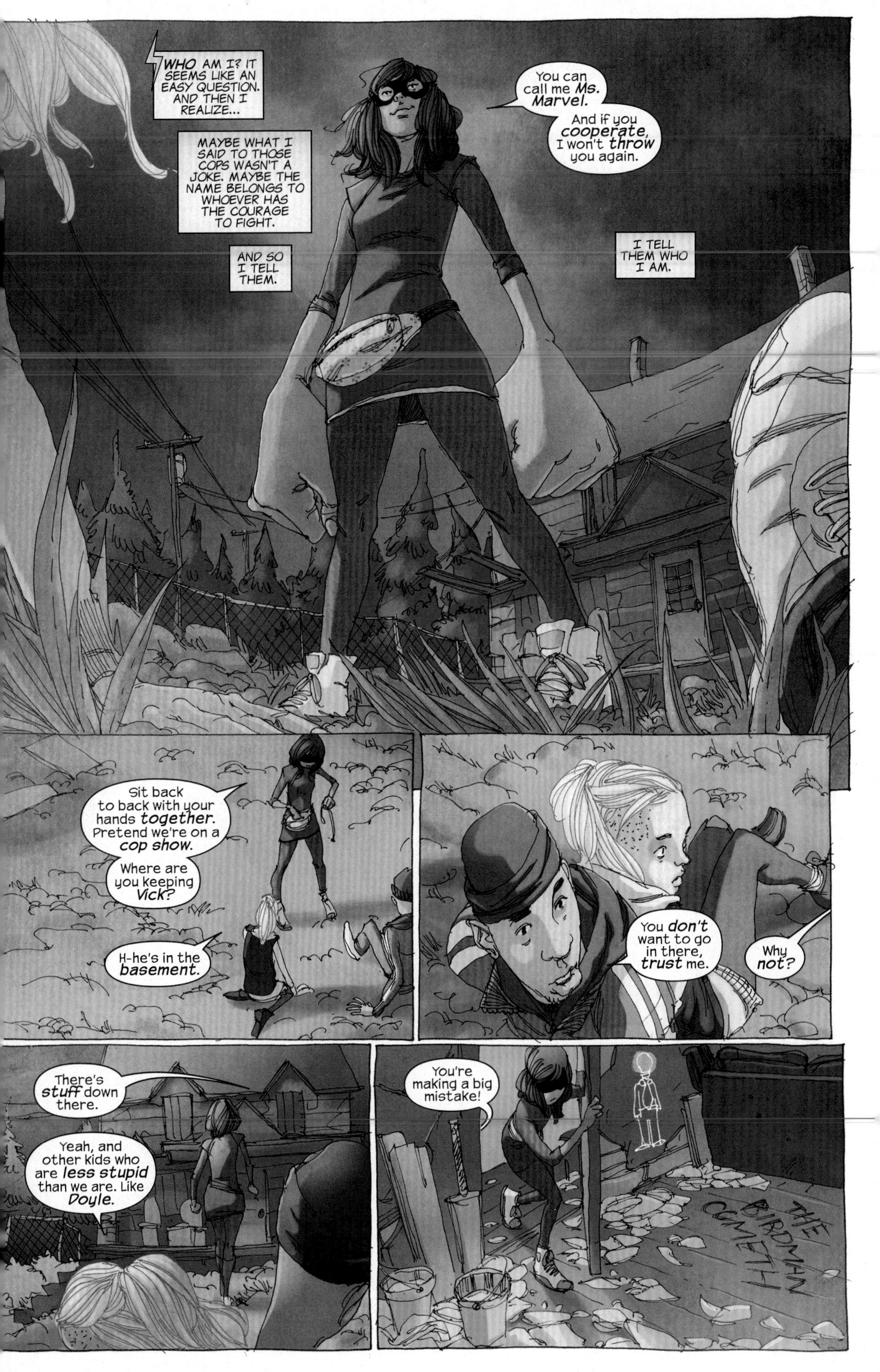
WHO AM I? IT SEEMS LIKE AN EASY QUESTION. AND THEN I REALIZE...
MAYBE WHAT I SAID TO THOSE COPS WASN'T A JOKE. MAYBE THE NAME BELONGS TO WHOEVER HAS THE COURAGE TO FIGHT.
AND SO I TELL THEM.
You can call me Ms. Marvel.
And if you cooperate, I won't throw you again.
I TELL THEM WHO I AM.
Sit back to back with your hands together. Pretend we're on a cop show.
Where are you keeping Vick?
H-he's in the basement.
You don't want to go in there, trust me.
Why not?
There's stuff down there.
Yeah, and other kids who are less stupid than we are. Like Doyle.
You're making a big mistake!
THE BIRDMAN COMETH

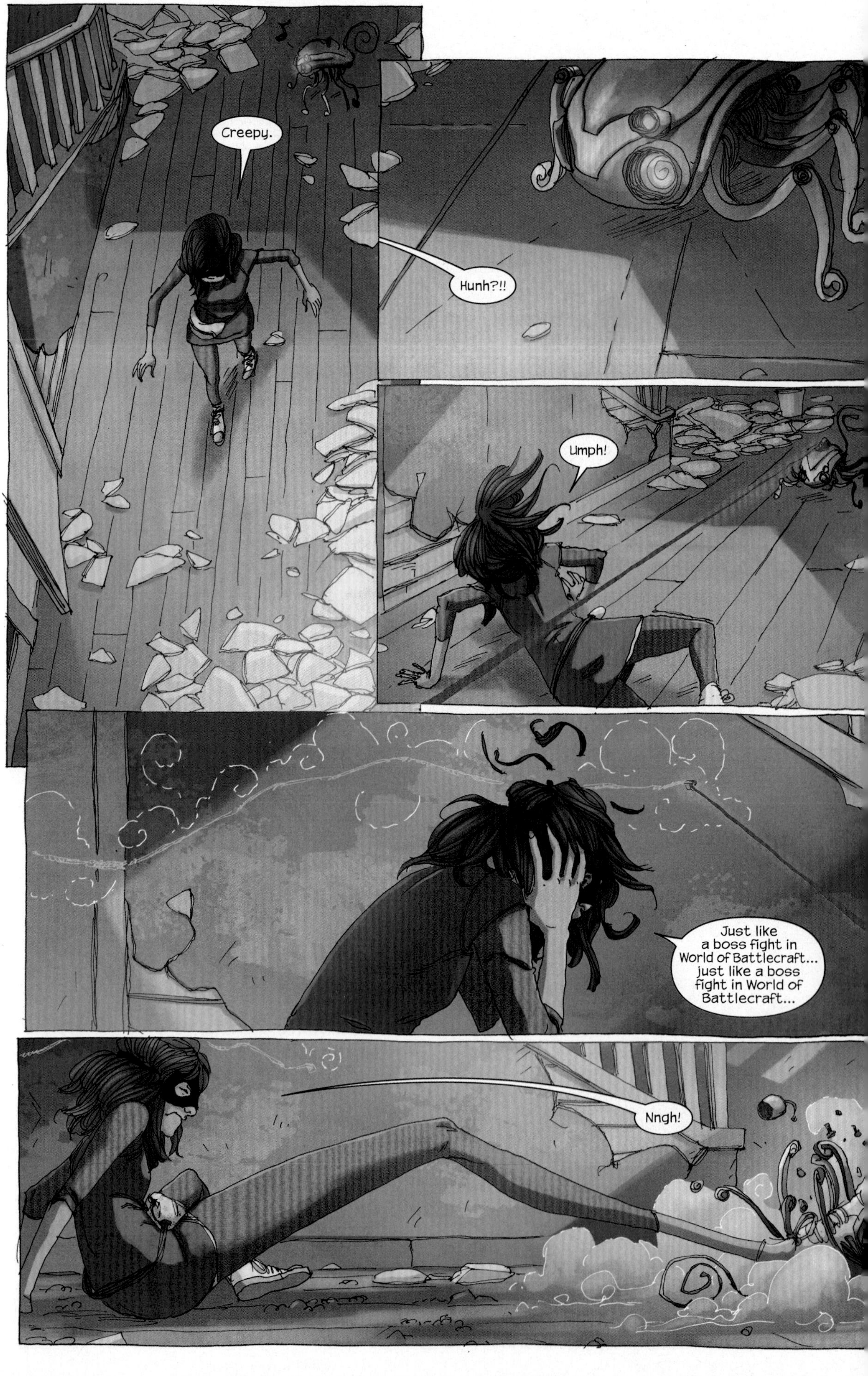
Creepy.
Hunh?!!
Umph!
Just like a boss fight in World of Battlecraft... just like a boss fight in World of Battlecraft...
Nngh!

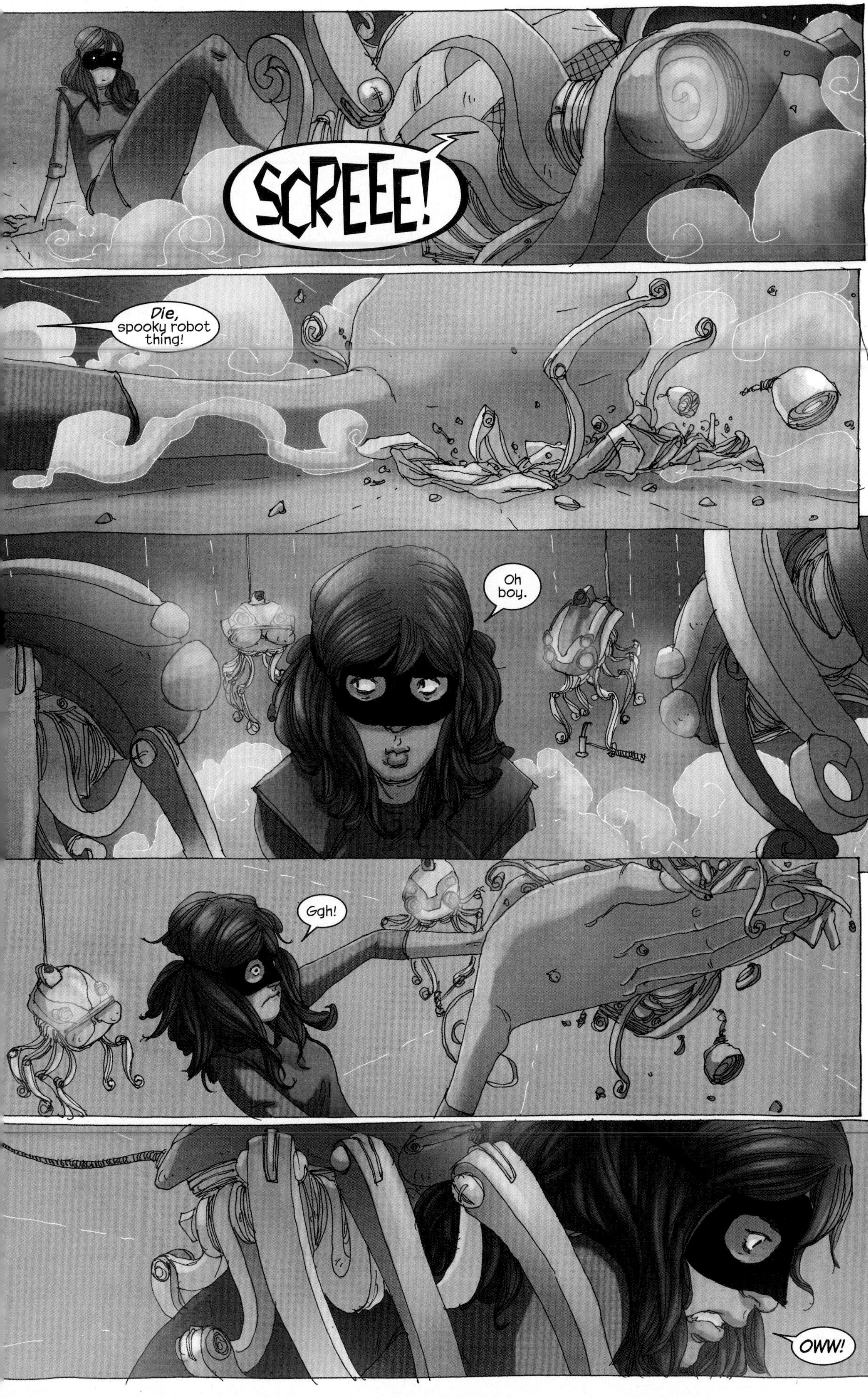
SCREEE!
Die, spooky robot thing!
Oh boy.
Ggh!
OWW!

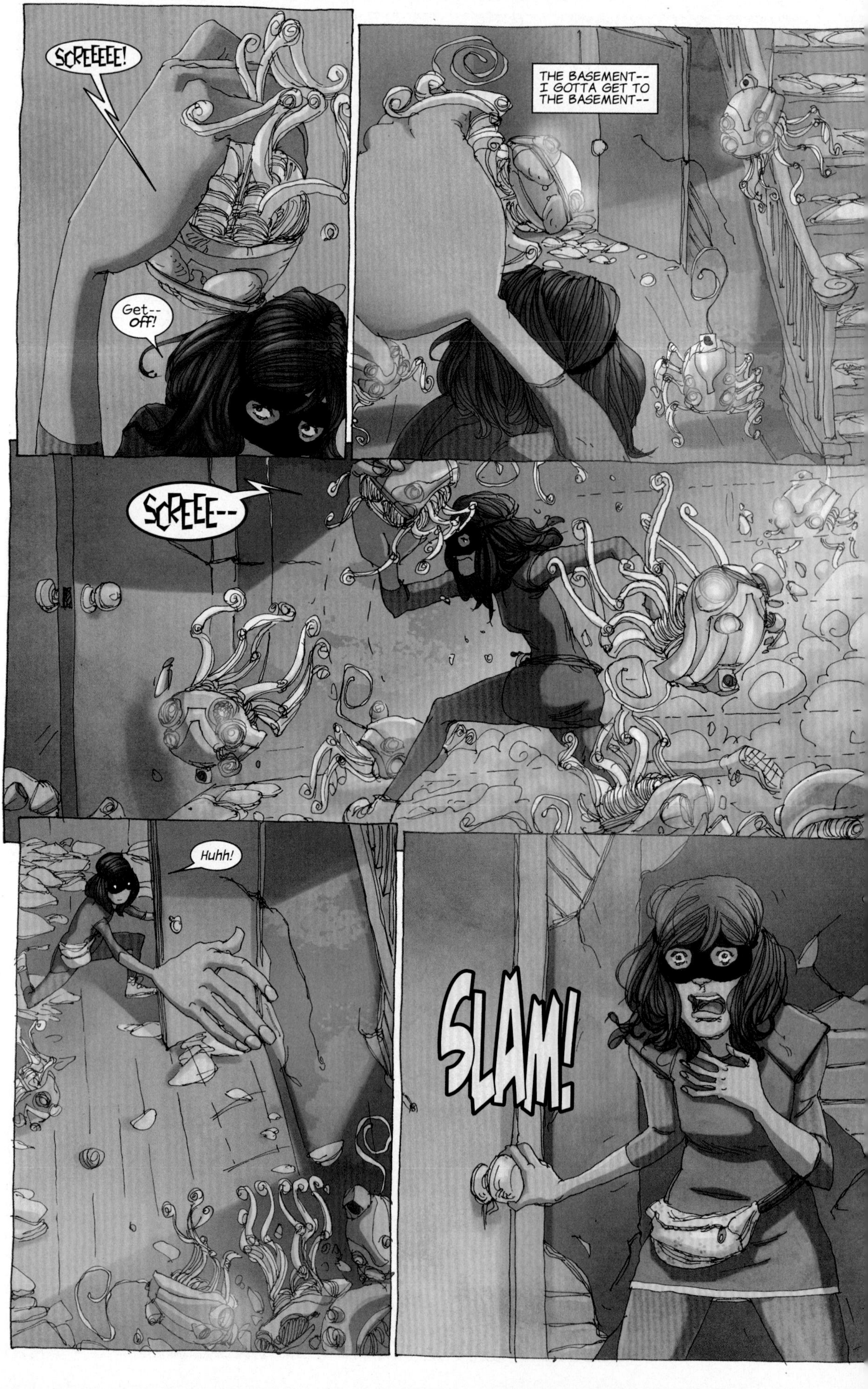
SCREEEEE!
Get-- off!
THE BASEMENT-- I GOTTA GET TO THE BASEMENT--
SCREEE--
Huhh!
SLAM!

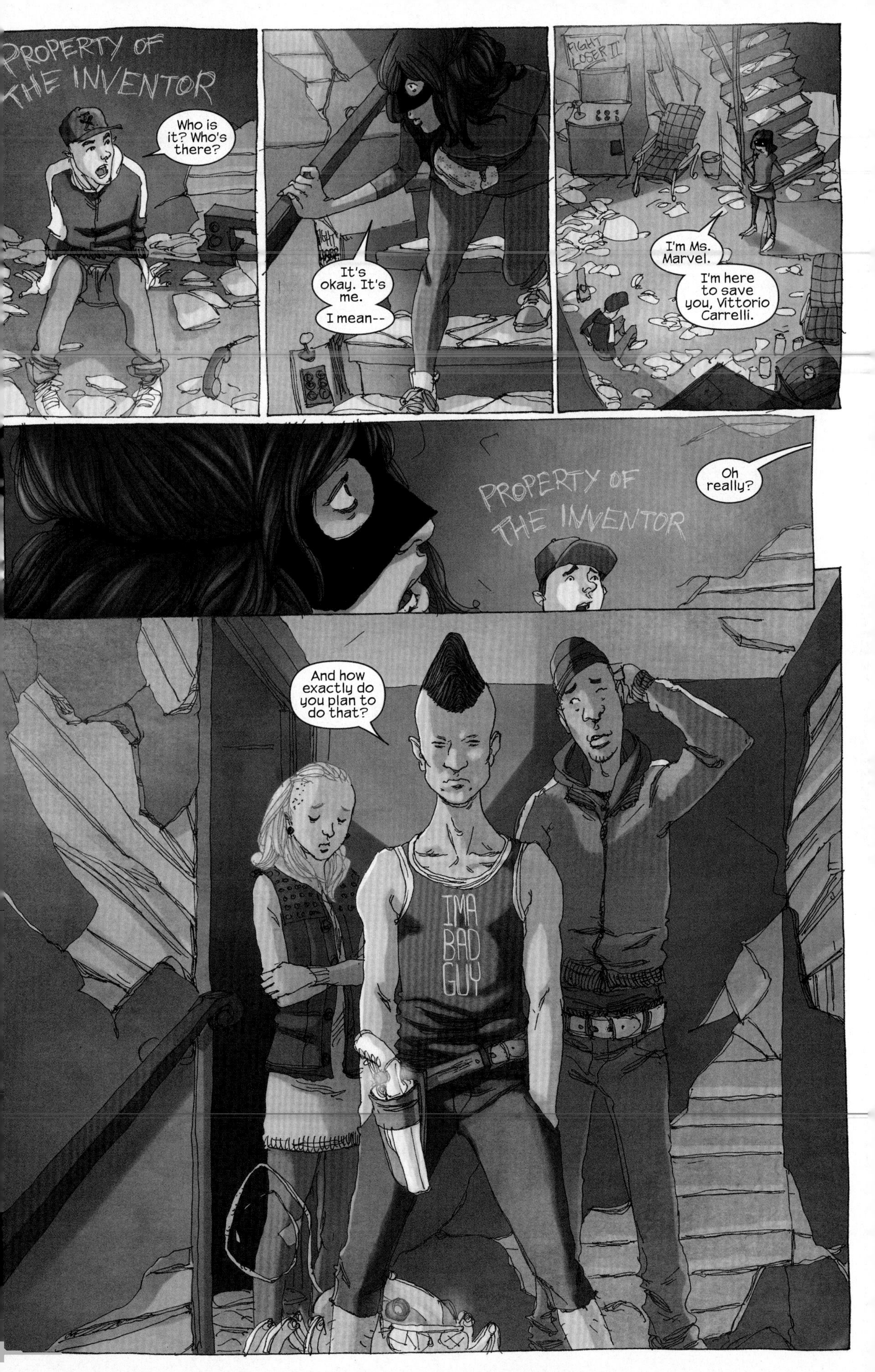
PROPERTY OF THE INVENTOR
Who is it? Who's there?
It's okay. It's me.
I mean--
FIGHT LOSER II
I'm Ms. Marvel.
I'm here to save you, Vittorio Carrelli.
PROPERTY OF THE INVENTOR
Oh really?
And how exactly do you plan to do that?
IMA BAD GUY

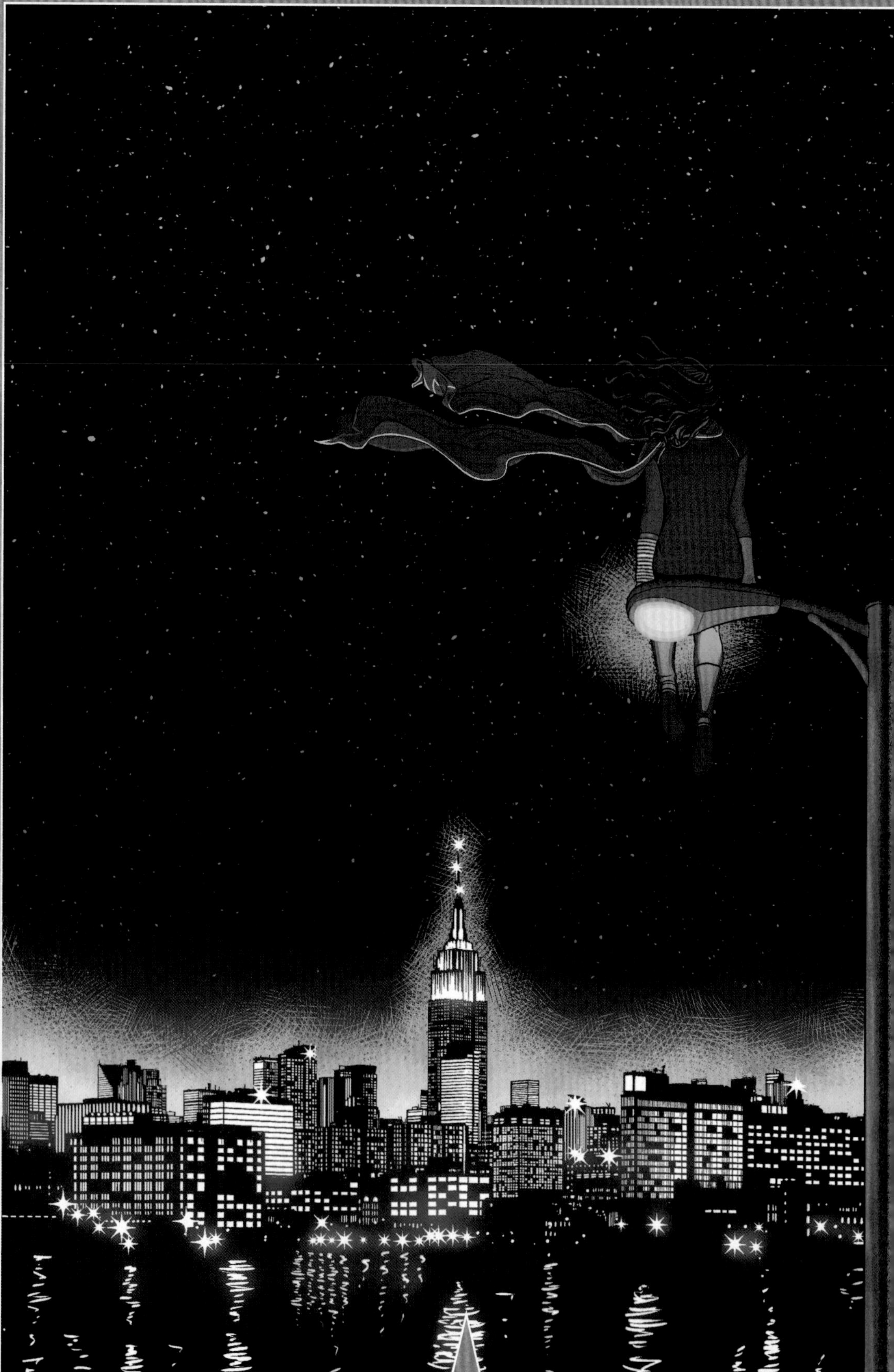
5

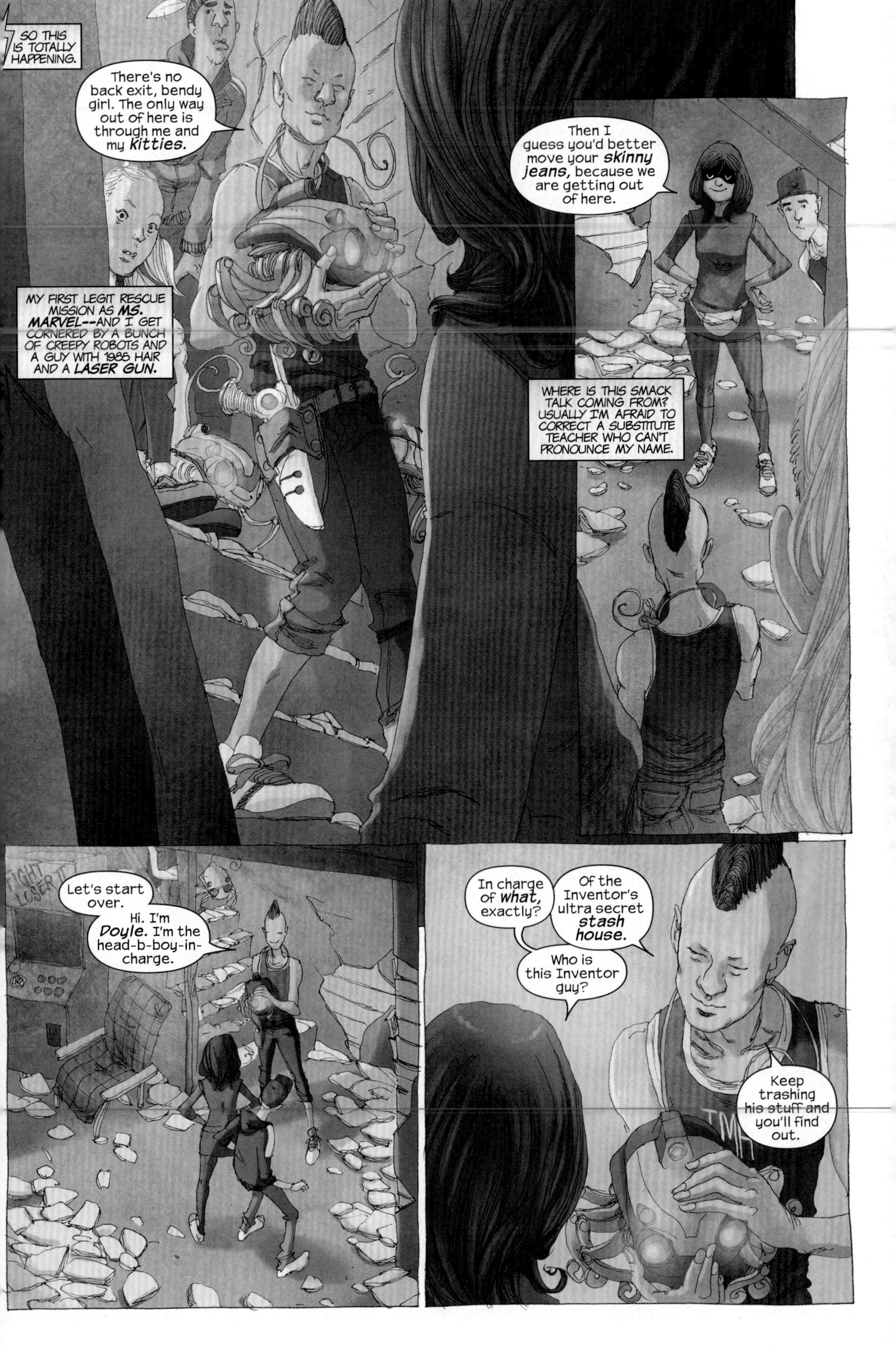

SO THIS IS TOTALLY HAPPENING.
There's no back exit, bendy girl. The only way out of here is through me and my kitties.
MY FIRST LEGIT RESCUE MISSION AS MS. MARVEL--AND I GET CORNERED BY A BUNCH OF CREEPY ROBOTS AND A GUY WITH 1985 HAIR AND A LASER GUN.
Then I guess you'd better move your skinny jeans, because we are getting out of here.
WHERE IS THIS SMACK TALK COMING FROM? USUALLY I'M AFRAID TO CORRECT A SUBSTITUTE TEACHER WHO CAN'T PRONOUNCE MY NAME.
Let's start over.
Hi. I'm Doyle. I'm the head-b-boy-in-charge.
In charge of what, exactly?
Of the Inventor's ultra secret stash house.
Who is this Inventor guy?
Keep trashing his stuff and you'll find out.

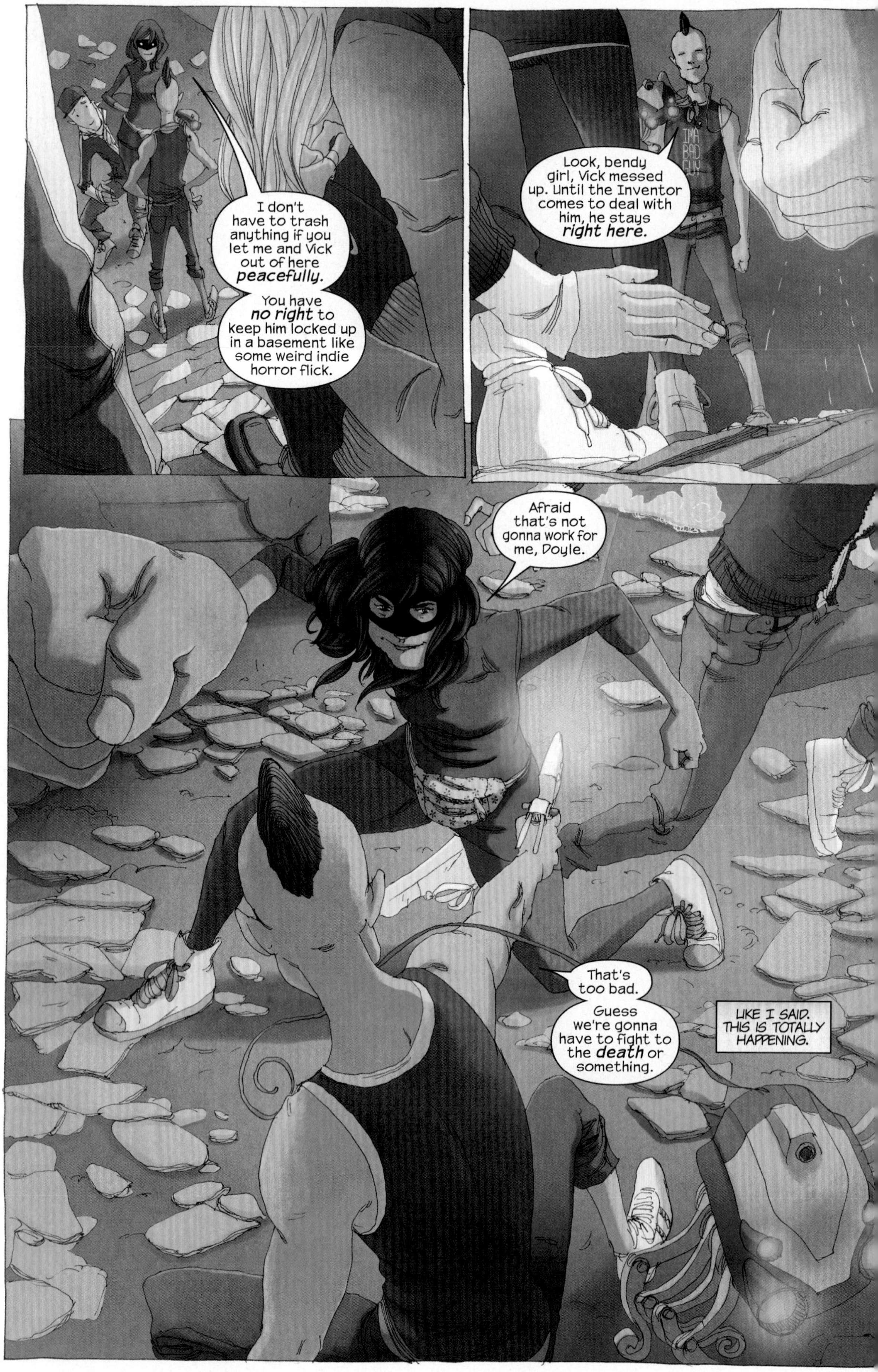
I don't have to trash anything if you let me and Vick out of here peacefully.
You have no right to keep him locked up in a basement like some weird indie horror flick.
Look, bendy girl, Vick messed up. Until the Inventor comes to deal with him, he stays right here.
IMA BAD GUY
Afraid that's not gonna work for me, Doyle.
That's too bad.
Guess we're gonna have to fight to the death or something.
LIKE I SAID. THIS IS TOTALLY HAPPENING.

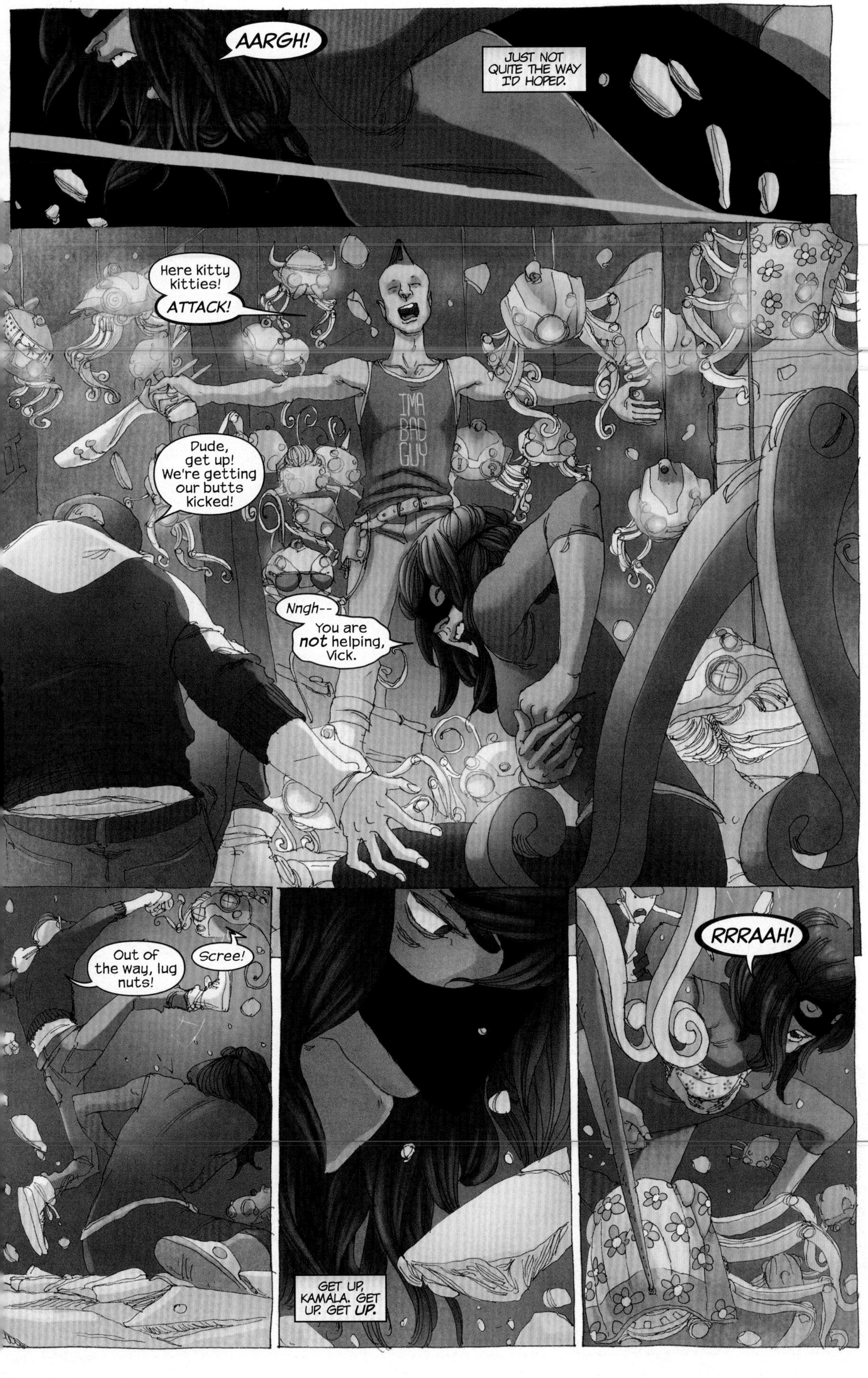
AARGH!
JUST NOT QUITE THE WAY I'D HOPED.
Here kitty kitties!
ATTACK!
IMA BAD GUY
Dude, get up! We're getting our butts kicked!
Nngh--
You are not helping, Vick.
Out of the way, lug nuts!
Scree!
GET UP, KAMALA. GET UP. GET UP.
RRRAAH!

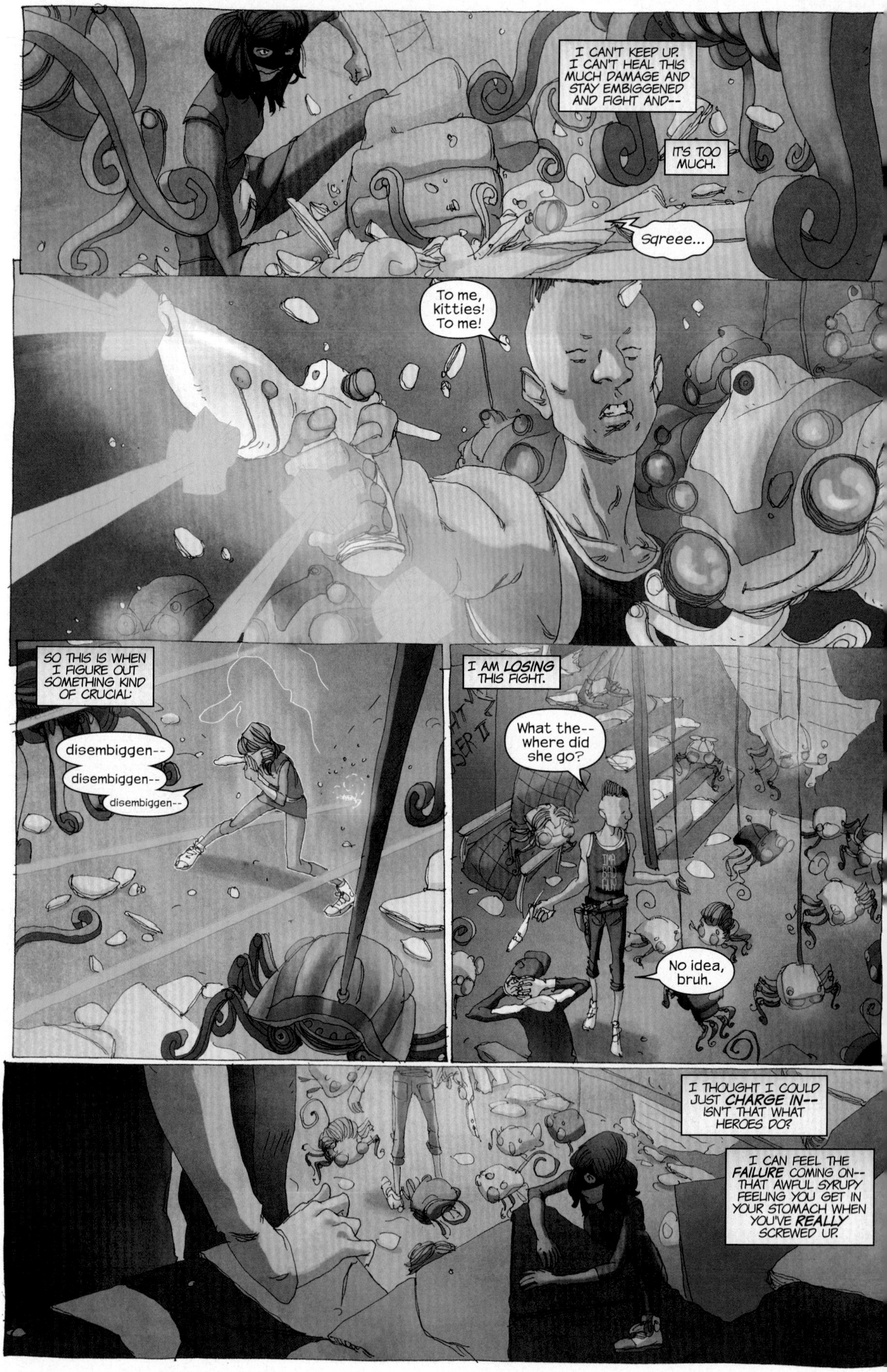

I CAN'T KEEP UP. I CAN'T HEAL THIS MUCH DAMAGE AND STAY EMBIGGENED AND FIGHT AND--
IT'S TOO MUCH.
Sqreee...
To me, kitties! To me!
SO THIS IS WHEN I FIGURE OUT SOMETHING KIND OF CRUCIAL:
disembiggen--
disembiggen--
disembiggen--
I AM LOSING THIS FIGHT.
What the-- where did she go?
No idea, bruh.
I THOUGHT I COULD JUST CHARGE IN-- ISN'T THAT WHAT HEROES DO?
I CAN FEEL THE FAILURE COMING ON-- THAT AWFUL SYRUPY FEELING YOU GET IN YOUR STOMACH WHEN YOU'VE REALLY SCREWED UP.

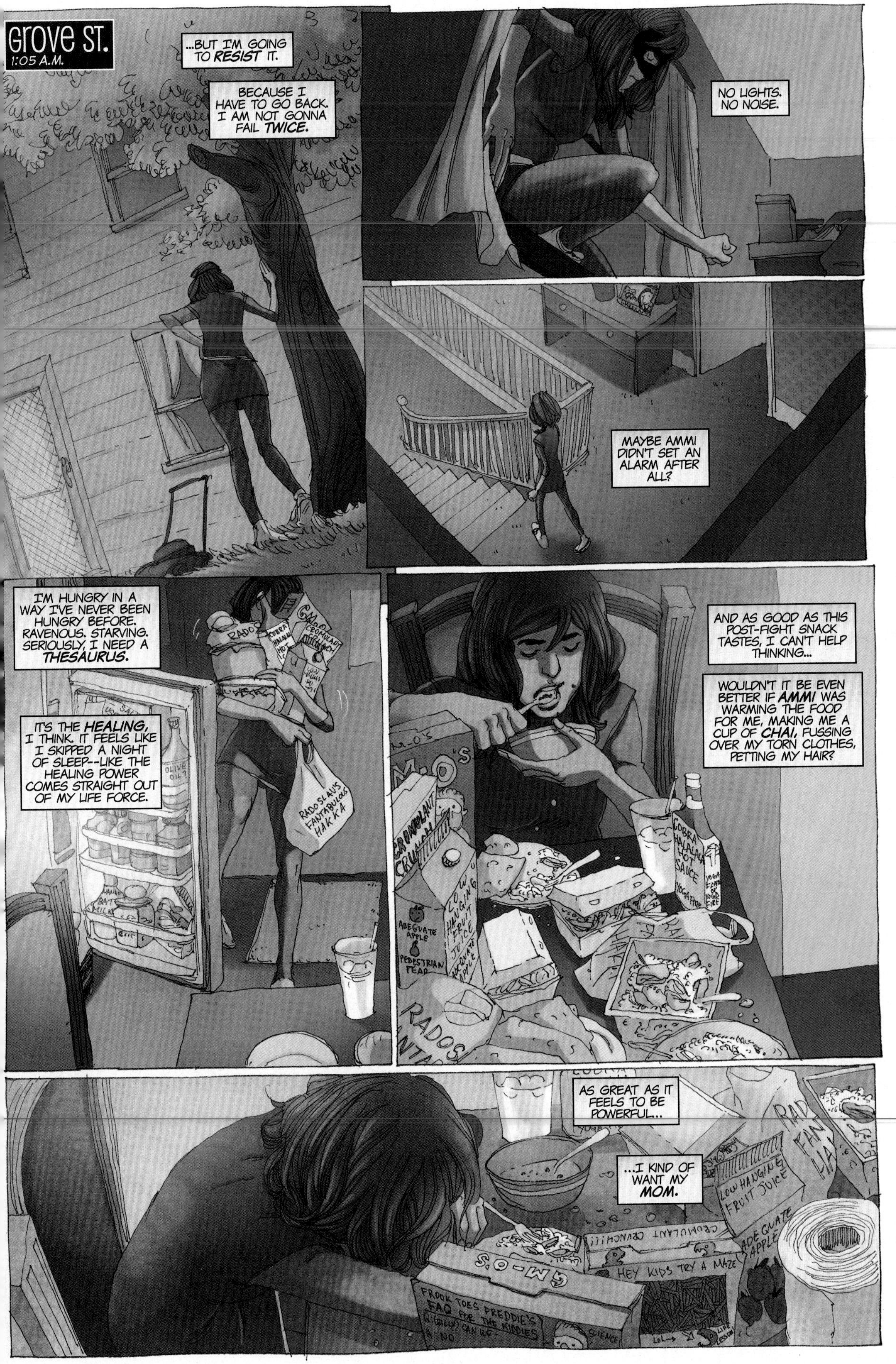

Grove St.
1:05 A.M.
...BUT I'M GOING TO RESIST IT.
BECAUSE I HAVE TO GO BACK. I AM NOT GONNA FAIL TWICE.
NO LIGHTS. NO NOISE.
MAYBE AMMI DIDN'T SET AN ALARM AFTER ALL?
I'M HUNGRY IN A WAY I'VE NEVER BEEN HUNGRY BEFORE. RAVENOUS. STARVING. SERIOUSLY, I NEED A THESAURUS.
IT'S THE HEALING, I THINK. IT FEELS LIKE I SKIPPED A NIGHT OF SLEEP--LIKE THE HEALING POWER COMES STRAIGHT OUT OF MY LIFE FORCE.
RADOSLAV'S FANTABULOUS HAKKA
OLIVE OIL
AND AS GOOD AS THIS POST-FIGHT SNACK TASTES, I CAN'T HELP THINKING...
WOULDN'T IT BE EVEN BETTER IF AMMI WAS WARMING THE FOOD FOR ME, MAKING ME A CUP OF CHAI, FUSSING OVER MY TORN CLOTHES, PETTING MY HAIR?
CROMULANT CRUNCH
COBRA HALALALA HOT SAUCE
LOW HANGING FRUIT JUICE
ADEQUATE APPLE
PEDESTRIAN PEAR
AS GREAT AS IT FEELS TO BE POWERFUL...
...I KIND OF WANT MY MOM.
LOW HANGING FRUIT JUICE
ADEQUATE APPLE
CROMULANT CRUNCH!!!
HEY KIDS TRY A MAZE
GM-O'S
FROOK TOES FREDDIE'S FAQ FOR THE KIDDIES

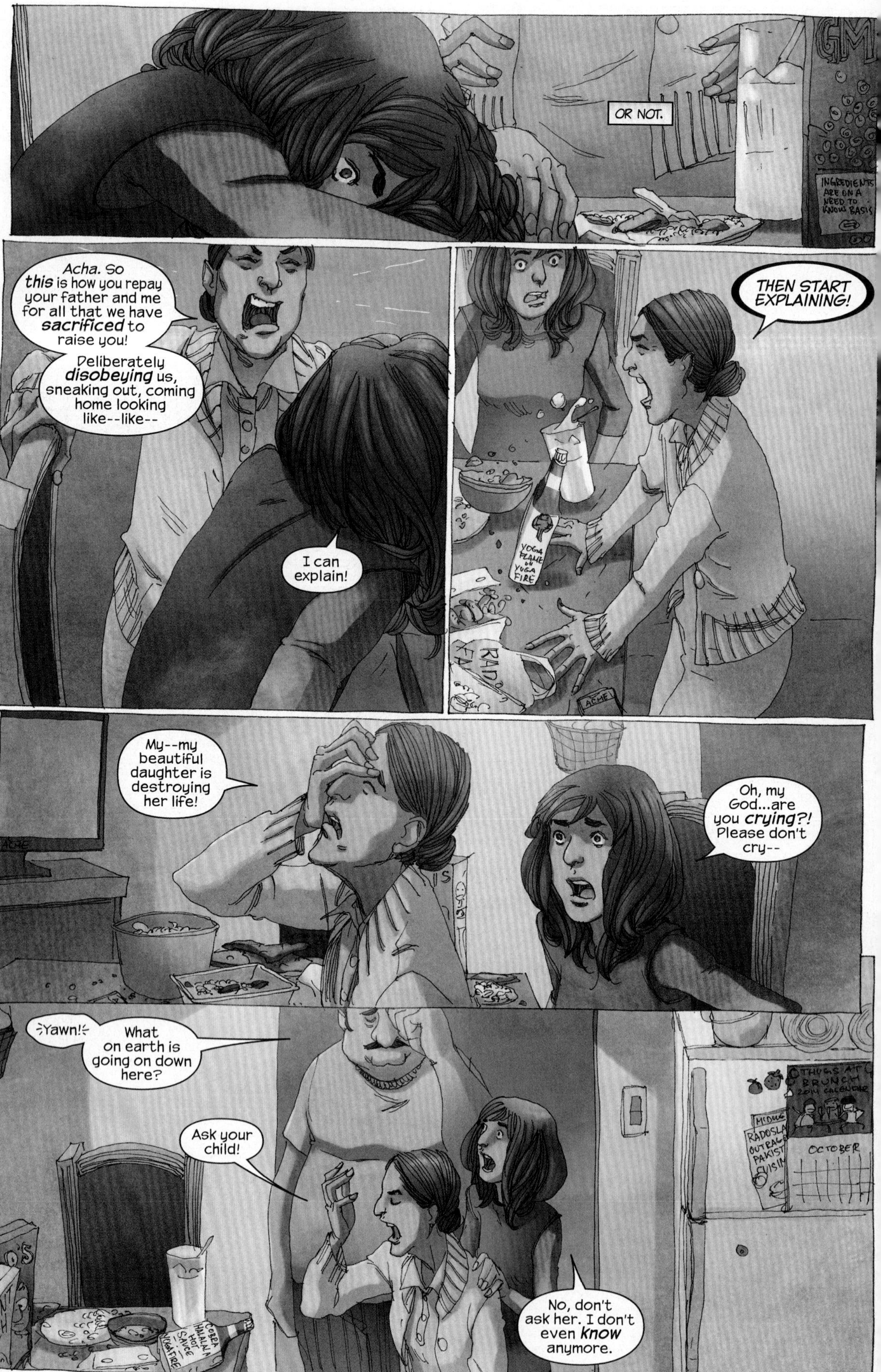
OR NOT.
INGREDIENTS ARE ON A NEED TO KNOW BASIS
Acha. So this is how you repay your father and me for all that we have sacrificed to raise you!
Deliberately disobeying us, sneaking out, coming home looking like--like--
I can explain!
THEN START EXPLAINING!
ACME
My--my beautiful daughter is destroying her life!
Oh, my God...are you crying?! Please don't cry--
Yawn!
What on earth is going on down here?
Ask your child!
OCTOBER
No, don't ask her. I don't even know anymore.

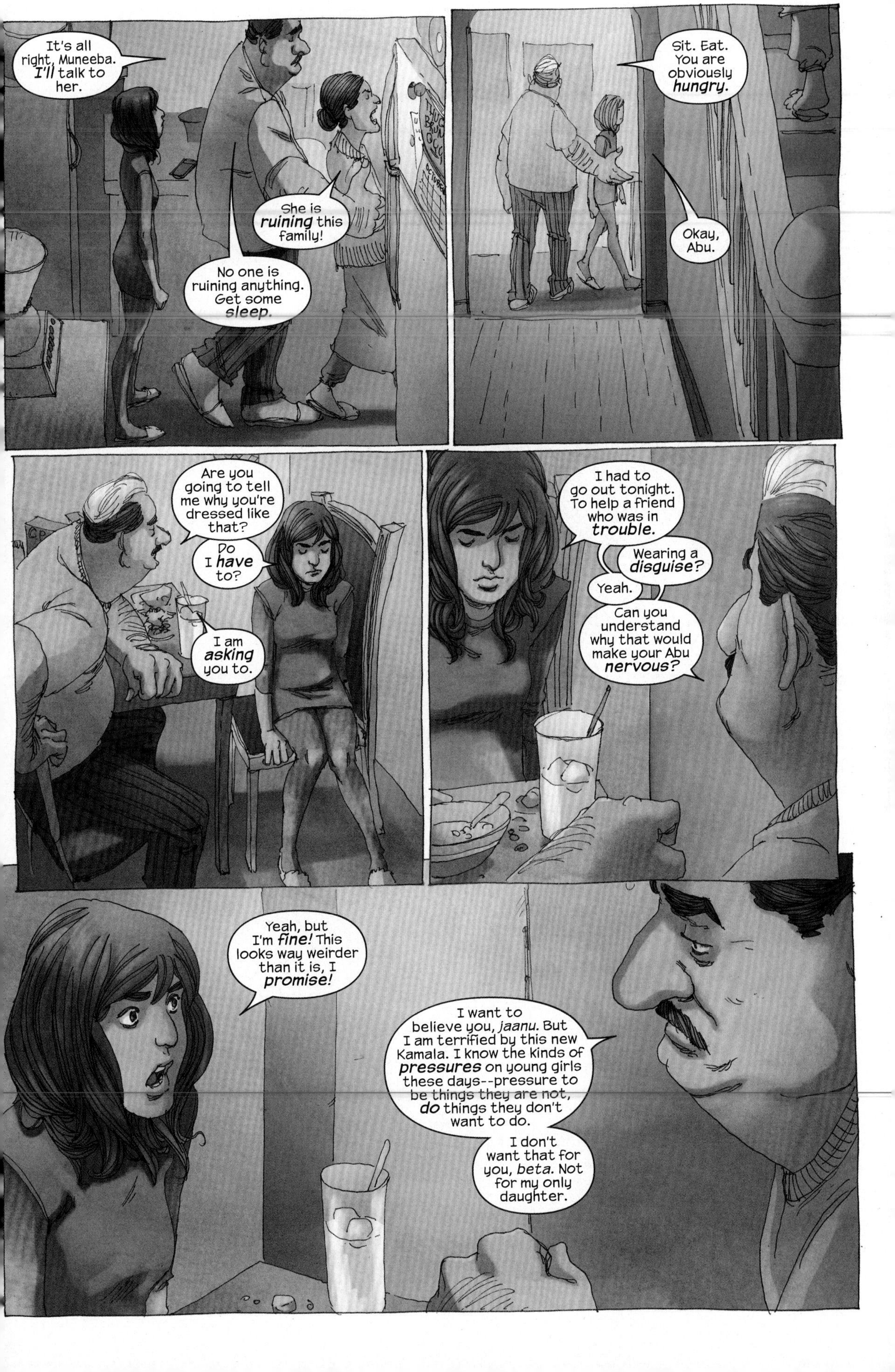

It's all right, Muneeba. *I'll* talk to her.
She is *ruining* this family!
No one is ruining anything. Get some *sleep.*
Sit. Eat. You are obviously *hungry*.
Okay, Abu.
Are you going to tell me why you're dressed like that?
Do I *have* to?
I am *asking* you to.
I had to go out tonight. To help a friend who was in *trouble*.
Wearing a *disguise?*
Yeah.
Can you understand why that would make your Abu *nervous?*
Yeah, but I'm *fine!* This looks way weirder than it is, I *promise!*
I want to believe you, *jaanu*. But I am terrified by this new Kamala. I know the kinds of *pressures* on young girls these days--pressure to be things they are not, *do* things they don't want to do.
I don't want that for you, *beta*. Not for my only daughter.

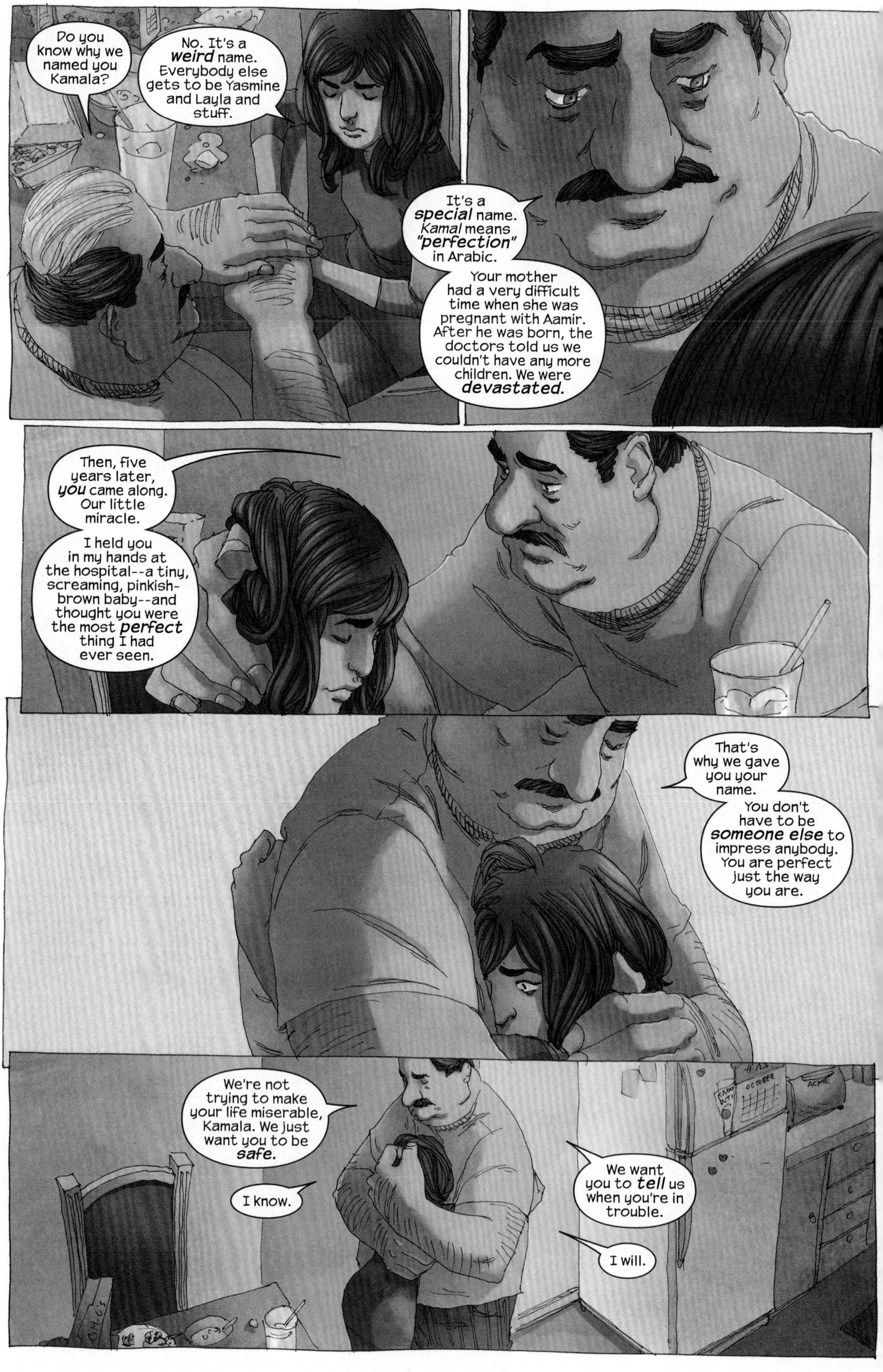
Do you know why we named you Kamala?
No. It's a *weird* name. Everybody else gets to be Yasmine and Layla and stuff.
It's a *special* name. *Kamal* means *"perfection"* in Arabic.
Your mother had a very difficult time when she was pregnant with Aamir. After he was born, the doctors told us we couldn't have any more children. We were *devastated.*
Then, five years later, *you* came along. Our little miracle.
I held you in my hands at the hospital--a tiny, screaming, pinkish-brown baby--and thought you were the most *perfect* thing I had ever seen.
That's why we gave you your name.
You don't have to be *someone else* to impress anybody. You are perfect just the way you are.
We're not trying to make your life miserable, Kamala. We just want you to be *safe.*
I know.
We want you to *tell* us when you're in trouble.
I will.

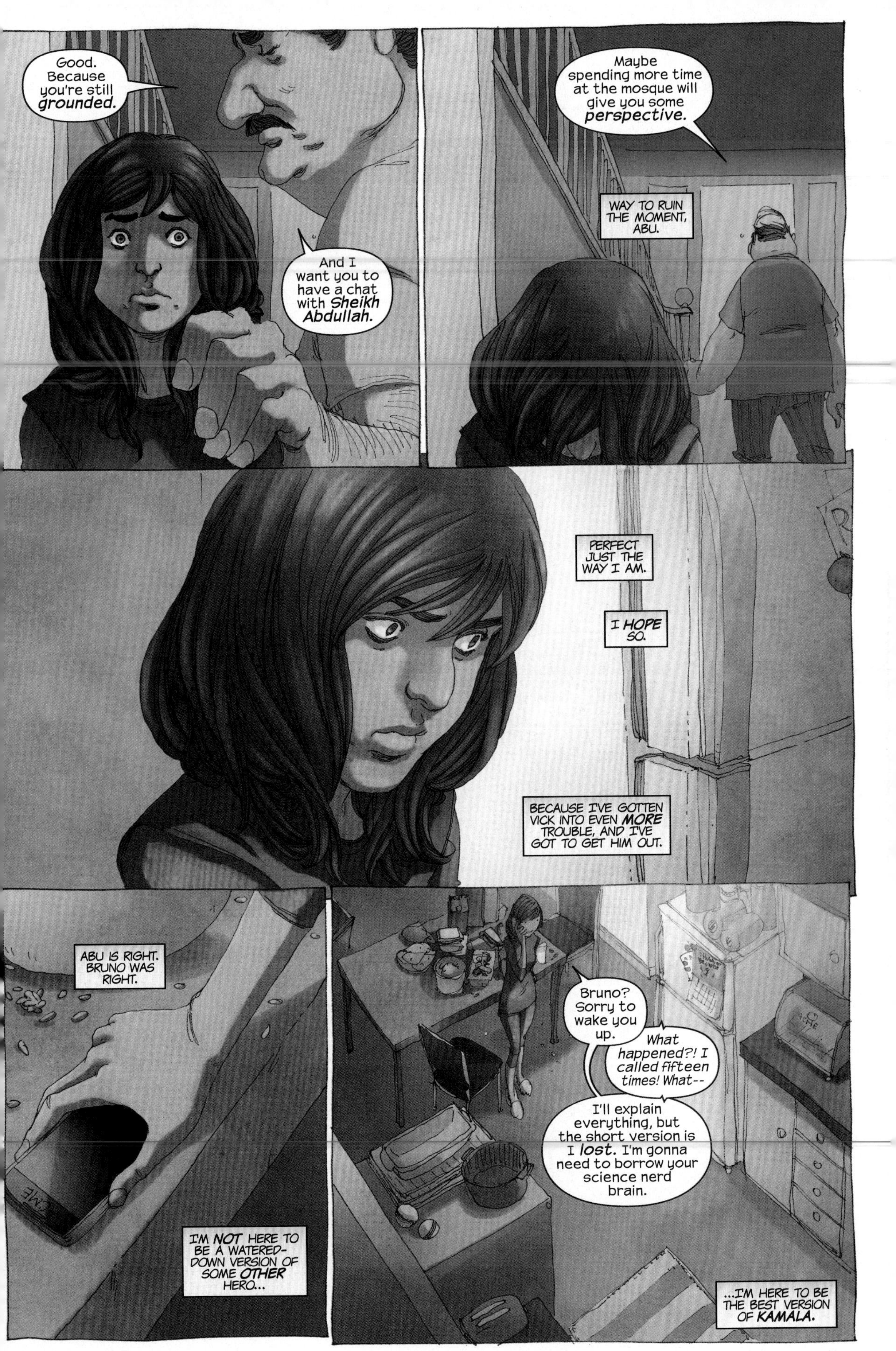
Good. Because you're still *grounded.*
And I want you to have a chat with *Sheikh Abdullah.*
Maybe spending more time at the mosque will give you some *perspective.*
WAY TO RUIN THE MOMENT, ABU.
PERFECT JUST THE WAY I AM.
I *HOPE* SO.
BECAUSE I'VE GOTTEN VICK INTO EVEN *MORE* TROUBLE, AND I'VE GOT TO GET HIM OUT.
ABU IS RIGHT. BRUNO WAS RIGHT.
I'M *NOT* HERE TO BE A WATERED-DOWN VERSION OF SOME *OTHER* HERO...
Bruno? Sorry to wake you up.
What happened?! I called fifteen times! What--
I'll explain everything, but the short version is I *lost.* I'm gonna need to borrow your science nerd brain.
...I'M HERE TO BE THE BEST VERSION OF *KAMALA.*

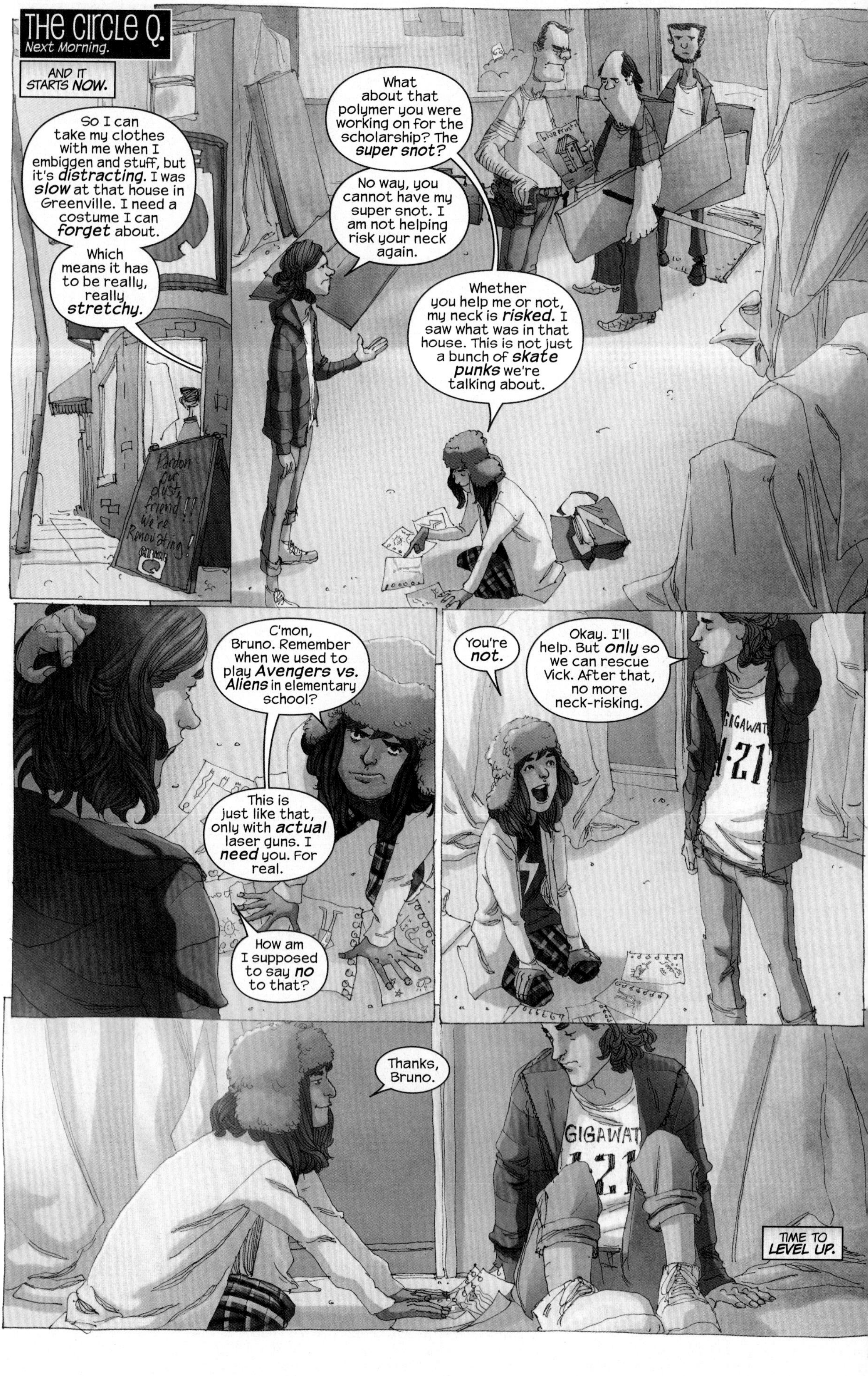
THE CIRCLE Q.
Next Morning.
AND IT STARTS NOW.
So I can take my clothes with me when I embiggen and stuff, but it's distracting. I was slow at that house in Greenville. I need a costume I can forget about.
Which means it has to be really, really stretchy.
What about that polymer you were working on for the scholarship? The super snot?
No way, you cannot have my super snot. I am not helping risk your neck again.
Whether you help me or not, my neck is risked. I saw what was in that house. This is not just a bunch of skate punks we're talking about.
Pardon our dust, friend!! We're Renovating!
C'mon, Bruno. Remember when we used to play Avengers vs. Aliens in elementary school?
This is just like that, only with actual laser guns. I need you. For real.
How am I supposed to say no to that?
You're not.
Okay. I'll help. But only so we can rescue Vick. After that, no more neck-risking.
GIGAWAT
Thanks, Bruno.
TIME TO LEVEL UP.

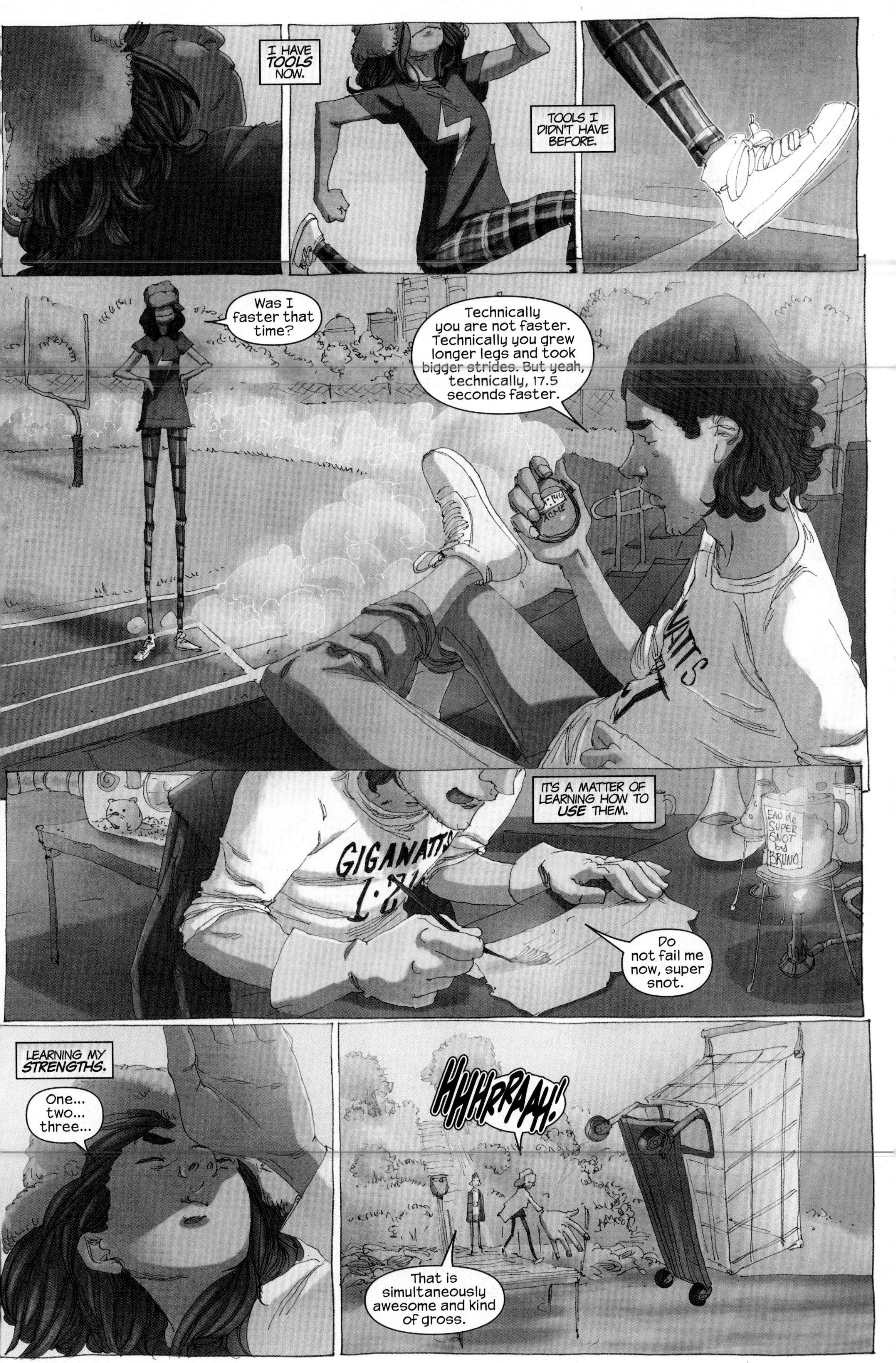
I HAVE TOOLS NOW.
TOOLS I DIDN'T HAVE BEFORE.
Was I faster that time?
Technically you are not faster. Technically you grew longer legs and took bigger strides. But yeah, technically, 17.5 seconds faster.
ACME
IT'S A MATTER OF LEARNING HOW TO USE THEM.
GIGAWATTS 1.21
EAU de SUPER SNOT by BRUNO
Do not fail me now, super snot.
LEARNING MY STRENGTHS.
One... two... three...
HHHRRAAH!
That is simultaneously awesome and kind of gross.

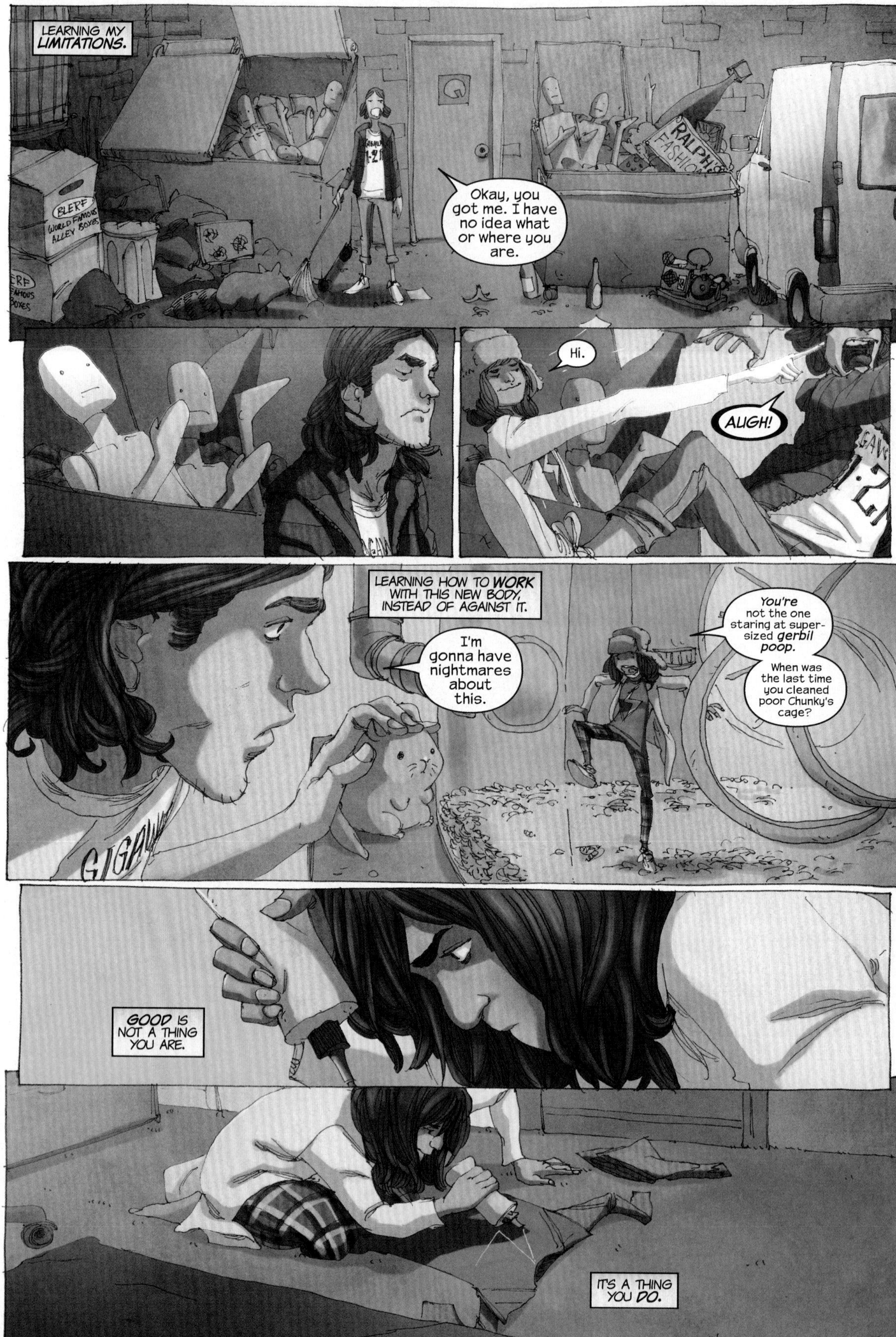
LEARNING MY LIMITATIONS.
BLERF WORLD FAMOUS ALLEY BOXES
RALPH'S FASHION
Okay, you got me. I have no idea what or where you are.
Hi.
AUGH!
LEARNING HOW TO WORK WITH THIS NEW BODY, INSTEAD OF AGAINST IT.
I'm gonna have nightmares about this.
You're not the one staring at super-sized gerbil poop.
When was the last time you cleaned poor Chunky's cage?
GOOD IS NOT A THING YOU ARE.
IT'S A THING YOU DO.

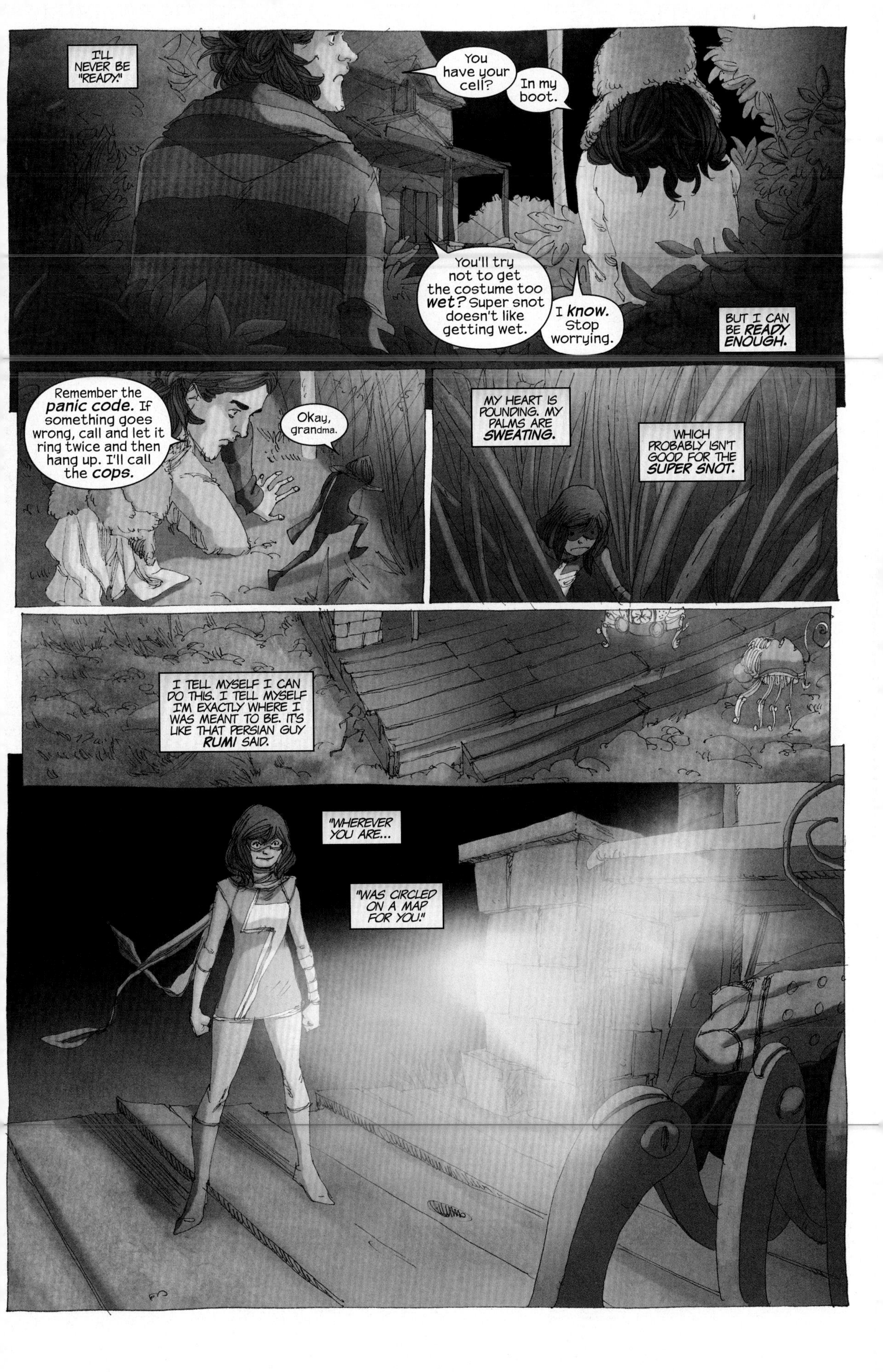
I'LL NEVER BE "READY."
You have your cell?
In my boot.
You'll try not to get the costume too wet? Super snot doesn't like getting wet.
I know. Stop worrying.
BUT I CAN BE READY ENOUGH.
Remember the panic code. If something goes wrong, call and let it ring twice and then hang up. I'll call the cops.
Okay, grandma.
MY HEART IS POUNDING. MY PALMS ARE SWEATING.
WHICH PROBABLY ISN'T GOOD FOR THE SUPER SNOT.
I TELL MYSELF I CAN DO THIS. I TELL MYSELF I'M EXACTLY WHERE I WAS MEANT TO BE. IT'S LIKE THAT PERSIAN GUY RUMI SAID.
"WHEREVER YOU ARE...
"WAS CIRCLED ON A MAP FOR YOU."

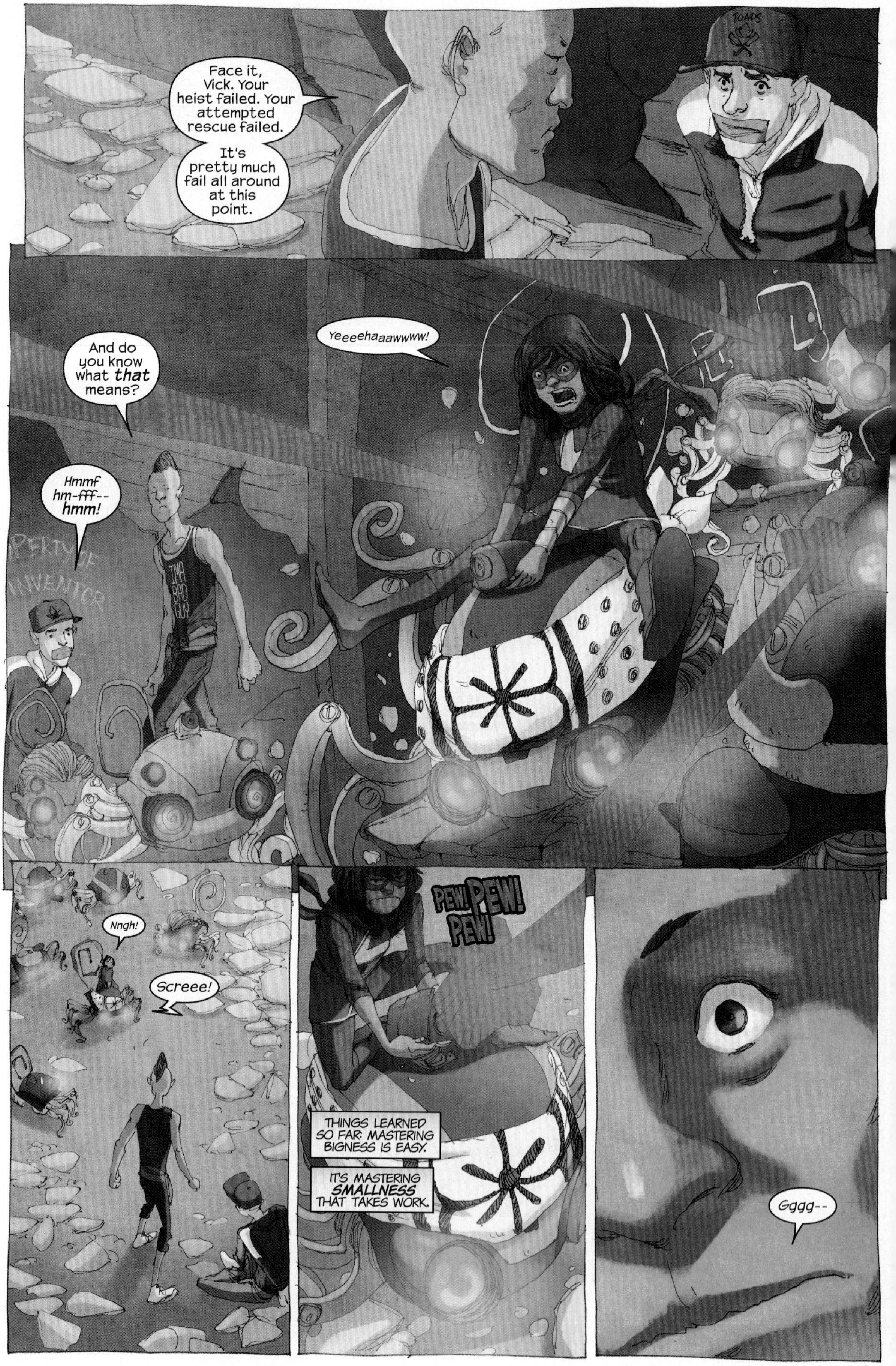
Face it, Vick. Your heist failed. Your attempted rescue failed.
It's pretty much fail all around at this point.
TOADS
And do you know what *that* means?
Yeeeehaaawwww!
Hmmf hm-fff-- **hmm!**
PERTY OF INVENTOR
IMA BAD GUY
Nngh!
Screee!
PEW! PEW! PEW!
THINGS LEARNED SO FAR: MASTERING BIGNESS IS EASY.
IT'S MASTERING ***SMALLNESS*** THAT TAKES WORK.
Gggg--

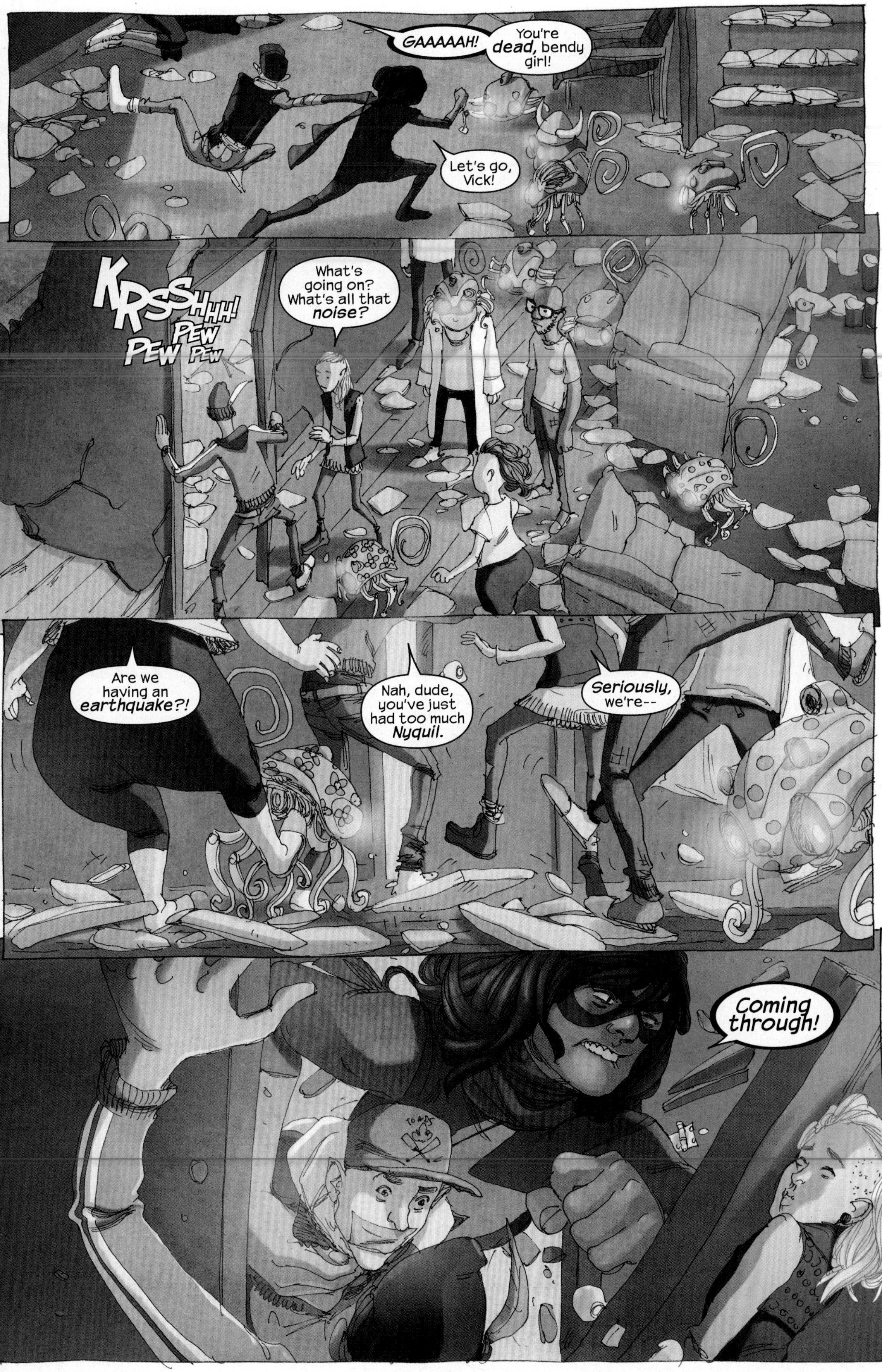
GAAAAAH!
You're dead, bendy girl!
Let's go, Vick!
KRSSHHH! PEW PEW PEW
What's going on? What's all that noise?
Are we having an earthquake?!
Nah, dude, you've just had too much Nyquil.
Seriously, we're--
Coming through!

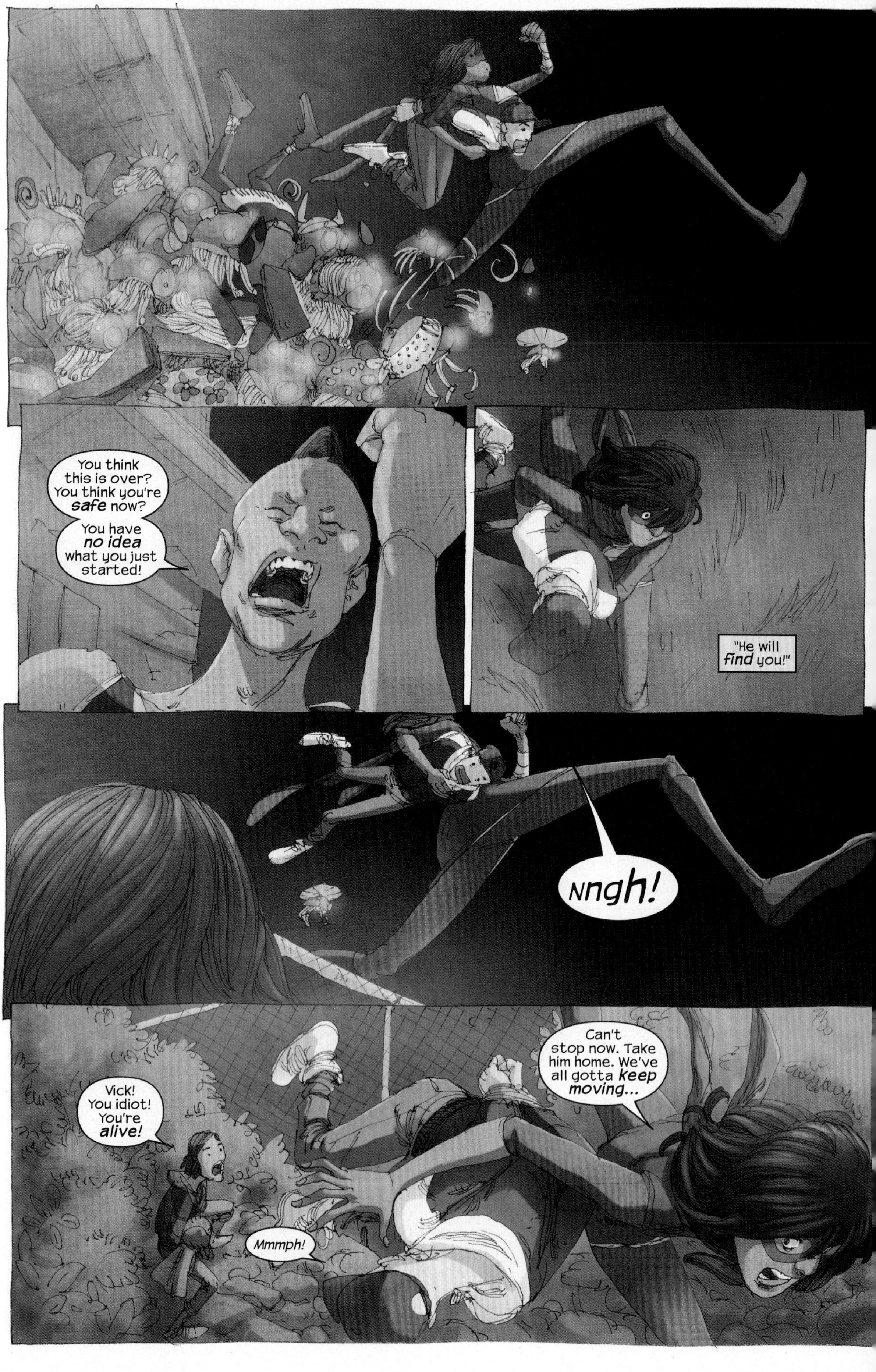
You think this is over? You think you're *safe* now?
You have ***no idea*** what you just started!
"He will *find* you!"
NNGH!
Vick! You idiot! You're ***alive!***
Can't stop now. Take him home. We've all gotta ***keep moving...***
Mmmph!

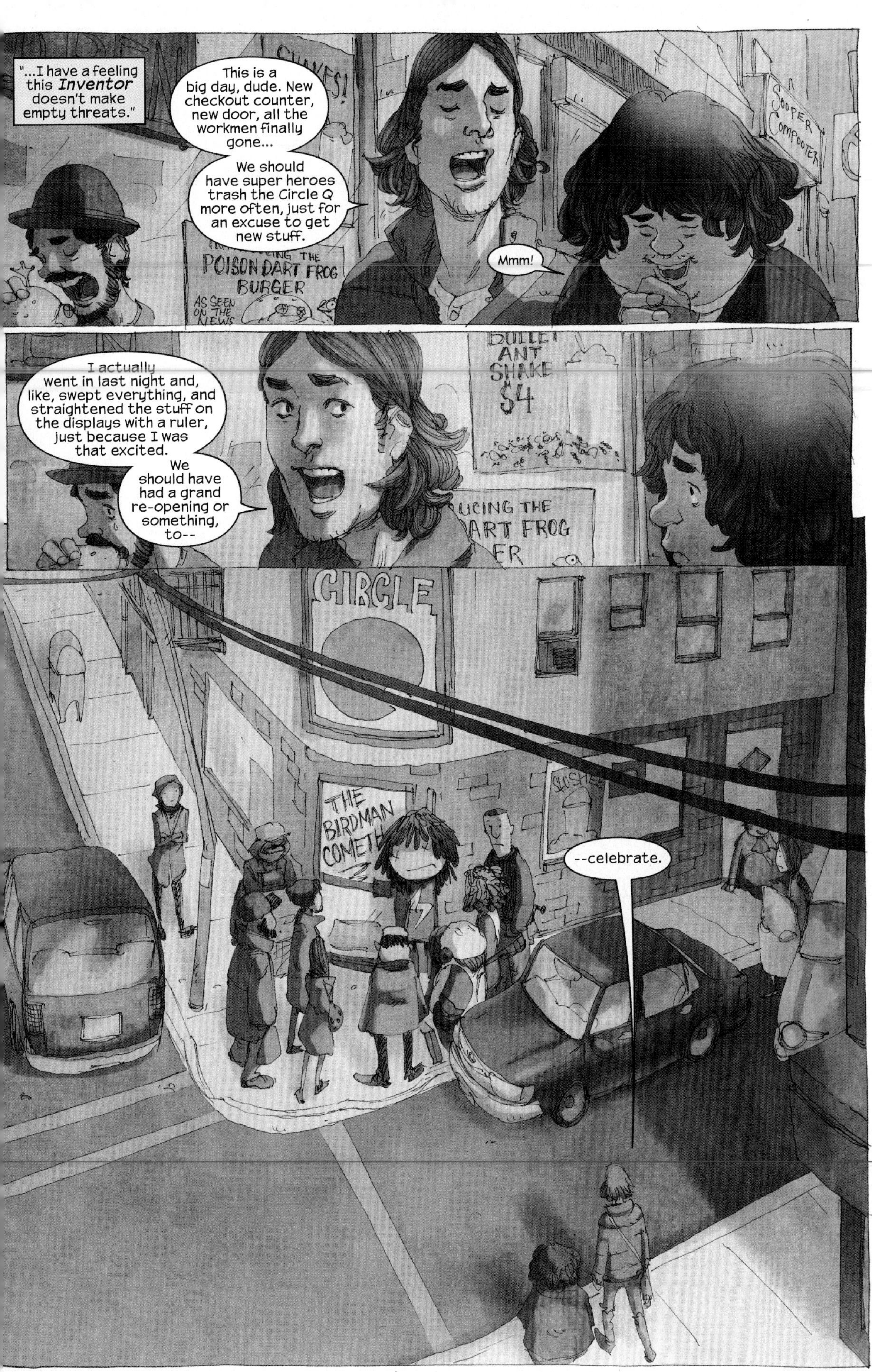
"...I have a feeling this *Inventor* doesn't make empty threats."
SHAKES!
This is a big day, dude. New checkout counter, new door, all the workmen finally gone...
We should have super heroes trash the Circle Q more often, just for an excuse to get new stuff.
SOOPER COMPOOTER
POISON DART FROG BURGER
AS SEEN ON THE NEWS
Mmm!
I actually went in last night and, like, swept everything, and straightened the stuff on the displays with a ruler, just because I was that excited.
We should have had a grand re-opening or something, to--
BULLET ANT SHAKE $4
CIRCLE
THE BIRDMAN COMETH
SLUSHEE
--celebrate.

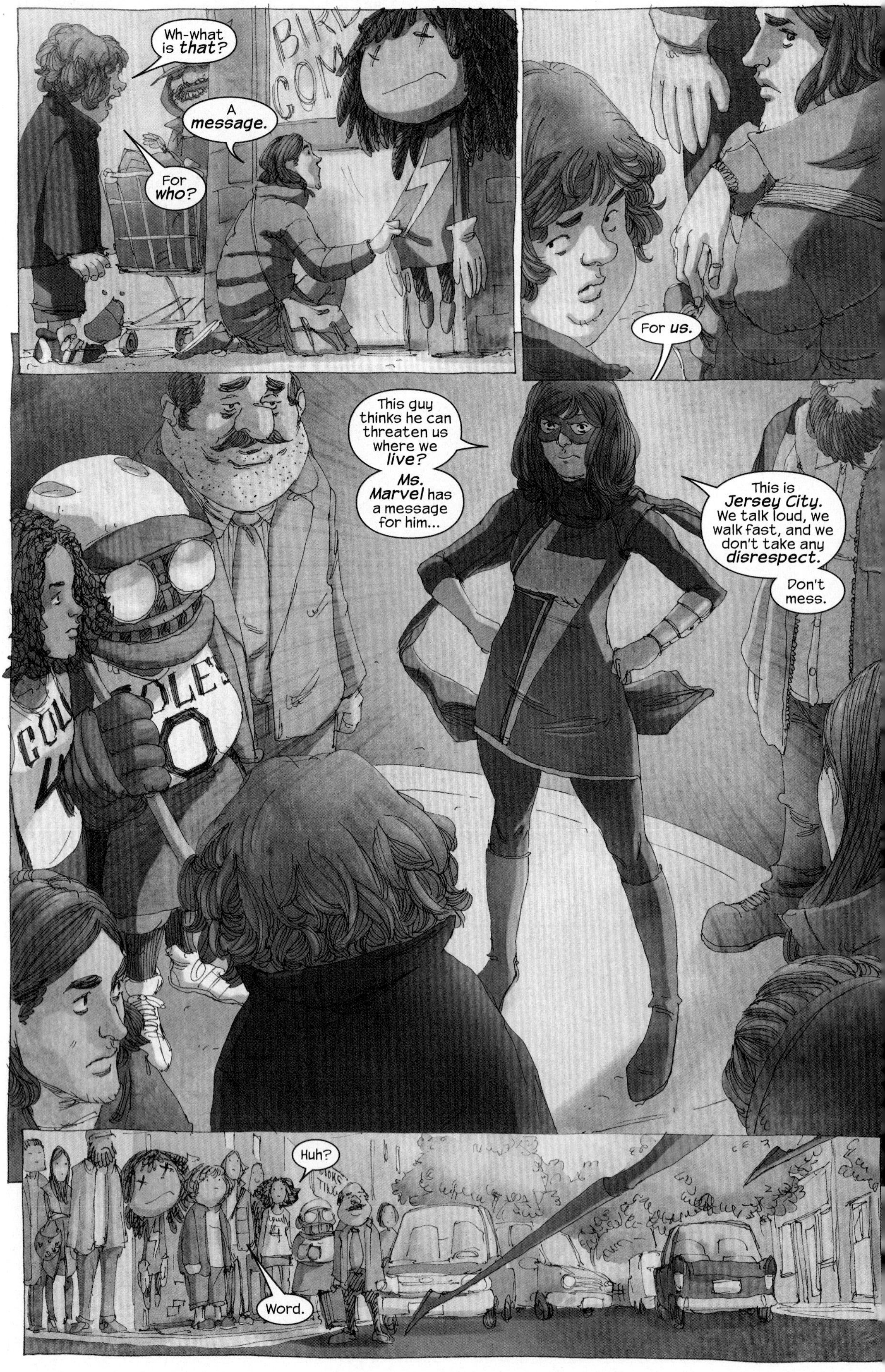

Wh-what is *that?*
A *message.*
For *who?*
For *us.*
This guy thinks he can threaten us where we *live?*
Ms. Marvel has a message for him...
This is *Jersey City.* We talk loud, we walk fast, and we don't take any *disrespect.*
Don't mess.
Huh?
Word.

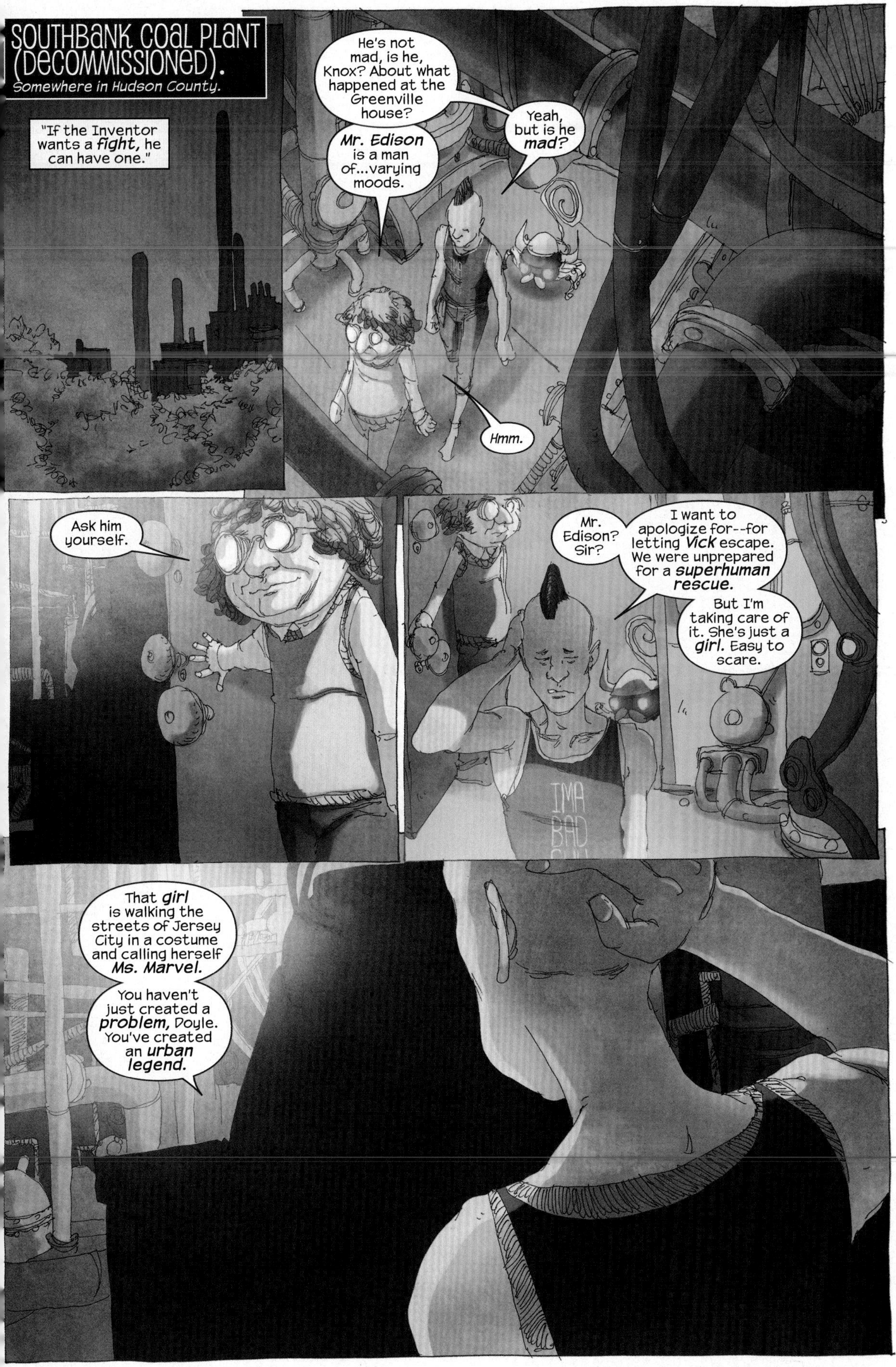

SOUTHBANK COAL PLANT (DECOMMISSIONED).
Somewhere in Hudson County.
"If the Inventor wants a fight, he can have one."
He's not mad, is he, Knox? About what happened at the Greenville house?
Mr. Edison is a man of...varying moods.
Yeah, but is he mad?
Hmm.
Ask him yourself.
Mr. Edison? Sir?
I want to apologize for--for letting Vick escape. We were unprepared for a superhuman rescue.
But I'm taking care of it. She's just a girl. Easy to scare.
IMA BAD
That girl is walking the streets of Jersey City in a costume and calling herself Ms. Marvel.
You haven't just created a problem, Doyle. You've created an urban legend.

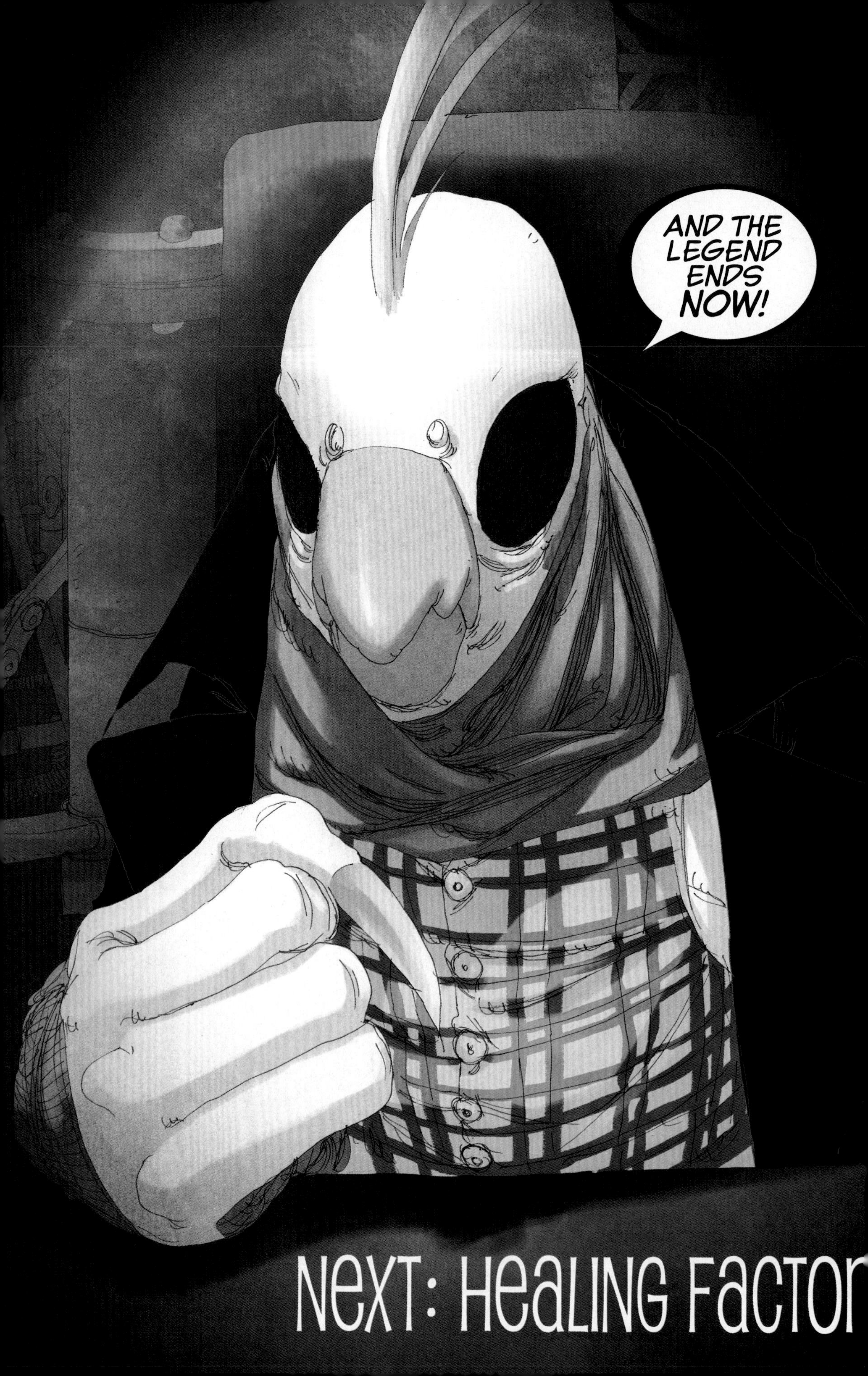
AND THE LEGEND ENDS NOW!
NEXT: HEALING FACTOR

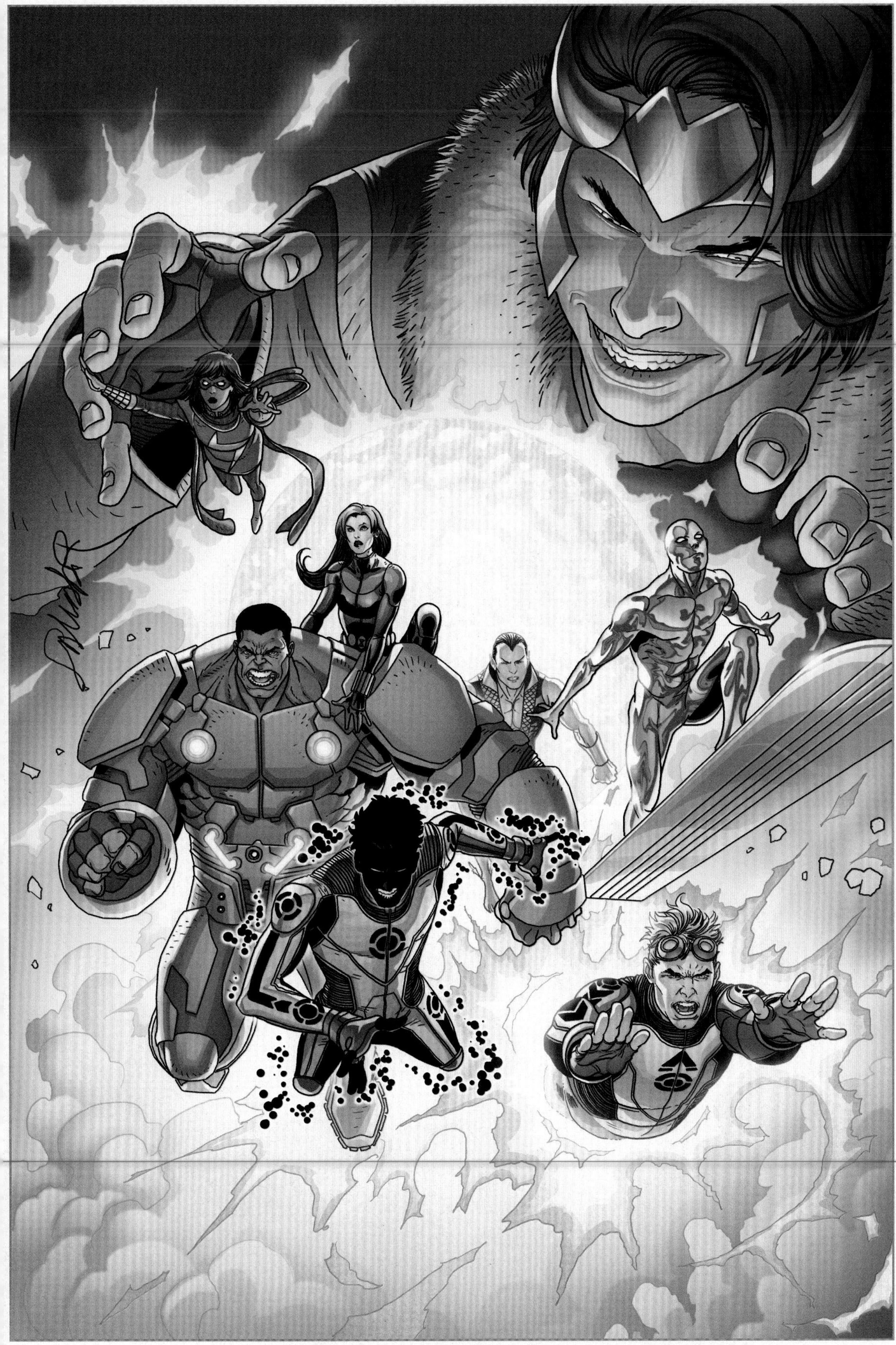

ALL-NEW MARVEL NOW POINT ONE #1
COVER BY SALVADOR LARROCA & LAURA MARTIN

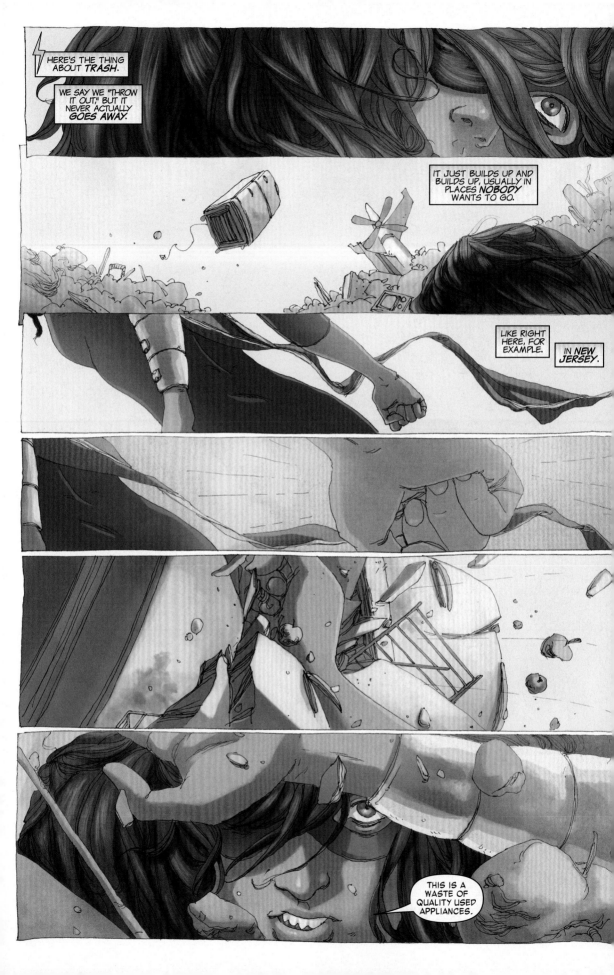

HERE'S THE THING ABOUT *TRASH.*

WE SAY WE "THROW IT OUT," BUT IT NEVER ACTUALLY *GOES AWAY.*

IT JUST BUILDS UP AND BUILDS UP, USUALLY IN PLACES *NOBODY* WANTS TO GO.

LIKE RIGHT HERE, FOR EXAMPLE.

IN *NEW JERSEY.*

THIS IS A WASTE OF QUALITY USED APPLIANCES.

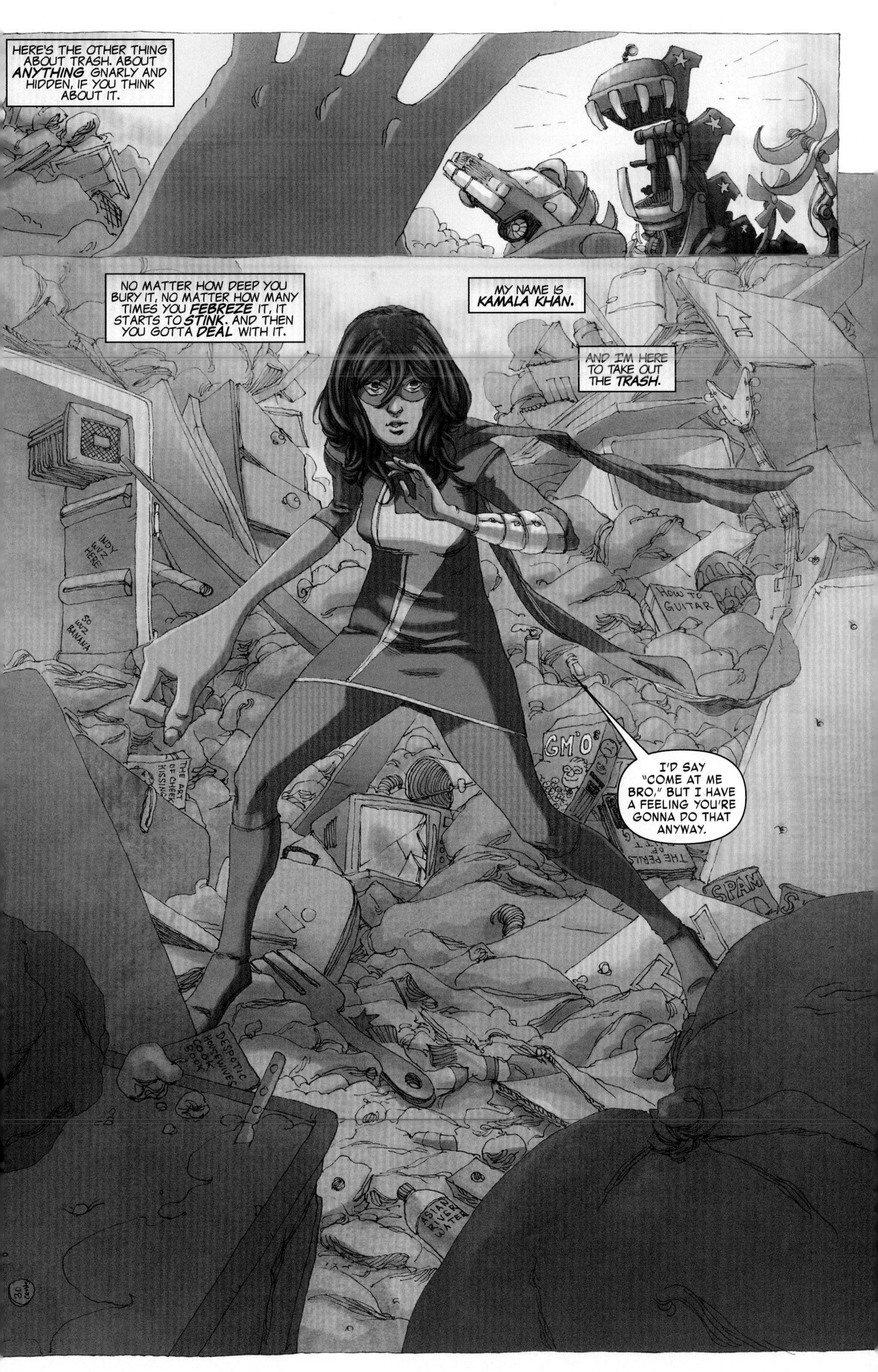
HERE'S THE OTHER THING ABOUT TRASH. ABOUT ANYTHING GNARLY AND HIDDEN, IF YOU THINK ABOUT IT.
NO MATTER HOW DEEP YOU BURY IT, NO MATTER HOW MANY TIMES YOU FEBREZE IT, IT STARTS TO STINK. AND THEN YOU GOTTA DEAL WITH IT.
MY NAME IS KAMALA KHAN.
AND I'M HERE TO TAKE OUT THE TRASH.
I'D SAY "COME AT ME BRO," BUT I HAVE A FEELING YOU'RE GONNA DO THAT ANYWAY.
INDY WUZ HERE
SO WUZ BANANA
HOW TO GUITAR
THE ART OF CHEEK KISSING
GM'O
SPAM
DESPOTIC HOUSEWIVES COOK BOOK
ASIAN RIVER WATER

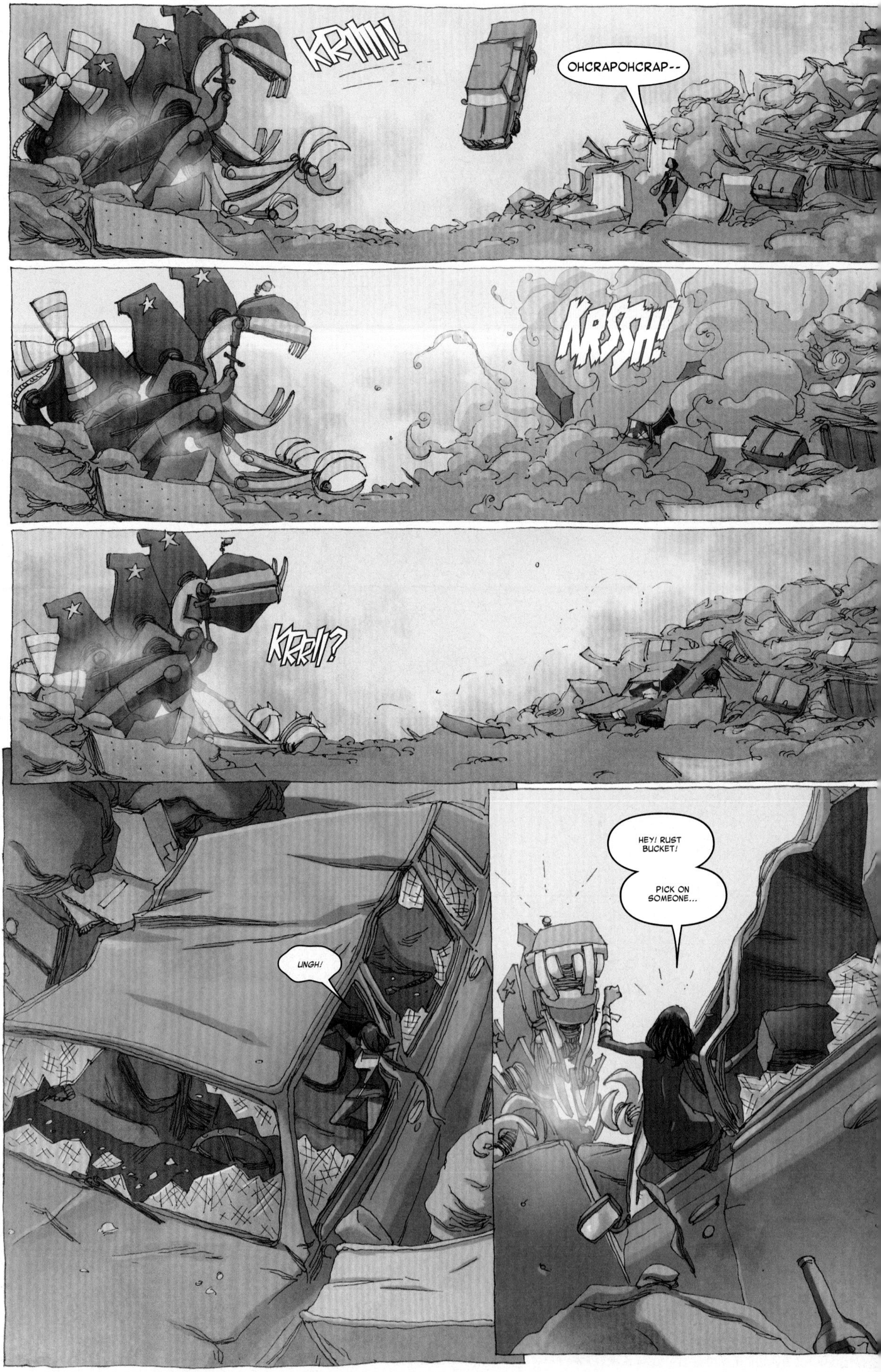
KRIIIII!
OHCRAPOHCRAP--
KRSSH!
KRRII?
UNGH!
HEY! RUST BUCKET!
PICK ON SOMEONE...

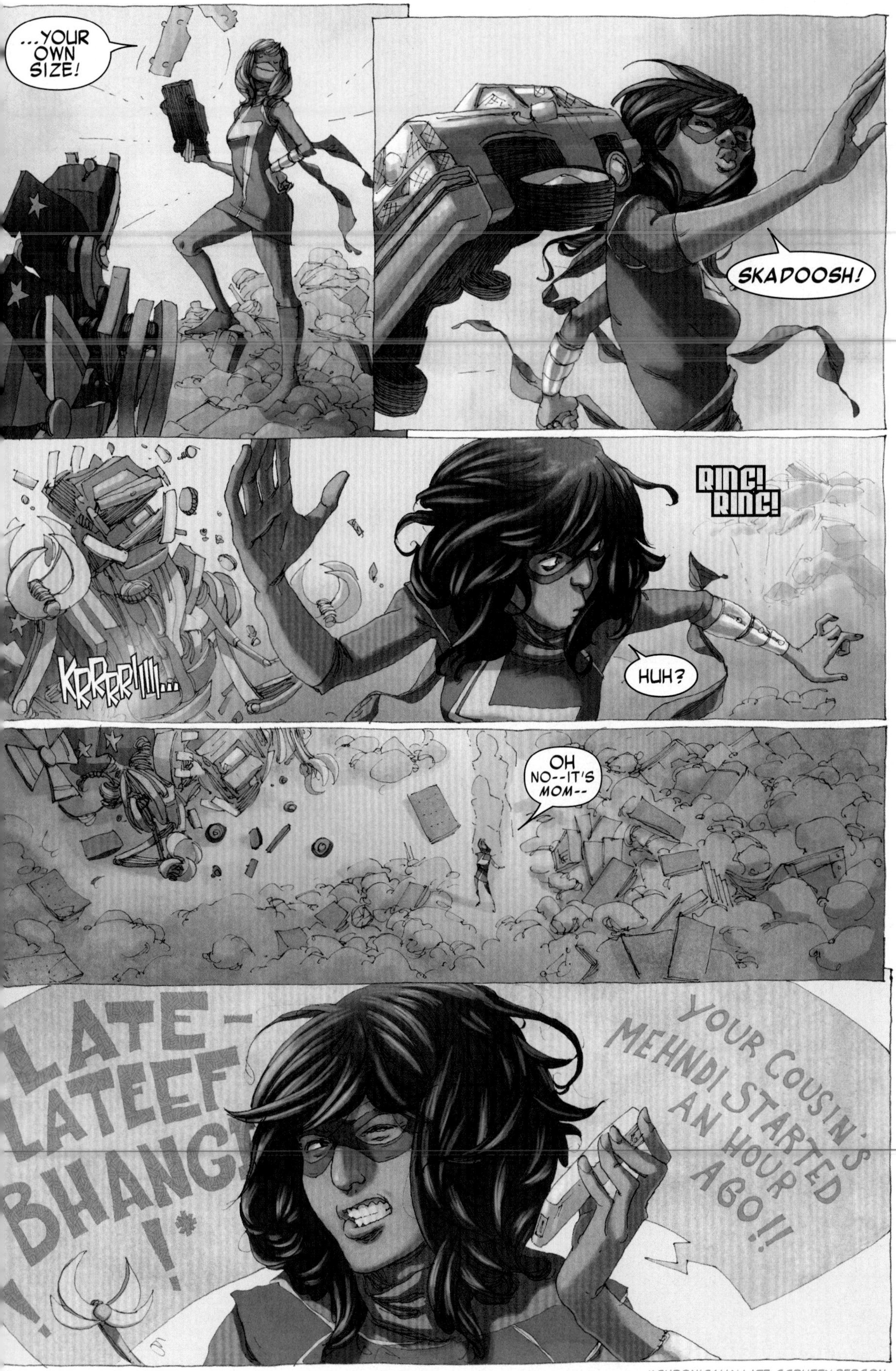
...YOUR OWN SIZE!
SKADOOSH!
RING! RING!
KRRRRRIIIIII...
HUH?
OH NO--IT'S MOM--
LATE-LATEEF BHANG!*!
YOUR COUSIN'S MEHNDI STARTED AN HOUR AGO!!

*CHRONICALLY LATE SCRUFFY PERSON.

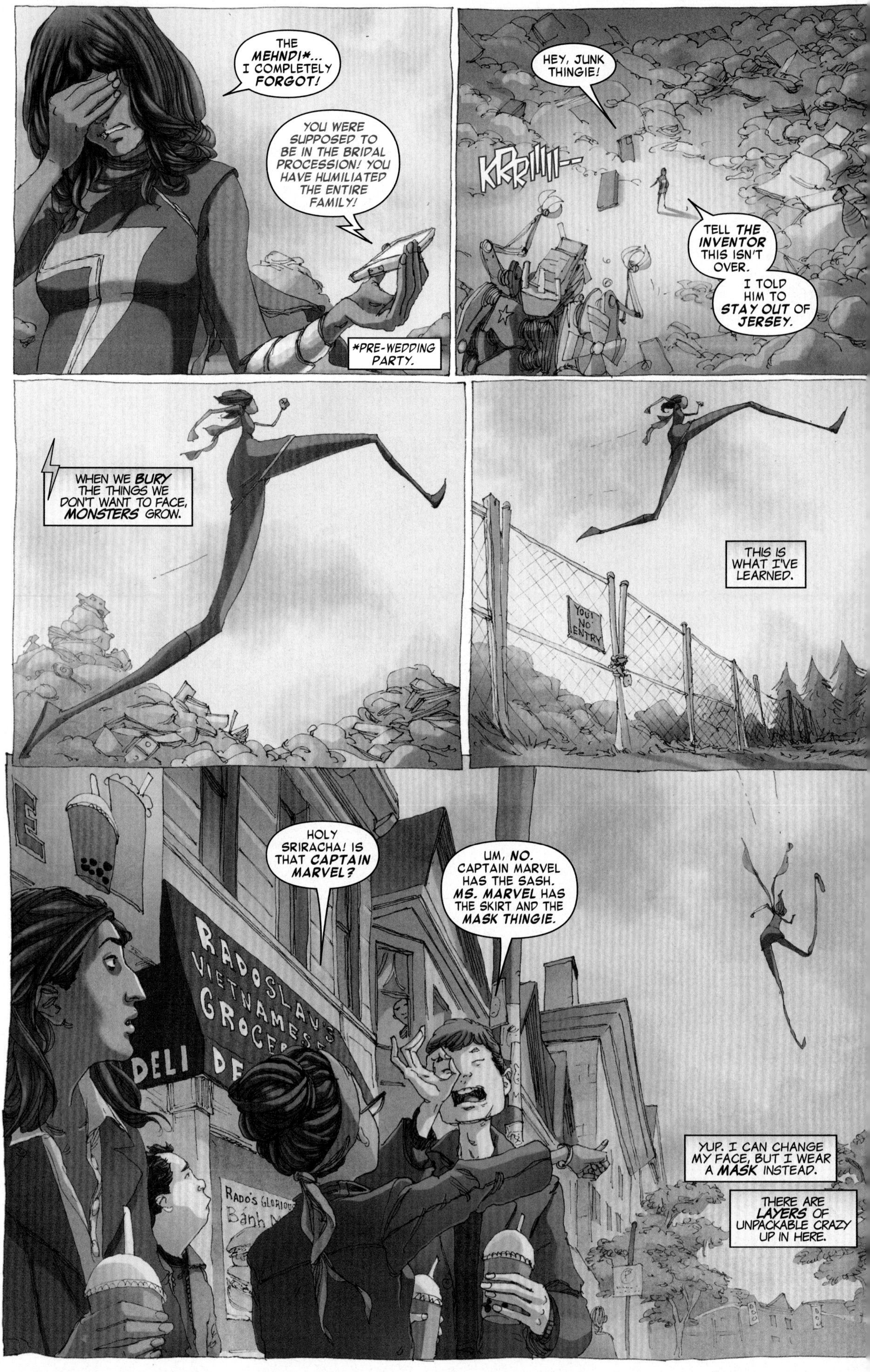
THE MEHNDI*... I COMPLETELY FORGOT!
YOU WERE SUPPOSED TO BE IN THE BRIDAL PROCESSION! YOU HAVE HUMILIATED THE ENTIRE FAMILY!
*PRE-WEDDING PARTY.
HEY, JUNK THINGIE!
KRRIIIIII-
TELL THE INVENTOR THIS ISN'T OVER.
I TOLD HIM TO STAY OUT OF JERSEY.
WHEN WE BURY THE THINGS WE DON'T WANT TO FACE, MONSTERS GROW.
THIS IS WHAT I'VE LEARNED.
YOU! NO ENTRY
HOLY SRIRACHA! IS THAT CAPTAIN MARVEL?
UM, NO. CAPTAIN MARVEL HAS THE SASH. MS. MARVEL HAS THE SKIRT AND THE MASK THINGIE.
RADOSLAV'S VIETNAMESE GROCER
DELI
RADO'S GLORIOU
Bánh M
YUP. I CAN CHANGE MY FACE, BUT I WEAR A MASK INSTEAD.
THERE ARE LAYERS OF UNPACKABLE CRAZY UP IN HERE.

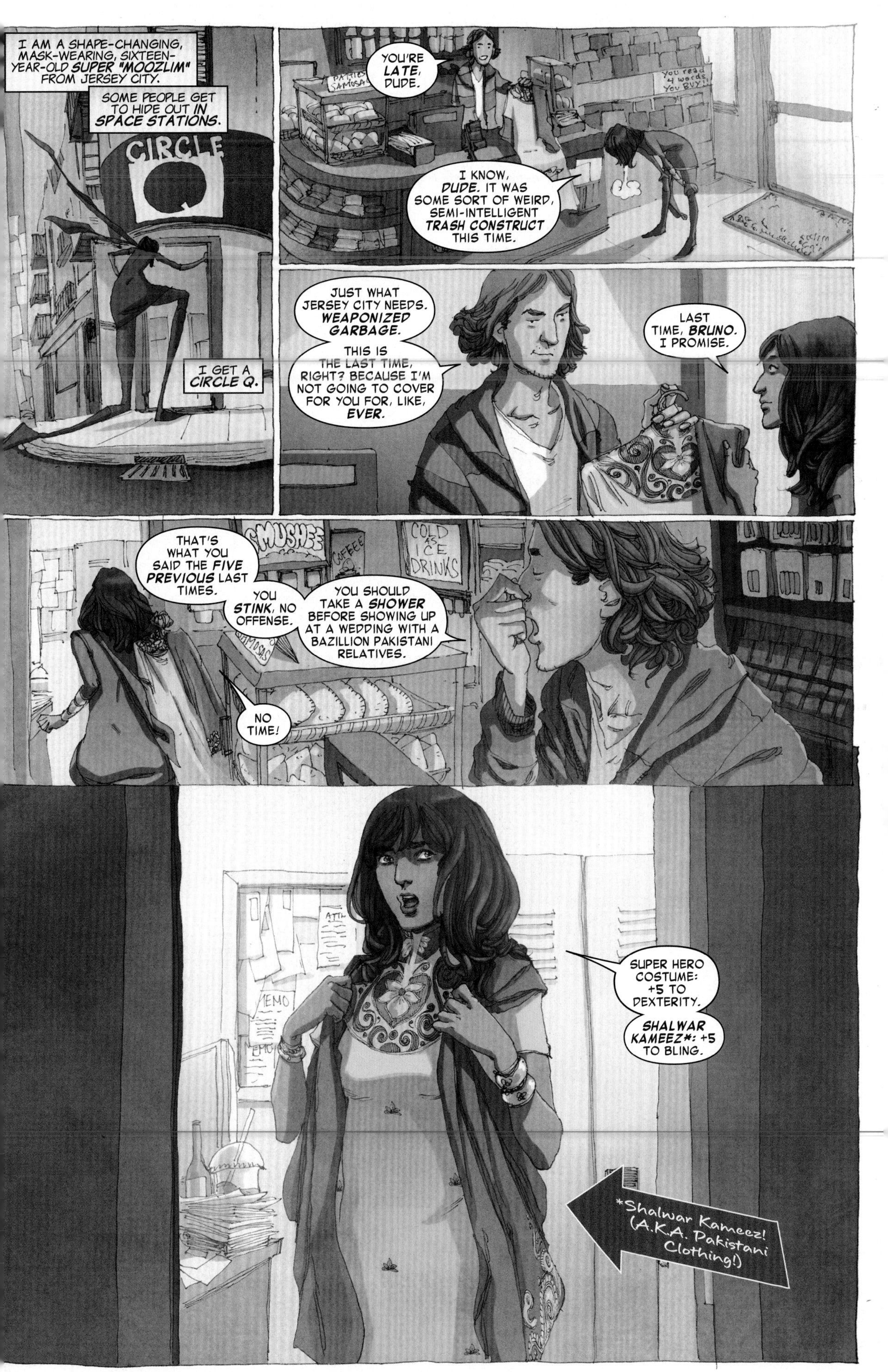
I AM A SHAPE-CHANGING, MASK-WEARING, SIXTEEN-YEAR-OLD SUPER "MOOZLIM" FROM JERSEY CITY.
SOME PEOPLE GET TO HIDE OUT IN SPACE STATIONS.
CIRCLE
I GET A CIRCLE Q.
YOU'RE LATE, DUDE.
I KNOW, DUDE. IT WAS SOME SORT OF WEIRD, SEMI-INTELLIGENT TRASH CONSTRUCT THIS TIME.
JUST WHAT JERSEY CITY NEEDS. WEAPONIZED GARBAGE.
THIS IS THE LAST TIME, RIGHT? BECAUSE I'M NOT GOING TO COVER FOR YOU FOR, LIKE, EVER.
LAST TIME, BRUNO. I PROMISE.
THAT'S WHAT YOU SAID THE FIVE PREVIOUS LAST TIMES.
YOU STINK, NO OFFENSE.
YOU SHOULD TAKE A SHOWER BEFORE SHOWING UP AT A WEDDING WITH A BAZILLION PAKISTANI RELATIVES.
NO TIME!
COLD AS ICE DRINKS
SUPER HERO COSTUME: +5 TO DEXTERITY.
SHALWAR KAMEEZ*: +5 TO BLING.
*Shalwar Kameez! (A.K.A. Pakistani Clothing!)

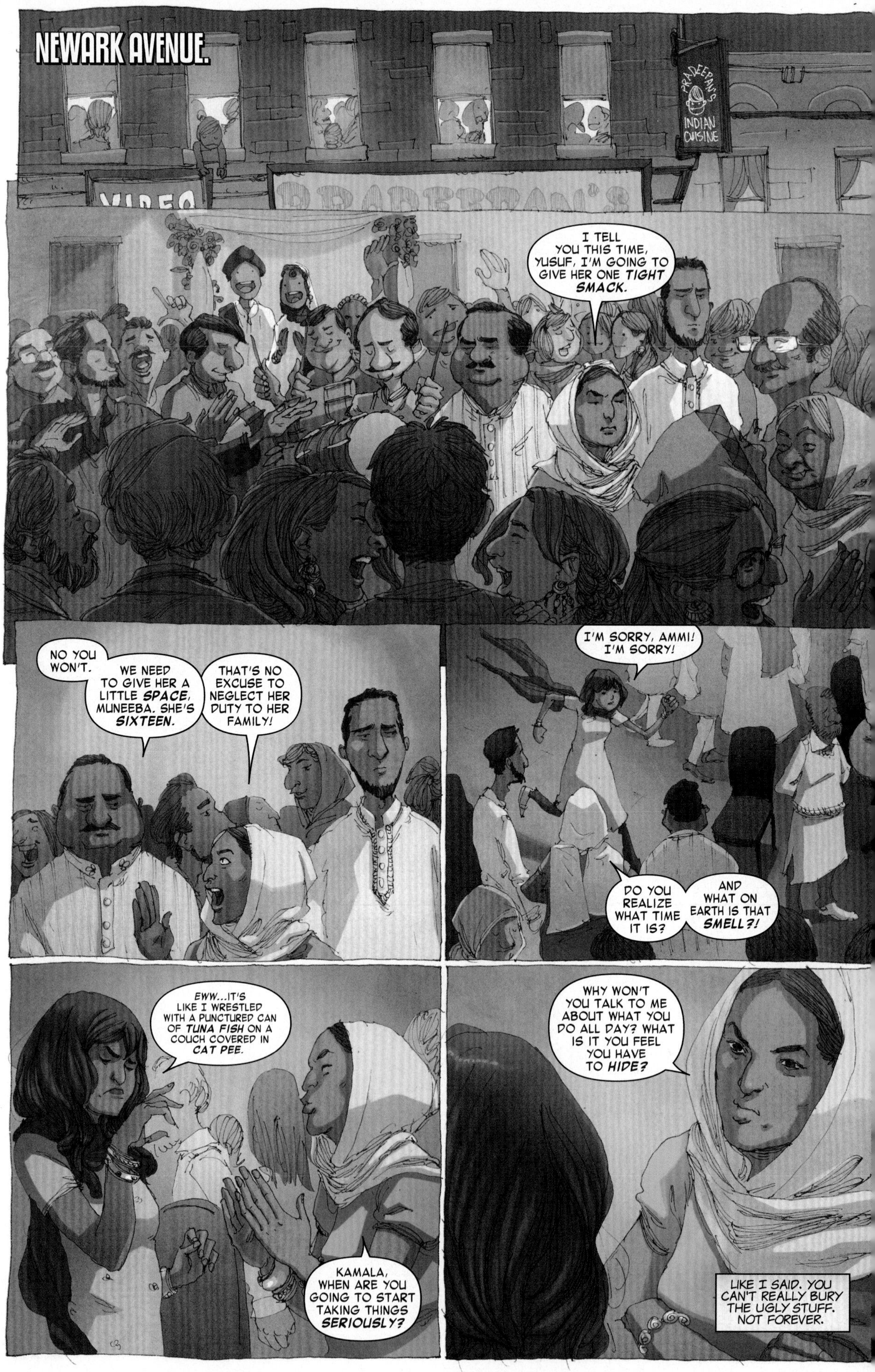
NEWARK AVENUE.
PRADEEPAN'S INDIAN CUISINE
VIDEO
I TELL YOU THIS TIME, YUSUF, I'M GOING TO GIVE HER ONE TIGHT SMACK.
NO YOU WON'T.
WE NEED TO GIVE HER A LITTLE SPACE, MUNEEBA. SHE'S SIXTEEN.
THAT'S NO EXCUSE TO NEGLECT HER DUTY TO HER FAMILY!
I'M SORRY, AMMI! I'M SORRY!
DO YOU REALIZE WHAT TIME IT IS?
AND WHAT ON EARTH IS THAT SMELL?!
EWW...IT'S LIKE I WRESTLED WITH A PUNCTURED CAN OF TUNA FISH ON A COUCH COVERED IN CAT PEE.
KAMALA, WHEN ARE YOU GOING TO START TAKING THINGS SERIOUSLY?
WHY WON'T YOU TALK TO ME ABOUT WHAT YOU DO ALL DAY? WHAT IS IT YOU FEEL YOU HAVE TO HIDE?
LIKE I SAID. YOU CAN'T REALLY BURY THE UGLY STUFF. NOT FOREVER.

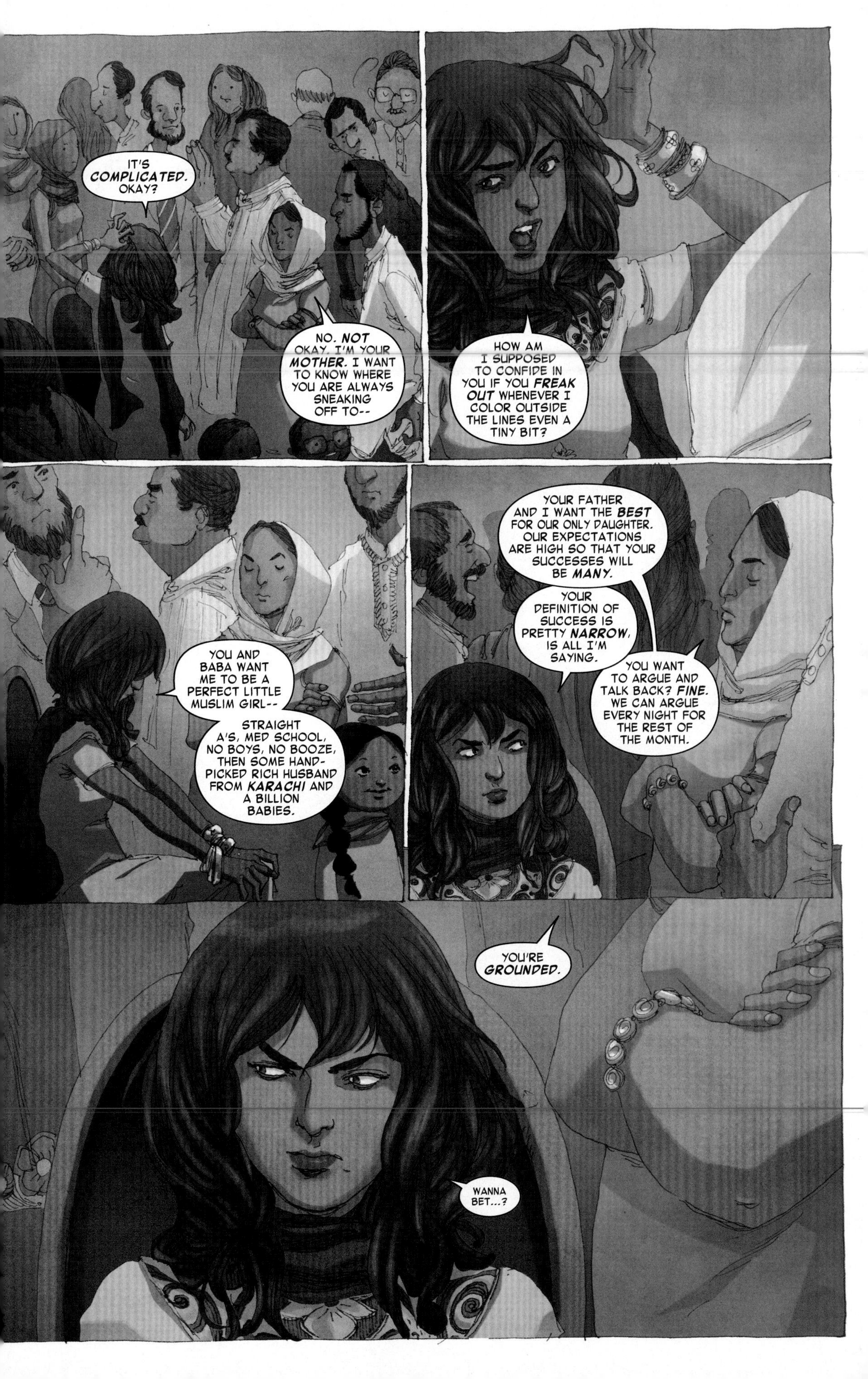
IT'S COMPLICATED. OKAY?
NO. NOT OKAY. I'M YOUR MOTHER. I WANT TO KNOW WHERE YOU ARE ALWAYS SNEAKING OFF TO--
HOW AM I SUPPOSED TO CONFIDE IN YOU IF YOU FREAK OUT WHENEVER I COLOR OUTSIDE THE LINES EVEN A TINY BIT?
YOU AND BABA WANT ME TO BE A PERFECT LITTLE MUSLIM GIRL--
STRAIGHT A'S, MED SCHOOL, NO BOYS, NO BOOZE, THEN SOME HAND-PICKED RICH HUSBAND FROM KARACHI AND A BILLION BABIES.
YOUR FATHER AND I WANT THE BEST FOR OUR ONLY DAUGHTER. OUR EXPECTATIONS ARE HIGH SO THAT YOUR SUCCESSES WILL BE MANY.
YOUR DEFINITION OF SUCCESS IS PRETTY NARROW, IS ALL I'M SAYING.
YOU WANT TO ARGUE AND TALK BACK? FINE. WE CAN ARGUE EVERY NIGHT FOR THE REST OF THE MONTH.
YOU'RE GROUNDED.
WANNA BET...?

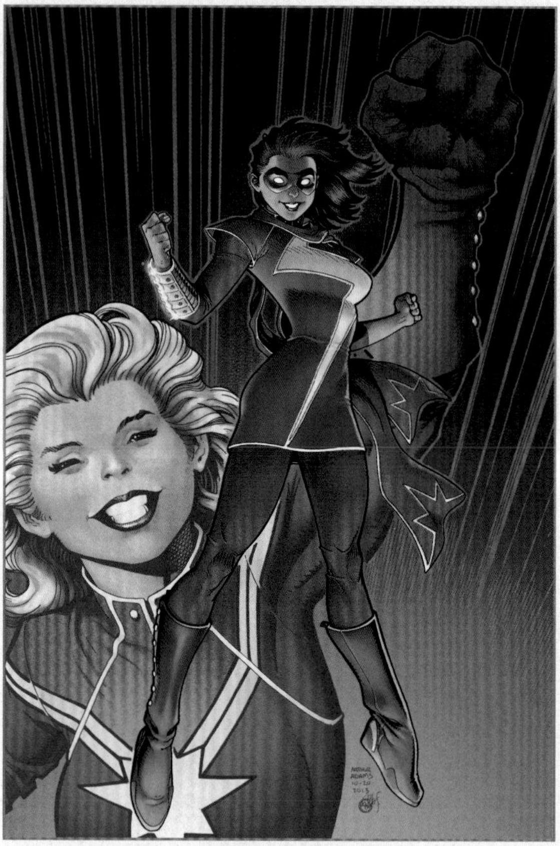

MS. MARVEL #1 VARIANT
BY ARTHUR ADAMS & PETER STEIGERWALD

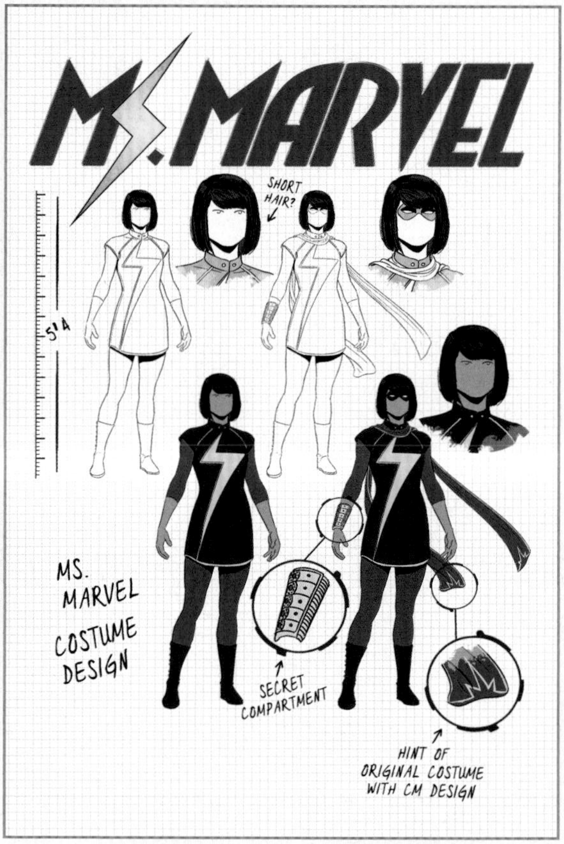
MS. MARVEL
SHORT HAIR?
5'4
MS. MARVEL COSTUME DESIGN
SECRET COMPARTMENT
HINT OF ORIGINAL COSTUME WITH CM DESIGN

MS. MARVEL #1 DESIGN VARIANT
BY JAMIE MCKELVIE

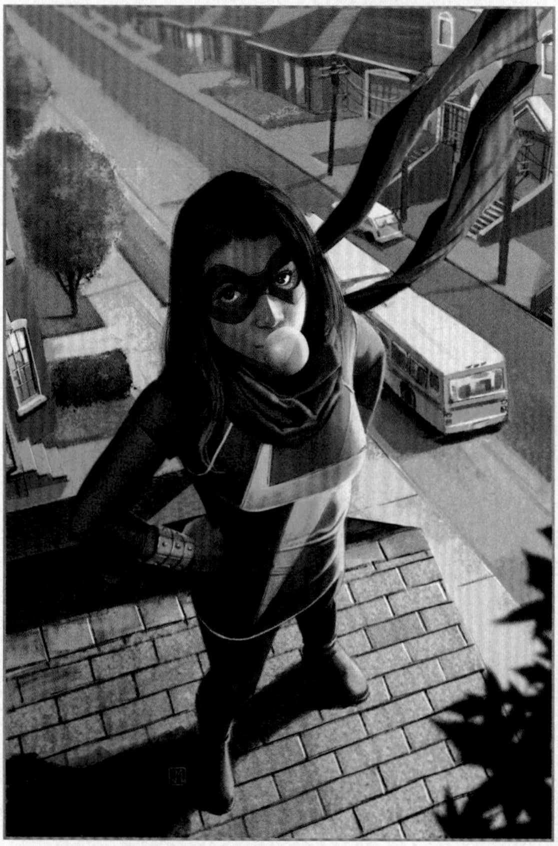

MS. MARVEL #2 VARIANT
BY JORGE MOLINA

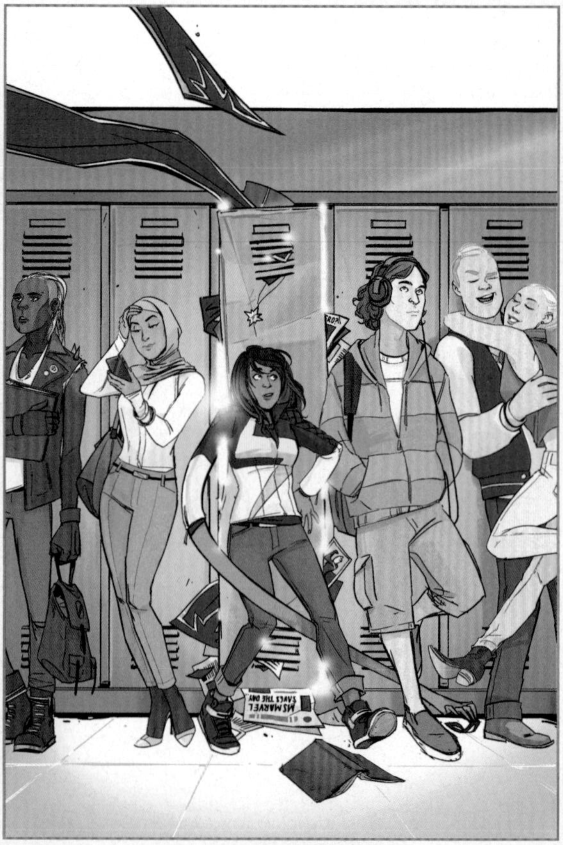

MS. MARVEL #3 VARIANT
BY ANNIE WU

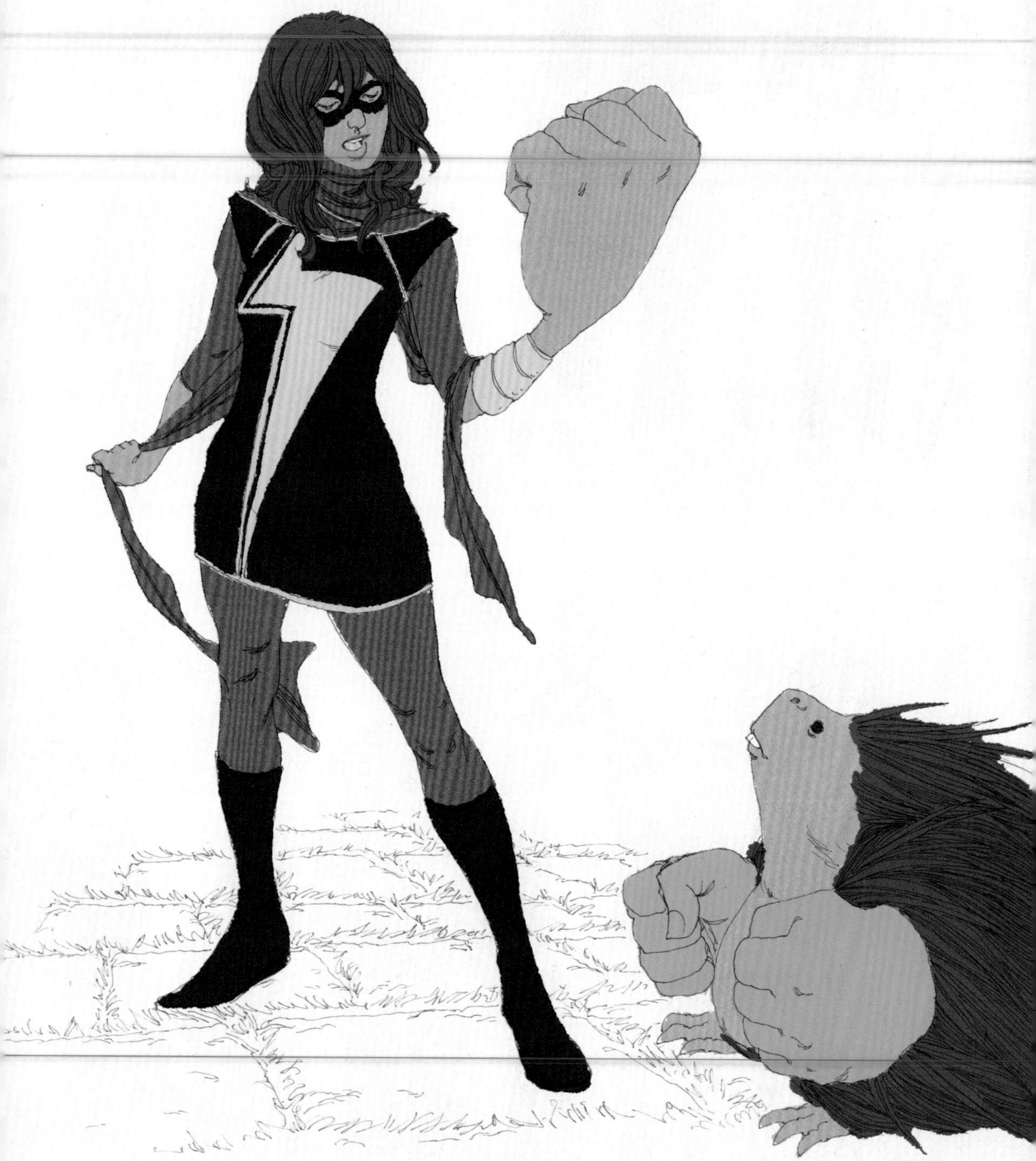

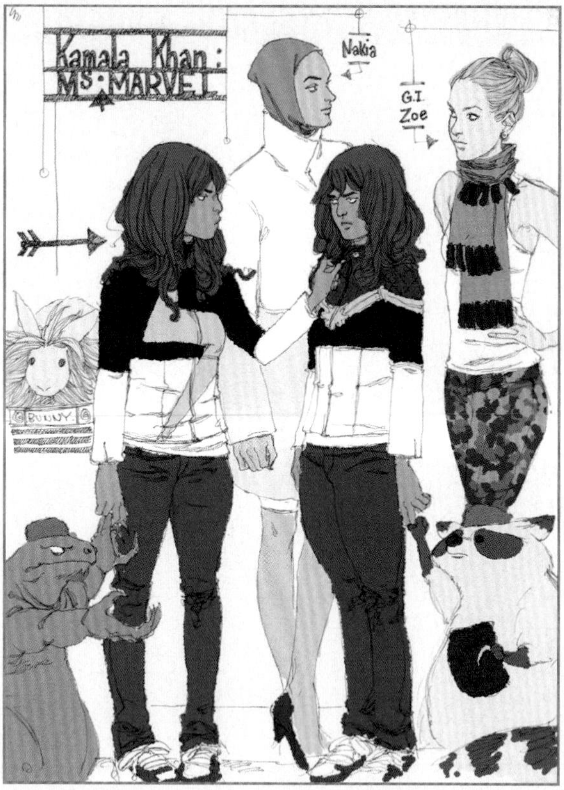
Kamala Khan:
Ms. MARVEL
Nakia
G.I. Zoe
BUNNY

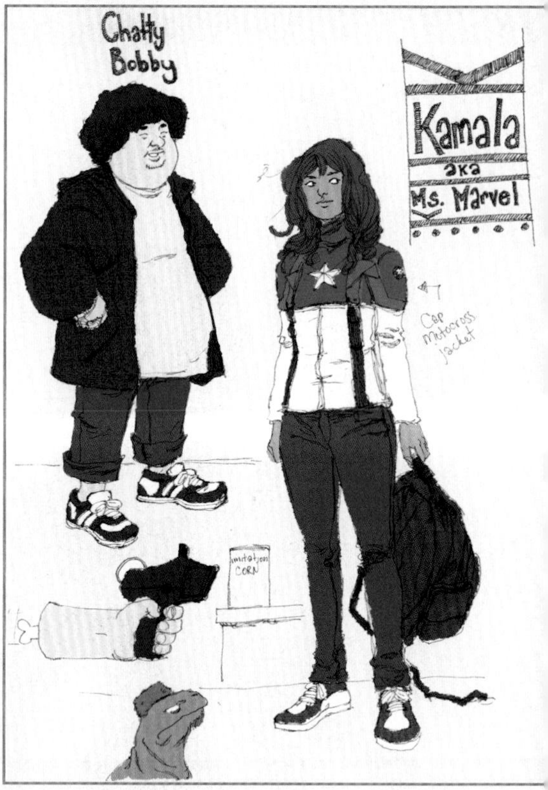
Chatty Bobby
Kamala
aka
Ms. Marvel
Cap motocross jacket
imitation CORN

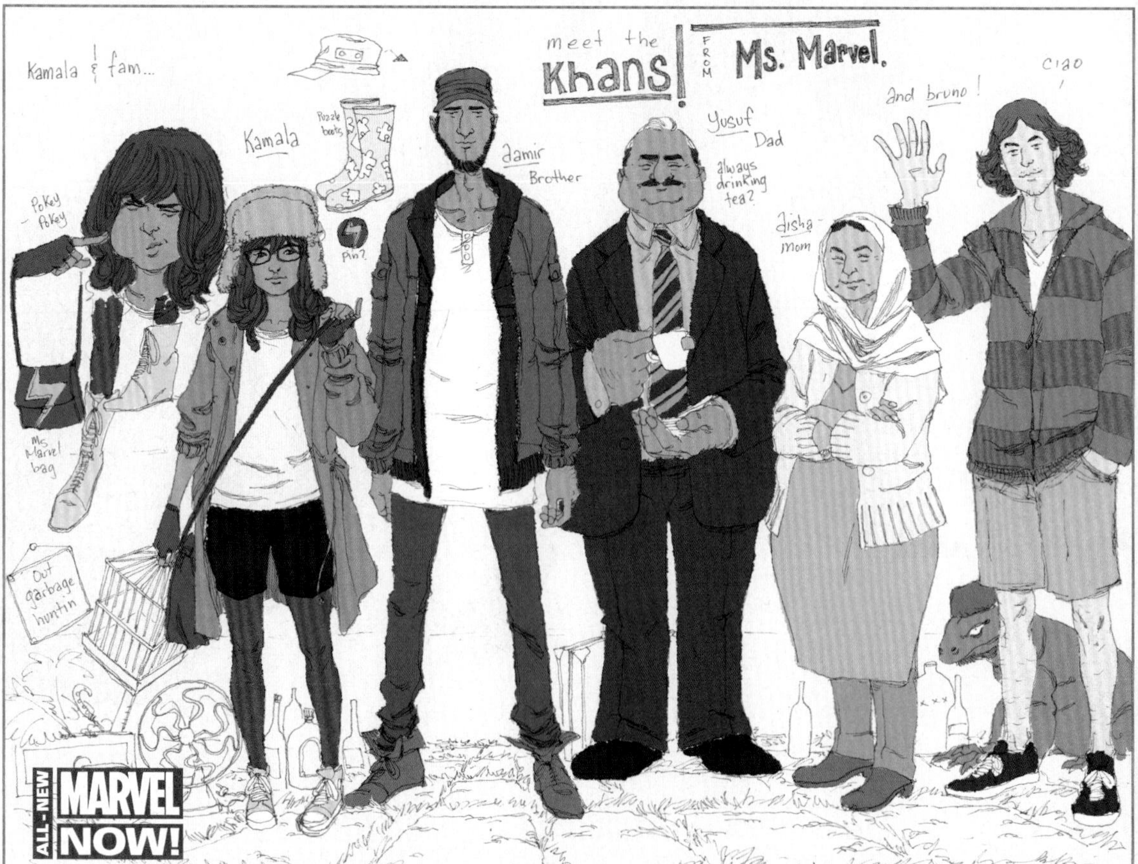
Kamala & fam...
meet the Khans!
FROM
Ms. Marvel.
ciao!
and bruno!
Kamala
Puzzle boots
Pokey Pokey
aamir
Brother
Pin?
Yusuf
Dad
always drinking tea?
aisha
mom
Ms Marvel bag
Out garbage huntin
ALL-NEW MARVEL NOW!

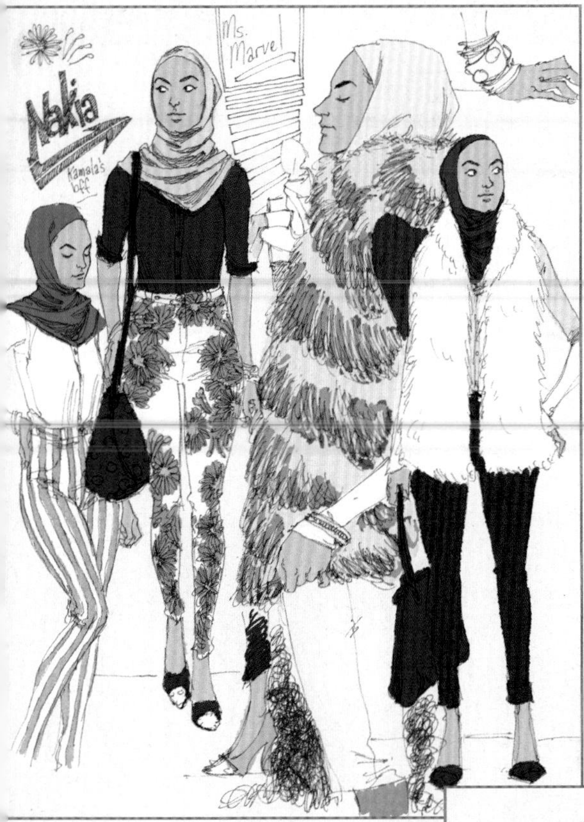
Nakia
Kamala's bff
Ms. Marvel

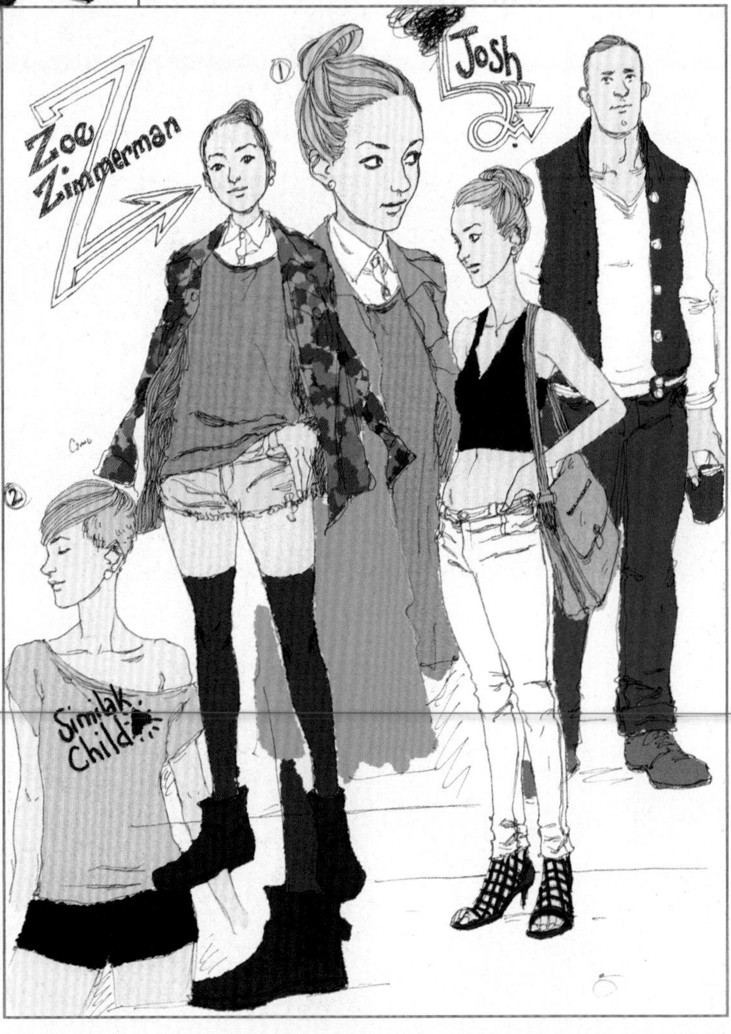
Zoe Zimmerman
Josh
1
2
Similak Child

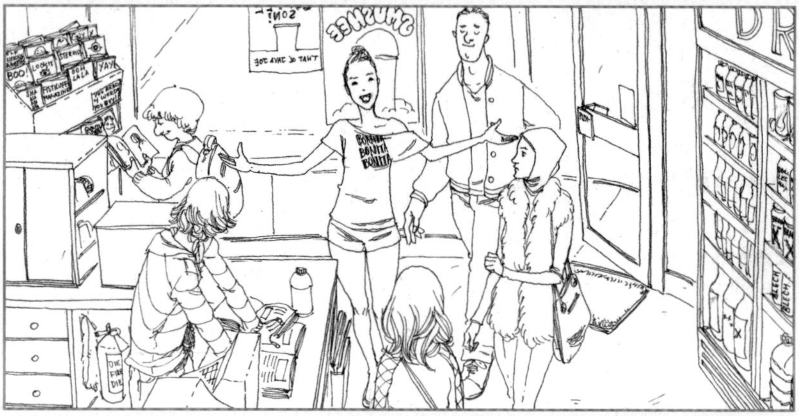
BOO!
YAY

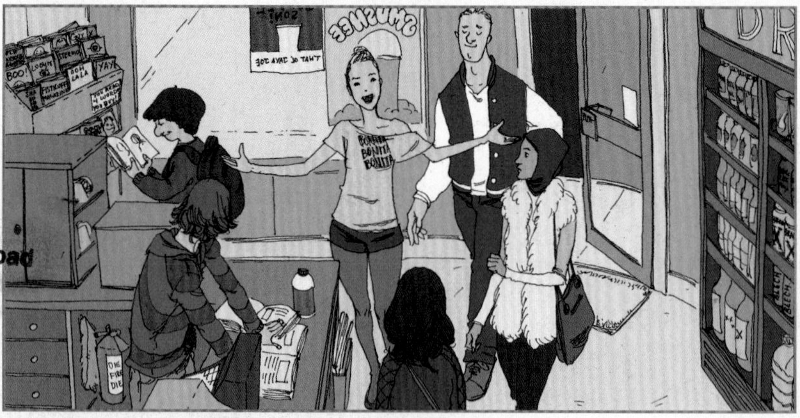

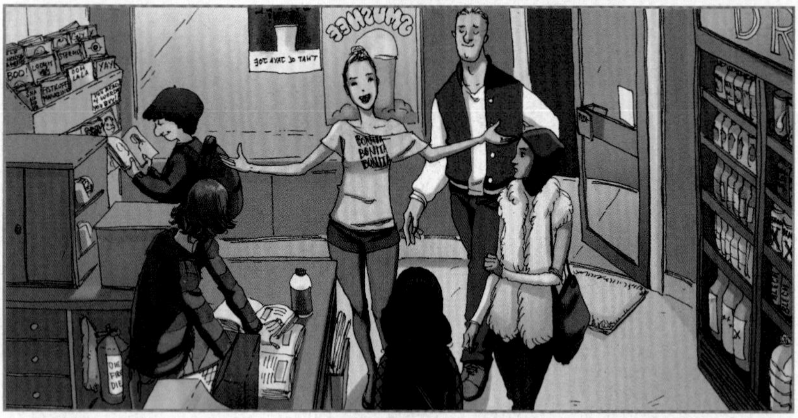

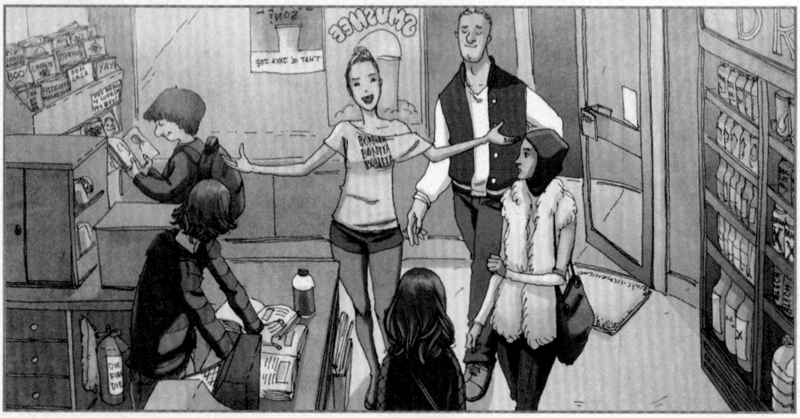